THE CHINESE LABOR MOVEMENT

BOOKS BY NYM WALES

THE CHINESE
LABOR MOVEMENT

NYM WALES, *pseud.*

Helen Foster Snow

THE JOHN DAY COMPANY

NEW YORK

For
REWI ALLEY

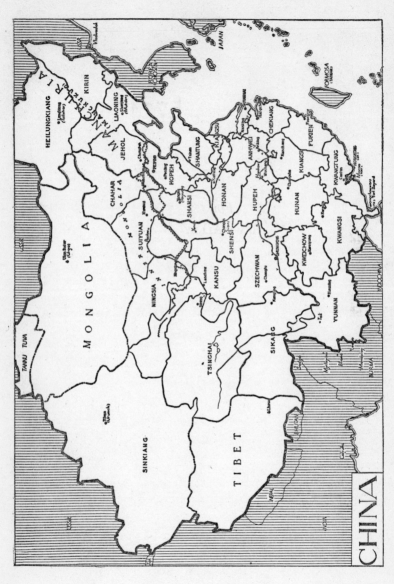

CHINA

Reproduced by permission from *A New Atlas of China* by Martha Rajchman (The John Day Company).

CONTENTS

APPENDICES

FOREWORD

THIS BOOK IS INTENDED as a general study and historical account of the organized labor movement in China, not as an analysis of industrial conditions, labor legislation, factory inspection, welfare work or kindred topics. As research on such matters is already available, I have only touched on the salient points. I have included, however, facts and figures essential to an understanding of labor organization.

As everyone familiar with the many problems of labor in China knows, this particular subject of organized labor is not an easy one on which to secure good information and a connected historical perspective. No history of the Chinese labor movement has been written. Of the few books on China's labor problems, each contains only short chapters on labor unions and labor activities. As these, with one recent exception, were all published in China and are not only out of print but difficult to get hold of, I have quoted pertinent comments which I thought would be particularly useful to the reader, for which I wish to make grateful acknowledgment. In fact, I have gone to some extra pains to trace back and indicate original sources wherever possible and to quote from various existing authorities, rather than giving my own judgment and keeping to a straightforward narrative. The three most recent and useful books are Lowe Chuan-hua's *Facing Labor Issues in China* (Shanghai, 1933), *Labor Legislation in China* (Peking, 1938), by Augusta Wagner, and *Life and Labour in Shanghai,* A Decade of Labour and Social Administration in the International Settlement, by Eleanor M. Hinder (New York, 1944). Few articles have been printed on labor unions in China in recent years. On the present wartime situation Israel Epstein's dispatches to the *Allied Labor News* are of special interest; he is now making a much-needed field study of industrial conditions and labor in China today for the Institute of Pacific Relations.

I have tried to encompass essential existing material on organized labor in China from the beginning of the movement following the first World War to the present, and to add what I have been able to gather from various sources out of an interest in the subject during the time I lived and traveled in China and the Far East from 1931 to 1940.

Authoritative and firsthand information on labor unions in China has always been difficult to secure. In the earlier periods this was partly due to the fact that so much of the organizational work was carried on by Communists. Most of their records have been lost and few of the original organizers survived to tell the inside story. During the civil war it was practically impossible for an outside Chinese or foreigner to get in touch with the underground labor leaders, and therefore public information was limited to external surveys and reports and to the "open sign-board" labor organizations.

As soon as the civil war stopped, I went to Yenan in 1937 for the purpose of obtaining firsthand information on the labor and peasant movements and similar subjects, spending five months interviewing all and sundry. I made a special point of getting detailed accounts from the labor leaders and experts, some of whom had been active organizers from 1919 on. Most important of these was Liu Hsiao-ch'i, Commissioner of Labor, and the leading expert on labor problems. I have directly quoted his statements in places on the 1922-1927 period during which he was a responsible organizer.

I also talked with Tsai Shu-fan, Commissioner of the Interior, who had been one of the labor organizers at Hanyehp'ing; with Wang Chên, an organizer of the Peking-Hankow Railway Workers' Union; Kuan Shang-yin, active in North China; Ho Ch'ang-kung, a worker in France who returned to lead the labor movement; Miss Tsai Chang, a "work-and-study" student in France and an important organizer of women workers and students; Miss Liu Chien-hsien, a leader from the Wusih textile factories, who was Director of National Mines and Factories when I met her; Miss Li Chün-chen, who had been head of a union of women "coolies" in Kwangtung and was Chief of the Soviet Women's Department when I talked with her, and several others who had led the labor movement. Of the above, several had been children of "coolie" families, such as Wang Chên, Miss Liu Chien-hsien and Miss Li Chün-chen. All of the above had been rank-and-file workers, except Liu Hsiao-ch'i and Miss Tsai Chang. They show the potentialities of the working people of China. It is note-worthy that nearly all the main Red armies had former labor leaders, of working-class origin, as political commissars and they dominated the political life of the armies. Today they are leading the anti-Japanese organizational and military work in guerrilla areas.

Except in limited investigations, statistical surveys are seldom kept up to date in China, so figures are unfortunately fragmentary and inadequate on many phases of China's labor problems.

All money quoted in the following pages is in Chinese currency unless otherwise noted. It is of little use to translate such figures into terms of foreign exchange, as local purchasing power at a given time is the essential factor in judging the real value of the Chinese dollar.

N. W.

THE CHINESE LABOR MOVEMENT

I. BACKGROUND OF THE LABOR MOVEMENT IN CHINA

THE LABOR movement in China is characterized by its dramatically rapid rise and surprising achievements during the five years from 1922 to 1927, and by its long subsequent period of depression. Chinese labor leaders divide it into six stages: (1) the initially successful wave of unionization and strikes during the year 1922, beginning with the Hong Kong Seamen's Strike in January, 1922, and ending with the suppression of the railway strike February 7, 1923; (2) the underground period from 1923 to the Second National Labor Congress on May 1, 1925; (3) the high tide of revolutionary activity from the May 30 Incident in 1925 to the split between the Kuomintang and the Communists in 1927; (4) the period of suppression during the civil war from 1927 to the outbreak of war with Japan; (5) the wartime period from 1937 to the present.

1. POLITICAL SETTING

The history of the Chinese labor movement is an integral part of the long and painful effort of China to achieve full national sovereignty, unity, and democracy. The pace and quality of the progress has varied greatly.

In analyzing the recent political development of China it must be remembered that, until the revolution of 1911, China was under the rule of the alien Manchu dynasty, which in its decadent latter years did little to oppose the constantly increasing depredations of the western powers and Japan. The attempt to overthrow the rule of the impotent Manchu regime finally came to a successful conclusion under Sun Yat-sen in the Wuhan revolt of October 10, 1911, with the birth of the Chinese Republic.

The early years of the Republic were stormy with the usual aftermath of disruptive change. The nominal government at Peking had little more than theoretical control over the opposing war lords throughout the country whose ephemeral power rose and fell as coalition succeeded coalition. In the recurrent struggles the partisans of Sun Yat-sen were replaced by different factions fighting in the name of the Republic largely for personal gain. The foreign powers generally were not anxious to extend aid or encouragement to the Chinese republican cause and were busy instead safeguarding the special privileges wrested from China under a system of unequal treaties.

Soviet Russia alone departed from this pattern to help China by announcing in 1920 her voluntary termination of her extraterritorial and other special privileges. This gesture of goodwill was followed by the dispatch of advisors and counselors to Sun Yat-sen and resulted in the careful reorganization of the Kuomintang Party early in 1924 for more effective military and political activity. Under the new plan, Communists were admitted to membership in the nationalist party.

The Kuomintang now established its base in Canton, recruited an army and trained officers in its new Whampoa Academy, modeled after the military schools of the Soviet Union. In 1926 the Nationalists started their famous Northern Expedition which was for the purpose of clearing away provincial war lords and the remnants of the corrupt Peking regime and establishing a democratic, sovereign, national government in central China. The Expedition successfully reached the Yangtze Valley at the end of 1926 and the Hankow government was immediately organized. At the height of victory, however, a split occurred between Right and Left elements, and the Rightists set up a rival government under Chiang Kai-shek in Nanking, which was soon recognized by the foreign powers. When the final split came between the Kuomintang Left wing and the Communists, the Hankow government collapsed, after only six months' existence. Ten years of civil war followed.

Now the military efforts of the Kuomintang on its northern march would probably have failed had there not been a great stirring in Chinese society itself, for it was at this time that the students and intellectuals were sounding the "anti-feudal, anti-imperialist" revolutionary slogan, which was taken up by the local labor and peasant organizations throughout the country. It was largely the big Hong Kong strike of 1925-1926 which had made it possible for the Kuomintang to maintain a firm base in Canton during the preparatory years. Once started, the way of the march was paved by labor and peasant movements so strong that, in Shanghai for ex-

4

ample, labor actually took control of the city before the armies arrived.

The very strength of these popular movements, encouraged and dominated as they were by the Communists, roused the fear of nationalist middle-class groups and of financial and industrial interests and became one of the causes of the 1927 split.

The effect of the split was to weaken and divide the three wings of the original revolutionary forces—labor, the peasantry, and the nationalist middle class. That effect was far-reaching and tragic as it left China open for the Japanese invasion which materialized ten years later.

In the 1927 realignment, the agrarian movement against land-lordism was led by the Communists, who organized the peasants and artisans in the interior provinces and established Soviet districts among a population of about nine million in Kiangsi, Hunan, Hupeh, Shensi, Anhui, Szechuan, and elsewhere. The Kuomintang, which more or less represented the middle-class elements except the students and Left-wing intellectuals, had primary bases in Nanking, Shanghai, and Canton, and co-operated with the feudal landlord power of the interior and with various interests to suppress these revolutionary agrarian and labor movements. Industrial labor, isolated from both the peasant and middle-class elements, was broken and submerged during the period of intense civil war that ensued. It has been unable to rise again from its difficult position.

Thus China was ill prepared for the Japanese attack in July, 1937. The three classes capable of leading mass resistance were still isolated from each other. The Communists, who had been driven to the northwest where they had established new bases in Shensi, Ninghsia and Kansu in 1936, had not yet had time to organize a new large-scale anti-Japanese peasant movement there. Nanking had failed to mobilize either the peasants or labor in the areas under its control. Even in the coastal cities labor was not organized to meet Japan's plans for taking over the industries.

Nevertheless when Japan attacked there was a great upsurge of patriotic activity throughout the country and the beginning of a real national people's war in 1937 and 1938. By the end of 1938, however, with the capture of Shanghai, Wusih, Tsingtao, Tientsin, Hankow, Canton, and other cities, Japan had either destroyed or

5

taken over about 90 per cent of China's modern industry. The capacity of labor to resist was therefore crippled almost at the outset, for the principal industrial city, Shanghai, had been captured in 1937. These large cities and industrial areas had had only about twenty-six years of semi-colonial Chinese sovereignty, from the fall of the Manchu dynasty in 1911 to their occupation by Japan in 1937 and 1938, which, in the interim, had been complicated by foreign concessions in the cities, and considerable foreign ownership of industry.

When the government moved to Chungking in 1939, the united front with the Communists began to deteriorate, and is still uncertain, threatening to turn into civil war unless a formula for democratic co-operation can be achieved. Established in Chungking, the Kuomintang government, cut off from its more progressive base in the modern cities, and now entirely dependent upon the reactionary semi-feudal landlord system of the interior, still fearful of the people, began active suppression of the people's movement. Too weak to fight on two fronts at once, the government decided that internal problems took precedence over the anti-Japanese war. A huge network of secret police and gendarmes was organized to prevent the rise of democratic tendencies and opposition. Dictatorship was intensified in all fields.

Recently, however, the Kuomintang has changed its tactics and is now openly substituting regimentation and organization for the former negative control and strict regulations. The San Min Chu I Youth Corps, patterned after the Hitler Youth Movement, has been started and a program of "thought control" for students and young people has been promulgated. Under the regulations aimed at labor, workers are forced to join and pay dues to "unions" under control of the Ministry of Social Affairs.

Whether the increased dictatorship will result in strengthening or weakening the Kuomintang is yet a question, but there is no question that it is causing widespread dissatisfaction, demoralizing the patriotic movement, and creating a strong undercurrent of democratic opposition. One spokesman for this opposition is Chang Lan, an old scholar now seventy-two, who is President of the Federation of Democratic Parties. In a recent statement he said: "China today is fighting shoulder to shoulder with the United Nations. But unless true democracy is carried out soon it will be

6

difficult for us to gain freedom, equality and independence either during or after the war. Because this is so closely connected with the destiny of China, all far-sighted persons are anxiously hoping that something will be done to carry it out."

Thus China is today divided into three spheres of influence: (1) the large cities and lines of communication under Japanese occupation; (2) the guerrilla areas organized by the Communists; and (3) the provinces in the interior under the Chungking government. Chungking troops have established an economic and military blockade around the guerrilla areas, isolating this region with its population of about fifty million from the rest of the country, making it not only more difficult for the people there to withstand the Japanese, but also cutting off this strategic area from co-operation with other anti-Japanese forces.

It may be that the above discussion, which was designed primarily to give the reader a brief orientation in the current political situation in China, has intimated too strongly that the course of the Chinese labor movement has been determined by the opposing political factions of China. Such of course is not the case, for labor movements do not wait for organized political action. The history of the labor movement in China does not fit into a purely political pattern, but rather it is the result of a combination of social and economic forces whose pattern is all the more confusing by virtue of the constantly changing forces at work in the broader background of China herself.

2. THE ECONOMIC AND SOCIAL FRAMEWORK

Among the artisans and workers of China there had for generations been both craft and regional guilds. The craft guilds were called *hongs,* the regional guilds *pongs*. As in Europe, these guilds were intended not primarily to serve the interests of the workers as a class but to promote the craft and guard its secrets. Both employers and employees were members, but the employers usually dominated the guild's activities. The guilds had ways of bringing pressure and strikes were occasionally used by them to secure better contract terms. One instance well remembered by foreigners in Peking was the time when the garbage collectors' guild refused to co-operate and the city became somewhat smelly.

7

In the breakup of the old society following the revolution, the guilds were gradually disintegrating. They no longer protected the trade, the workers or the employers and some attempt at new forms of organization became necessary. Various methods were tried. In some cases separate workers' and employers' associations were established. In other instances these attempts resulted in a reversion to the guild form dominated by the employers. Where labor was strong, the reorganized guilds became authentic unions, where labor was weak, the "unions" retained certain old features and became a kind of company union. In the older cities and interior towns, the guilds were naturally more enduring. However, as elsewhere in the world, these guilds proved inflexible for real labor organization and completely inadaptable to large modern factories or industries.

Labor in China never went through the slow period of organization that occurred in many other countries, but was born in the chaos of revolutionary emergencies. It cannot be understood if one views it as a mere trade-union development. Rather it was a revolutionary mass movement of the infant working class struggling to free itself from the bondage of semi-feudal and semi-colonial conditions. Such conditions have not existed in modern capitalist countries since the early stages of the industrial revolution.

One must not think of this struggle in terms of collective bargaining and legal safeguards, as in the framework of stable, democratic government, but rather in terms of street barricades, the *sans-culottes* or the various uprisings against Czarism in 1905. There were never any Terence V. Powderlys or Samuel Gompers in China; the pace was too rapid. Su Chao-jen, the famous seaman, leaped from being active in a sailors' welfare society in 1920 to leading the Chinese Seamen's Union strike of 50,000 men in Hong Kong in 1922; from that to Chairman of the All-China Labor Federation of nearly three million members. Finally he became Minister of Labor in the Hankow government in 1927. His fall was equally rapid, however, and in 1929 he was no longer alive.

There are many reasons for the unusually rapid rise of the Chinese labor movement.

(1) Modern industry in China did not develop gradually as during the industrial revolution in capitalist countries. It had a quick growth during and after the World War, though successful modern

8

industry dates from the opening of the first cotton mill in 1890 in Shanghai. Cotton is the principal industry, and China had fifty-four cotton mills in 1920 and 119 in 1927; spindles increasing from 1,650,000 to 3,612,000. During this period the number of factories of all kinds employing over thirty workers increased from 673 to 1,347 (excluding Tientsin). Machinery imported into China during 1917 was valued at 5,439,770 Hk. Tls. (Haikuan Taels), the customs unit. In 1919 it was valued at 14,591,635 Hk. Tls. and reached a peak of 56,578,424 Hk. Tls. in 1921, dropping to 27,141,059 Hk. Tls. in 1923.

(2) The workers, mostly fresh from the country, had not yet been beaten down into passive wage slaves with no hope for better living conditions. In 1916 there were estimated to be approximately a million industrial workers, and this number is said to have doubled by 1922.[1]

[1] In 1927 the figure was estimated at 2,750,000 by Su Chao-jen and handicraft workers at 12,160,000, while organized union membership under the All-China Labor Federation was given as 2,800,000. Total figures are always very rough and inaccurate in China, especially before 1930. For reference, however, I include here one of the earliest estimates available, taken from Su Chao-jen's "Report on the Labor Movement in China," *Proceedings of the Pan-Pacific Trade Union Conference, 1927.* Su Chao-jen was then Minister of Labor in the Hankow government. As can be seen, these figures include postal workers, policemen, and municipal employees, as well as "rice-selling workers," etc.:

NUMBER OF INDUSTRIAL WORKERS IN CHINA IN 1927

Electrical Workers	80,000
Textile Workers	280,000
Silk Workers	160,000
Miners	540,000
Seamen	160,000
Railway Workers	120,000
Wharf Workers	300,000
Metal Workers	50,000
Building and Construction Workers	200,000
Postal Workers	90,000
Municipal Employees and Policemen	250,000
Salt Workers	250,000
Tobacco Workers	40,000
Rice Selling Workers	60,000
Printers	50,000
Other Manufacturing Workers	120,000
Total	2,750,000

(3) Industrial workers were concentrated principally in five coastal provinces, Kiangsu, Liaoning, Hopei, Kwangtung, Shantung, and in Hupeh in the interior. Factory workers were concentrated in a few cities, chiefly in Shanghai and Wusih, Tientsin, Tsingtao, Hankow, Canton and British Hong Kong, and in Dairen in Manchuria (in Japanese-leased territory in Liaoning). Geographically, therefore, workers were easily organizable both into local and general unions. Strategically, they were also more easily united into a compact political force as compared with other scattered elements of the population.

The picture was well presented in an authoritative study by H. D. Fong.[2] He found that "industrialization is confined chiefly to six provinces, namely, Kiangsu, Liaoning, Hopei, Kwangtung, Shantung and Hupeh. These six provinces, which have a total area of 10 per cent and a total population of 36.3 per cent, possess 55.1 per cent of China's mining industry, 64.9 per cent of China's coal mining, 64.4 per cent of China's iron mining, 93 per cent of China's cotton spinning, 92.6 per cent of China's silk reeling, 86 per cent of China's oil pressing, 87.6 per cent of China's electric power capacity, 84 per cent of China's whole trade, 92.5 per cent of China's foreign trade, 91.9 per cent of China's transit trade, 53.4 per cent of China's railways, 42.1 per cent of China's motor roads and 42 per cent of China's telegraph wires."

H. D. Fong also analyzed the first basic government survey of modern industrial workers made by the Ministry of Industries in 1930, which included nine provinces and twenty-nine cities, showing that of a total of 1,204,318 industrial workers, 47 per cent (566,301) were in textiles, 14.7 per cent in food factories, 6.6 per cent in clothing, 6.5 per cent in building, 6 per cent in chemicals, 5.4 per cent in machinery, 4.9 per cent in education (printing, etc.). The concentration in a few industries made possible cohesive industrial unionism.

(4) The fact that in China the railways and various key industries were owned by the "government," and controlled by whatever militarist happened to be in power, *ipso facto* made the workers

[2] *China's Industrialization, a Statistical Survey,* pamphlet by H. D. Fong, Institute of Pacific Relations, Shanghai, 1931. *See also* China Year Book, 1933, p. 382.

a factor in the struggle for power and a strong anti-feudal force in breaking the control of the militarists. In many cases, the provincial governor or militarist actually owned a large part of the industries in his region. Labor disturbances immediately weakened his position. Until 1927 labor activities were important in this respect. The failure of the Kuomintang to mobilize labor for this purpose after 1927 was one reason why it could not unify the country and break the power of the provincial militarists. In 1928 some attempt was made by the Kuomintang in Peking and Tientsin to form labor unions out of the old guilds, but it was half-hearted.

The same situation exists today in Chungking. If labor were democratically mobilized instead of alienated by the Kuomintang, it could be effective in helping to establish stable, democratic government in China under central control. At present, however, as after 1927, anti-labor policies antagonize labor, and it considers itself as well off if not better under provincial authorities as under Chungking. Regimentation and Fascist policies only serve to create its opposition.

(5) The presence of Communists and others just returned from abroad where they had learned something about labor organization and strike methods provided the necessary leadership in a situation already ripe for action. They were only a spark set to tinder, and it was almost spontaneous combustion. The Chinese are peculiarly capable of cohesive organization, and the workers had been held back largely by sheer lack of information. Once the ideas and methods were supplied by the Communists, they learned quickly and were loyal to their cause, hence few splits occurred in their ranks. Except for the old guild tradition, chiefly in handicrafts, they were virgin territory for a strong class movement. Labor was wide open and "in flux," as the saying is. The organizers had only to build, not to destroy first.

It is commonly said that "the students organized the Chinese labor movement." What actually happened is very interesting. One student was enough to kindle the fire in hundreds of workers. The student merely told the workers what unions and strikes were and the workers acted. The whole organizational movement was empirical. The Labor Secretariat members in Shanghai who directed

11

it were inexperienced and most of the organizers it sent out were very young, very amateurish and not always very practical. They supplied the ideas and the overall strategy, but the workers organized themselves. Their role was important because most of the workers were illiterate, but it does not take a college professor to see the need for a living wage, and it takes only a few minutes to learn the principles of organized action if one's rice bowl depends upon it.

(6) Working conditions were overdue for improvement in 1922 and the workers lived at a bare subsistence level. Hours and wages in handicrafts had carried over into the factories and the seven-day week was the custom. This may be tolerable in small workshops where slow methods are the time-honored protection of the worker against his own physical destruction, but in a factory such conditions cannot be easily endured for more than a few years by a normal person. Labor revolted against these medieval conditions, and once realizing their power to improve their livelihood even in small ways, the Chinese workers stood firmly together and made the most of it. To understand the situation, one would have to study the appalling circumstances surrounding labor in the early days of the industrial revolution in other countries.

A picture of conditions in 1923 is shown in the following: [3]

"In machine industries the hours are still frequently as much as 14 to 17 per day, though it is becoming usual in the large factories to work 12-hour shifts, generally with no fixed or regular break.

"Steel workers are employed for from 12 to 18 hours, and other engineering runs from 10 to 14 hours a day."

This article reports further: that in Shanghai women workers averaged $8 a month in wages, older children 18 cents to 30 cents per day or $6 a month. Unskilled workmen averaged $9 monthly and skilled workmen $20. In central China a new cotton mill paid $4.50 to $6 monthly to the unskilled and $14 to $15 to skilled workers. In central and north China an ordinary unskilled workman received 15¢, 18¢ and 20¢ a day. One study in Shanghai is quoted as showing that "some 40% of the workers are living below the poverty line."

[3] "Labour and Industry in China," by W. T. Zung and J. B. Tayler, *International Labour Review,* July, 1923. (J. B. Tayler is now active in the industrial co-operative movement in China.)

Another study by M. T. Tchou in 1923 showed that in 1922 the average monthly wage for unskilled men was $9, for women $7.50, for children $4. Skilled men in cotton received $16 and women $12. "In Wuhan (the Hanyehp'ing mines and steel works) the steel laborers work from 12 to 18 hours a day." The hours for men, women, and children averaged 12; in cotton they were from 11 to 13½. The seven-day week was usual except in Christian establishments.

An immediate reason for labor unrest was the rise in the cost of living that followed the World War. M. T. Tchou quoted figures from the Ministry of Agriculture and Commerce showing that from 1914 to 1922 the price of rice had risen 100 per cent, and the price of polished rice in Shanghai 135 per cent. Wholesale prices in Shanghai had increased 140 per cent and wages only 80 per cent, causing great hardship to wage-earners. "During nine months last year (1922), over 50 strikes took place in the two cities of Canton and Chaochow alone. . . . Increases in wages range from 10% to 40% of the original amount. . . . From March to September, over 60 labor unions were formed in Shanghai alone, and over 50 strikes, large and small have occurred, generally ending favorably for the workers."

(7) Two other causes for the revolt of labor in China showing the need of good unionism may be mentioned, the apprentice system and the labor contract system. The apprentice system in China is largely a method of obtaining free labor and of keeping adult wages down. During the period of "training" the apprentice receives no wages at all or only enough to keep the individual alive, though his food and clothing are provided for. Often when he has served several years of apprenticeship and is entitled to wages, he is dismissed to avoid payment of wages and a new apprentice taken on.[4]

The labor contract system operates in this way: In the textile industry, agents go out into the country to recruit girls for a period of from one to three years, at the end of which time they are to pay

[4] *Facing Labor Issues in China* by Lowe Chuan-hua, China Institute of Pacific Relations, Shanghai, 1933. Mr. Lowe stated that "In the overwhelming majority of modern factories in China the working day is still between ten and twelve hours, while in the handicraft industries the working day even goes up to fifteen hours, seven days a week."

the girl's family a small sum of money. Lowe Chuan-hua states: "It is estimated that after paying for the girls' food and shelter, the recruiting agents can often retain over 60% of the girls' earnings." He continues: "It has been estimated that of the 2,000,-000 mining population in China no less than 80% are affected by the labor contract system. . . . The contractor usually deducts 10% and sometimes 20% of the miners' wages as his commission, and in some cases where the operation and management of the mine is entirely entrusted to the contractor, his commission runs up as high as 60% of the compensation for the work agreed upon."

The labor contract system also functions among hotel and restaurant waiters, wharf coolies, seamen and railway workers. Lowe Chuan-hua reported: "Organized into powerful gangs, the labor-contractors and their subordinates usually retain 60 to 80% of what the steamship companies pay for the loading or unloading of cargo. When one bears in mind that in Shanghai alone, no less than 70,000 to 80,000 wharf coolies are under the domination of the labor-contractors and gang leaders, one may easily realize what an immense sum of money the wharf coolies have been losing year in and year out."

3. CHARACTERISTICS OF THE CHINESE LABOR MOVEMENT

In considering the rise of the Chinese labor movement, those conditions peculiar to the labor situation in China must be borne in mind.

(1) China was a semi-colonial country, with foreign concessions in Shanghai, Tientsin, Tsingtao, Hankow, and other treaty ports, and Hong Kong a British colony. A large percentage of modern industries were owned by foreigners, chiefly the British and Japanese, while the railways had been financed with foreign capital. In 1930 80 per cent of the total shipping business of China (including coastal trade) was done by foreign-owned vessels. Of the 128 cotton mills in China in 1932, 84 were owned by Chinese firms, 41 by Japanese and 3 by British. H. D. Fong estimated in 1932 that less than half the $288,328,138 local currency reported to be then invested in the cotton mills was Chinese-owned. The figures

14

given were $126,008,222 for Chinese investment; $148,919,916 for Japanese; and $12,500,000 for British investment.[5]

Cotton textiles constituted the principal large-scale factories. A good picture of the situation may be seen from a 1937 survey which showed that there were 143 cotton mills, employing 232,846 workers. Though 95 of these were Chinese-owned, a little less than half the spindles, more than half the looms and a third of the workers were employed in foreign-owned mills, chiefly Japanese.

The following statistics were given:

	Spindles	Looms	Workers
Chinese	2,746,392	25,503	145,176
British	221,336	4,021	12,221
Japanese	2,135,068	28,915	75,449

These mills were competing with those in Japan, England, the United States and other countries, and in order to do so successfully the workers were ground down to the "cheapest" labor terms possible. Protective customs tariffs were not instituted until 1928 but even then were not increased effectively.

From the above it can be seen that Chinese labor was capable of becoming a strong anti-imperialist force, even in its economic struggle, and this was a powerful factor in rousing it to action. So long as it was directed against foreigners, Chinese industrial interests did not object, and the Kuomintang supported it. When it became strong they opposed it, fearing the economic threat to themselves. One must also remember the peculiar compradore nature of capitalism in China, so that its loyalties were always divided, especially in the financial world.

(2) Light industries have developed in China rather than heavy industry, most machinery being imported. Therefore, the fundamental political position of labor was weak as compared with other countries where basic heavy industry exists as a key center from which labor can bring pressure and achieve its demands. In fact, the railways were the chief vital center for labor action, yet even here strikes did not paralyze either the industry or trade of the

[5] *Cotton Industry and Trade in China,* by H. D. Fong, Nankai Institute of Economics, Industry Series, Bulletin No. 4, Tientsin, Nankai University, 1932.

15

country as they might in other countries, because the chief industrial centers were dependent upon ocean or river transport, and foreign imports of machinery and, to a large extent, of raw materials. Rather than paralyzing or embarrassing native industry, a strong labor movement among transport workers in China served to increase the cost of the distribution of foreign-produced consumers' goods, which have been principally Japanese, serving as a protection to native industry in interior cities where the market has been local. As the basic political power in an industrial country is largely in the hands of those who own and control its key heavy industries, neither capital nor labor in China enjoyed this power but was comparatively weak and semi-colonial, dependent upon foreign production. This weakness is a dominant characteristic of both Chinese capital and labor, and no nation or class can be independent which does not control its own key industries.

The predominance of light industry and lack of heavy industry has also resulted in another essential characteristic of Chinese labor that has affected the movement: the high percentage of girls, women, and children employed in factories and workshops. On the one hand this has weakened the position of organized labor in China and kept down wages, but on the other hand women and children have been among the most militant and self-sacrificing and have not been spared in the tragic story of suppression. The situation is shown by the following figures: "According to a compilation by the former Ministry of Agriculture and Commerce, woman labor occupied for the period 1914-1920 from 47 to 65 per cent in textile factories, from 31 to 43 per cent in food and drink factories, from 11 to 23 per cent in miscellaneous factories, from 12 to 22 per cent in chemical factories, from one to four per cent in metal factories, and about one per cent in special factories." [6]

Another survey in Shanghai showed the following: "According to a census made by the Bureau of Public Safety in the autumn of 1928, out of the entire population, the working class in the 47 different industries amounted to an aggregate of 237,574 persons, of which 33.9 per cent were male workers, 58.7 per cent female workers, and 7.4 per cent child workers. The majority of the factory workers in Shanghai was shown to be female workers. This

[6] *Extent and Effects of Industrialization in China,* by Franklin Ho and H. D. Fong, Nankai University, Tientsin, China, 1929, p. 29.

is due to the fact that as many as 124,752 female workers were employed in the textile industry, which constituted 89 per cent of the total female workers and 52 per cent of the total number of factory workers in Shanghai." [7]

In 1930 a Ministry of Industries survey of 799,912 workers in 28 cities and nine provinces showed that 46 per cent were men, 46.6 per cent women, and 6.9 per cent children. Nankai University researchers analyzed the survey further and showed that of 964,953 workers, 49 per cent were men (468,728 workers), 45 per cent women (432,940 workers) and 6 per cent children (63,287 workers). [8]

D. K. Lieu found that women and children in cotton spinning and weaving in Shanghai worked over twelve hours a day in 1929, and that boys in type printing presses worked thirteen and a half hours sometimes, and over twelve hours in lithographing. Child workers averaged eight to nine hours a day.

The best study of woman's role in Chinese industry was made by Miss Cora Deng in an unpublished thesis prepared in 1941, "Economic Status of Women in Industry in China." She was Industrial Secretary of the Y.W.C.A. and had worked among the factory girls for ten years. During four or five months of 1937, an intensive study was made of 368 women and girls employed in 102 Shanghai factories, representing 19 different kinds of industry. They were selected from Y.W.C.A. classes.

Miss Deng found that 42.4 per cent of the girls were between 18 and 21 years of age; 25.3 per cent between 14 and 17; 16.6 per cent between 22 and 25. Of the total, 84.3 per cent were from 14 to 25 years of age. The median age was 19. Only two of the girls were 12. Of the total, 83 per cent were single and 16.5 per cent married.

Monthly wages [9] ranged from $11 to $20.99 as an average; the median was $14.50 and the average $14.75. Of the total 42 per cent ranged from $11 to $15.99 monthly, and 25 per cent from $16 to $20.99 (two-thirds or 67 per cent of the group). The highest

[7] *Standard of Living of Shanghai Laborers,* Bureau of Social Affairs, City Government of Greater Shanghai, 1934, pp. 86-87.

[8] *Nankai University Weekly Statistical Service,* IV, No. 9, March 2, 1931, 53.

[9] Miss Deng gives the exchange rate for 1937 as approximately $3 for $1 U.S.

17

paid individual received $50 a month in a foreign tobacco company. The highest average individual wage per month was $42 in a tobacco factory. Tobacco workers were the highest paid in the field of industrial employment in Shanghai.

These wages were much higher as compared with 21 girls in hand workshops at the same time. None earned above $13 to $14.99 per month.

Among cotton mill workers, both spinning and weaving, the individual median monthly wage was found to be $14.50—exactly representative of the whole group, which as a whole earned $14.50 a month.

If we take these figures as representative, the average Chinese woman worker before the war was an unmarried girl of 19, receiving $14.50 a month (U. S. $4.83). She probably could not read nor write. "The women and girls of this study were generally without education. For the few who were able to read there were almost no newspapers or magazines or books to read," Miss Deng reported.

I must add a footnote here, however, to clarify the picture, that I talked with several of these same girls in Shanghai a few months after the survey was made, and went to classes and discussion groups among similar factory girls. I was amazed at their knowledge and intelligence and how they kept up with the news. Several had read the translation of my husband's book *Red Star Over China*, for example, and knew all about the subject. They also knew all about Han Ying's guerrillas who were operating near Shanghai, and later on quite a number joined these guerrillas. The few who were able to read seemed to keep the others well informed. I venture to remark that two or three of those particular ones I talked with were a little in advance of the average American girl of nineteen in progressive political ideas.

(3) Unlike most capitalist countries where labor movements have recently developed, China has a large number of handicraft workers.[10] Nor are they to be ignored in the story of organized labor. While labor in the cities had its spectacular successes and defeats, primarily as a semi-colonial movement against imperialism, within the framework of infant capitalist development, another process has been going on against feudalism in the villages and towns. By

[10] One study of small-scale industry is given in *Land and Labour in China,* by R. H. Tawney. Others have been made by Nankai University researchers.

18

the end of 1926 and early 1927 organization had only begun to reach the handicraft workers, notably in Hunan and Hupeh, where *hsien* unions had begun to affiliate with the provincial federation. Even so thousands among the 2,800,000 union members had already been organized. The handicraft workers were among the strongest leading elements in the Soviet movement for ten years, and are now active in the anti-Japanese movement in guerrilla areas. Among the 300,000 men and 10,000 women in the Soviet trade unions in 1934, a large percentage were handicraft workers. Others then swelled the ranks of the Red armies, as now the present guerrilla forces. Of the million labor union members claimed for the guerrilla areas in 1944, probably at least 25 per cent are handicraft workers, 20 per cent to 25 per cent "industrial workers," and the rest agricultural wage laborers.

Another interesting development is the Chinese Industrial Co-operatives, which, though originally led by engineers and advanced industrial workers, on the whole represents the handicraft type of industry in a newly organized modern form.

At present in Free China and guerrilla areas, the handicraft worker is the base of the labor force, and this subject takes on new interest since these areas were cut off from the industrial cities by the Japanese.

It was and is impossible remotely to estimate the number of handicraft workers in China. These industries were disintegrating long before 1922 as imported goods came in, and factories were established. Yet as one travels through interior towns and villages, the streets are lined with little workshops busily producing for the local market. Augusta Wagner believed in 1938 that "for her manufactures China relies chiefly on handicraft production." Rewi Alley, who spent several summers walking through the countryside and studying handicrafts, always told me that decline in handicrafts was proceeding rapidly.

One must always remember, however, that even city workshops used handicraft methods. The Ministry of Industries reported in 1933 one figure of 370,731 "factories," employing 2,190,409 workers, and further that the Factory Act could apply only to 2,787 factories and 786,716 workers (i.e., those which employed over 30 workers or used motive power). Even this is considered an overstatement by most authorities.

A brave attempt was made by Su Chao-jen in 1927, estimating the handicraft workers as 12,160,000. Another was published by a Kuomintang magazine in 1931,[11] presumably from some kind of government estimate, which I include here for what it may be worth:

NUMBER OF HANDICRAFT WORKERS IN CHINA

Spinning and weaving workers	320,000
Native miners	600,000
Building workers	600,000
Tailors	850,000
Tea workers	350,000
Net workers	80,000
Straw hat braiders	120,000
Porcelain workers	250,000
Firecracker workers	200,000
Barbers	240,000
Metal smiths	160,000
Shoemakers	300,000
Paper makers	150,000
Coolies	1,200,000
Salt workers	420,000
Rice sellers	240,000
Shop employees and apprentices	1,600,000
Boatmen	1,200,000
Printers	80,000
Other handicraft workers	3,000,000
Total	11,960,000

4. PRELIMINARY STAGE: TO 1922

In general, until 1920 and 1921 the workers were groping in the dark for new forms of organization to meet their needs and the rising cost of living. The old type of mutual welfare society was a common method, aside from the guild. In 1919 and especially in 1920 and 1921 many workers' clubs were organized in China, for educational and welfare purposes ostensibly, but also for group co-operation and protection. These were the real forerunners of the labor union movement, especially among the unorganized work-

[11] Taken from *The Way of Light*, Shanghai, April 16, 1931, and quoted in Lowe Chuan-hua, *Facing Labor Issues in China*, 1933.

ers who had no guild background. At the same time, circles for the study of Marxism, labor problems and other revolutionary theories were in vogue among the students and intellectuals and they began to make contacts with the workers.

Strikes reported before 1922 were frequently strikes among the guilds, sometimes referred to carelessly as "unions" by Chinese writers. For example, I note that the mechanics' guild in the south is often called a "union," though it did not even change its name until 1926.

Actually, in Canton in 1923 there were only 80 unions, and Hong Kong had only 100 unions in 1925. In both cases, many guilds were included as "unions" by Chinese writers. Such figures included all kinds of organizations, some of which were still guilds and mutual benefit societies not only in fact but in name, especially in Canton where handicrafts predominated. Others were the *"hui,"* or societies, organized among all classes of the population for various purposes. Some were temporary strike committees or workers' clubs that may have called themselves "unions." The wave of strikes in 1919 included merchants' guilds as well as employers and employees in other guilds, and unorganized workers.

The earliest strike reported in a modern industry occurred in 1912 among the workers on the Tsing-yang Railway on the Lunghai line. In 1912, following the fall of the Manchu dynasty, Kuomintang members tried to organize a "National Labor Party" which had 700 members in Tongshan, chiefly among the Kwangtung Guild workers who had emigrated from the south. In the same year, however, the leaders were expelled and the party dissolved. The railway workers and a few rickshamen in Peking were said to have been organized by students and teachers in Peking. The first ricksha pullers' union, however, was organized by a lawyer, Ssŭ Yang, in Hankow in 1920. In 1916 an attempt was also made to create a "Farmers' and Laborers' Federation" in Shanghai by "a Kuomintang leader returned from Russia in 1916," according to one reference, but it came to nothing.

In 1919 came the first conscious semi-organized stirrings of labor, influenced by the May Fourth student movement in Peking. In this year an attempt was made to organize employees of the Peking-Mukden railway and the Kailan mines, and several strikes occurred in the north. However, in 1922 the Kailan workers were

21

still agitating for the right to form workers' clubs, not unions.

There was a general stoppage of work in Shanghai during four days in June, 1919, as a demonstration against the Peace Conference at Versailles. Strikes occurred in the Nantao and Chapei districts, and included the Commercial Press Guild, the workers of the Chung Hwa Book Company, the Nanyang Brothers, the British-American Tobacco Company, and some public utilities. Li Li-san reported: "As to the working class, we see in the Fourth of May Movement the beginnings of definite and conscious participation in the anti-imperialist struggle. So, for example, the Peking and Tongshan railway workers, the Shanghai seamen and wharf coolies and other sections of the Chinese proletariat played no inconsiderable part in that struggle." [12]

According to the figures of the time, about 6,500 workers took part in strikes in 1918, 91,500 in 1919, and 108,000 in 1921.

In one of the earliest articles on the subject in 1923,[13] it is stated that the "student agitation of the spring of 1919 led to the formation of 26 labour organizations ... It is said that some two hundred have been formed in Hongkong and three hundred in Canton in the last three or four years. ... In a list of 25 strikes in Canton in 1921, 19 led to increases in wages of from 15 to 50 per cent. ... There are more than 50 labour unions in Shanghai."

The year 1920 may be said to mark the first permanent type of modern labor union. Labor Day was first celebrated on May 1, 1920, in Shanghai, with a demonstration of workers and students. In that year or early in 1921 the "Chinese Seamen's Philanthropic Society" was reorganized into the "Chinese Seamen's Union." The first ricksha pullers' union was organized by Ssŭ Yang in Hankow, and others appeared on the scene. The "All-China Mechanics' Guild," first organized in 1909, in Canton, did not change its name to the "Kwangtung Mechanics Union" until 1926, and was still a guild in policies at that time. The "Commercial Press Guild," formed in 1917, did not become the "Commercial Press Employees' Union" until June 21, 1925. The B.A.T. Company workers had only a recreation club until its union was formed in 1925.

[12] Report on the Labor Movement in China, "Proceedings of the Pan-Pacific Trade Union Conference," Hankow, 1927, p. 11.

[13] "Labour and Industry in China," by W. T. Zung and J. B. Tayler, *International Labour Review,* July, 1923.

During 1920 the first significant strike in south China occurred, on April 20, known as the "Hong Kong Mechanics' Strike," in which about 9,000 workers took part. This was directed against the British, and wage increases of from 20 per cent to 32 per cent were won. It was organized by the Hong Kong Chinese Engineering Institution, an affiliate of the All-China Mechanics' Guild in Canton, which had been reorganized in June, 1918, to include workers in Hong Kong as well as Canton, and Chinese in the South Sea areas.

Until 1921 and 1922, when students began to return from abroad, only a few Chinese knew the principles of modern union organization. Strikes in China, even very large ones, up to the present have been frequently organized either spontaneously or by a few individuals, without any union or permanent type of organization, the "ringleaders" being often kept secret from the employers and police. Sometimes the demands are presented and negotiations carried on through "third parties." In other cases, strikes have been organized by the Kuomintang or Communists through their own party setup without separate workers' organizations.

A systematic program for unionizing labor along modern lines did not come into effect until 1921 and 1922, when the "Secretariat of the China Labor Organization," which had been created by the Communists for this purpose, planned and directed the strike movement of 1922. Previously, labor agitation had been carried on mostly by individuals, not always agreed on policies. By 1919 Professor Ch'ên Tu-hsiu and his close followers of the famous "New Youth" magazine already considered themselves Marxists. Early in 1920, Ch'ên Tu-hsiu gathered together in Shanghai a group of seven, later fifty, people who called themselves Communists. At the same time, other groups were formed in Peking under Li Ta-chao, Teng Chung-hsia and Chang Kuo-t'ao; in Hankow under Teng Pi-wu and Chen Tan-chiu; in Hunan by Mao Tsê-tung [14] and others, and later in other places.

---

[14] Mao Tsê-tung stated: "In the winter of 1920, I organized workers politically, for the first time, and began to be guided in this by the influence of Marxist theory and the history of the Russian Revolution. During my second visit to Peking I had read much about the events in Russia, and had eagerly sought out what little Communist literature was then available in Chinese." *Red Star Over China,* by Edgar Snow.

The Shanghai group published a newspaper for workers in 1920, the first of its kind, and also began organizing unions among mechanics, printers and textile workers during subsequent months. In July, 1921, the First Congress of the Chinese Communist Party was held in Shanghai, marking the founding of that party. Some of these "Communists" were anarchists, and the Canton branch was in their hands for a while, attempting to carry on activities among labor in Canton. In 1920 anarchists had also organized a big strike in a Changsha textile mill. Their policies, however, did not fit in with either the old guild tradition in Canton, nor with the disciplined unionism advocated by the Communists. Some broke away from the Communist Party, others were expelled, and little was heard of their activities among labor after 1921.

The Socialist Youth had been formed in 1918 among students and this joined the Communist Youth International in 1920, after which it began to recruit workers in its membership. At the First Congress of Youth Leagues held in Canton in May, 1922, the Youth Leagues had a membership of 4,000, including working-class members. These young people had been active in the 1919 movement.

During all this time and until 1924 and 1925, the Kuomintang had had little to do with organizing the modern labor movement or the youth movement, having worked with guilds chiefly in the south. It was considered an "old-fashioned" apparatus and the young people had formed innumerable "Hsin Min Hsüeh Hui" and societies of their own, groping for a national form of activity. Not until the radical reorganization of the Kuomintang in 1924 were the students or labor recruited under its banner. In the meantime, however, Sun Yat-sen had always had connections chiefly in a conspiratorial relationship with the old *pongs* and *hongs,* both those overseas and in Canton. Sun Yat-sen had never ignored labor but was merely not alive to its possibilities until he and Liao Chung-k'ai were influenced by the Marxists. For example, he could have made good use of the railway strikes of 1922 had he realized their possibilities.

Sun Yat-sen had early connections with two labor organizations in particular, one among seamen and the other in Canton and Hong Kong. In 1914 he established a branch of his party among Chinese seamen on foreign ships who helped in carrying messages overseas for the revolutionaries, and later sponsored the Seamen's Mutual Benefit Society and the formation of the Chinese Seamen's Union in 1920. He also supported the Hong Kong Seamen's Strike in 1922.

The other connection was with the Mechanics' Guild and railway workers in Canton and Hong Kong. From 1920 to 1923 the mechanics and railway workers of Canton supported the Kuomintang in its attempts to control the city. The Hong Kong Mechanics' Strike in 1920 was also supported by Sun Yat-sen.

Curiously enough, one of the main inspirations for effective modern forms of labor organization among Chinese originated in France, a direct result of the World War. China sent a Labor Corps [15] of about 140,000 workers to France as her contribution to the Allied war effort. These were mostly "Shantung coolies," noted at home for their strength and endurance, but included also a number of skilled workers. These were recruited by the British government under contract for three years of non-military service on a ten-hour day. They were employed by the British at the rate ` of from 1 to 1.50 francs per day, and accounts were also established for them in China for an additional Ch. $10 to $15 monthly. The first contingent left Weihaiwei January 18, 1917, and the second a month later. The initial effect was the voluntary cutting off of queues, presently followed by other modern ideas.

In January, 1920, a Labor Federation for Chinese Workers in France was registered with the French government. It had 6,000 members and 36 branches with headquarters at Paris. In the meantime, other laborers already returned to China formed the Chinese Returned Laborers' Association in Shanghai in September, 1919. (In 1920 there was also in Canton the Chinese Overseas Labor Association, started in 1917.) Many of these laborers who returned from France with new ideas and a knowledge of the outside world served as a leavening agent in the rise of the labor movement at home. One of them, for example, whom I met later, Ho Ch'ang-kung, became an active labor organizer and was in 1937 one of the directors of K'ang Ta University in Yenan.

About the same time a group of Chinese students who later played leading roles in promoting labor unions in China were

[15] A reference for this is "The Story of the Chinese Labor Corps," by B. Manico Gull, *The Far Eastern Review,* April, 1918, XV, No. 4, 125.

trained in France. These included Chou En-lai, Li Li-san, Lo Man, Miss Tsai Chang, Li Fu-chen, Nieh Jung-chen, and Fu Chung, who are still alive. Others executed after 1927 were Tsai Ho-sheng, Miss Hsiang Chin-yü, the two sons of Ch'ên Tu-hsiu—Ch'ên Chao-nien and Ch'ên Yen-nien—Miss Kuo Nung-chen, and Chao Shih-yen.

These students went to France as part of a "work-and-study in France" project for poor students organized by Mao Tsê-tung and Tsai Ho-sheng in 1919. Studying part time, they worked in factories and joined unions. There were 3,000 of these work-and-study students in France after the war, aside from other independent students and those sent by the Chinese government and the Boxer Indemnity. The majority of the work-and-study students were political-minded, and their leaders were divided at first into three factions, Socialists, Anarchists and Social-Democrats. The active Socialists became Communists after that party was formed in China in 1921, and this movement was soon absorbed by them, together with a majority of the Anarchists and some of the Social Democrats. The other Anarchists and Social Democrats apparently did not transplant to Chinese soil successfully, and took little interest in the labor movement, with the result that their influence was felt only in intellectual circles. However, many were active as individuals in the 1925-27 revolution, though third party attempts were doomed to failure after 1924.

In 1923 the Chinese Communist Party branch in France had 500 members, mostly workers, according to Miss Tsai Chang, who gave me this information. Upon their return to China they provided a nucleus more or less experienced in organizing for the Chinese labor movement. In 1922, 104 left-wing leaders of the work-and-study students were ordered back to China by the French police after a demonstration of one thousand Chinese students which they had led. They seem to have wasted little time after their arrival.

Previous to this a few other students with ideas about organizing labor had returned from France and the U.S.S.R.[16]

[16] An article, "Communist Policy and the Chinese National Revolution," by Maurice T. Price, *Annals of the American Academy of Political and Social Sciences,* Vol. 152, Nov., 1930, states that "From 1920 on, individual students were selected and sent to Russia in batches of at least sixty per year." By January 1, 1922, the university in Moscow had 587 Chinese students, he says.

II. THE FIRST STAGE OF THE CHINESE LABOR MOVEMENT: FROM 1922 TO FEBRUARY 7, 1923

THE FIRST stage of the organized national labor movement in China began with the Hong Kong Seamen's Strike in January, 1922, and ended with the suppression of the railway strike on February 7, 1923, known in China as "Wu Pei-fu's Massacre of Railway Workers," or sometimes as the "Pinhan Incident." This was the high tide of the labor movement prior to the 1925-1927 revolutionary period.

The Hong Kong Seamen's Strike, which lasted fifty days, was led by Su Chao-jen and Lin Wei-ming, two seamen who achieved their fame as labor leaders during this strike. Lin Wei-ming was later elected first chairman of the All-China Labor Federation and Su Chao-jen his successor in 1926. Chinese seamen had never received equal pay with foreign seamen. In 1919 foreign seamen had received a 15 per cent increase, while most of the Chinese were still paid at prewar rates. The cost of living in Hong Kong after the war had risen higher than in other cities in China. Since 1914 the cost of polished rice in Hong Kong had risen 155 per cent; in Shanghai 125 per cent.

The Chinese Seamen's Union had been organized early in 1921. It set up a committee to study the wage problem in 1921. About the end of that year the union sent two requests to the shipping companies for wage increases; both were ignored. On January 12, 1922, the union demanded a reply to its third petition within twenty-four hours. Receiving no satisfaction, on January 13 about 1,500 deck hands and stokers went on strike. In response to this the British Governor of Hong Kong declared the union an unlawful organization and ordered its sign-board taken down. This caused a general sympathetic strike in the colony. By January 27, 30,000 workers were on strike, representing most of the trades of the city. By February 1, about 50,000 were involved, including domestic and office employees, especially in British homes and firms. This labor activity, or rather inactivity, affected fourteen

27

steamship companies and 166 vessels. Negotiations resulted in an agreement on March 5, 1922, granting a wage raise of 20 per cent to 30 per cent. The Governor also rescinded his order against the Seamen's Union. The union's sign-board was replaced by the same policeman who had taken it down. (This was one of the fine points of the controversy.)

This strike had repercussions even in the House of Commons in London where Winston Churchill reported on it, defending the Governor, and was attacked by labor M. P.'s. Hong Kong, of course, was one of the great shipping ports in the Orient, and the life of the city had been practically paralyzed during the strike. Teng Chung-hsia said that 200,000 Chinese celebrated the victory of the strike on the streets of Hong Kong.

One of the important results of this strike was to interest the Kuomintang in labor for anti-British purposes. According to Teng Chung-hsia it was not organized by the Kuomintang, but received financial aid ($100,000) from Li Chi-sen after it was started by militants among the seamen.

Following the strike, the Kwangtung Provincial authorities repealed the local application of Article 224 of the Provisional Penal Code of the Peking government which had in effect made strikes illegal, providing that: "When workmen in the same business combine in a strike, the ringleader shall be punished with imprisonment for a period of not severer than the fourth degree or detention or a fine of not more than 300 dollars, and the others shall each be punished with detention or a fine of not more than 30 dollars."

The Hong Kong strike was also notable for the fact that workmen on the railways supported it with strike funds and a sympathetic attitude, marking a new feeling of solidarity among labor. Northern railway workers on the Peking-Hankow, Tientsin-Pukow, Peking-Mukden, and Peking-Suiyuan railways contributed one day's pay to the support of the seamen's strike.

Though many strikes occurred in 1922 (Chen Ta reported incomplete figures of 91 strikes during the year, in which 139,050 workers were involved in 30 cases reported), the important feature of this first stage of the labor movement was the railway strikes which laid the foundation for the whole national development that followed. The railway workers were the connecting link between activities in north, south, and central China, carrying messages, and keeping the various cities informed of all labor developments. These railway strikes were organized by the Labor Secretariat with headquarters in Shanghai.

On May 1, 1922, the Secretariat called the First Labor Congress in China. It was attended by over one hundred delegates, from Hong Kong, Hankow, Changhsintien, Hunan and other places, representing approximately 70,000 workers, according to information given by Liu Hsiao-ch'i, who was a member of the Secretariat and helped to organize the congress.[1] The Congress drew up a manifesto supporting the eight-hour day, but failed to establish a national labor organization. It voted that the next conference would be called by the Secretariat. Another point was that the delegates decided unions should be organized on an industrial rather than a craft basis whenever possible. This was one reason for the strength of the movement that developed later.

This Secretariat was rather interesting. It had been organized by the Chinese Communists either in 1920 or 1921. I have not been able to ascertain the exact date, but apparently it was created before the Communist Party was officially founded in July, 1921, and later reorganized. Again nobody seems to know the day of the month for this latter event, and it has been lost to history.[2]

The Secretariat in 1922 was made up "mostly of students just returned from the U.S.S.R. and France, with some from Peking colleges." Liu Hsiao-ch'i did not tell me the exact number, nor all the names, but said they were all Communist Party members and

[1] Figures seldom agree in China. According to Chen, whose sources were second-hand: "The trade union movement of a really national character dates from the First National Labor Conference held at Canton from 1 to 6 May, 1922, at which 162 delegates from 200 unions in 12 cities, representing about 400,000 workers were present." See "The Labor Movement in China," by Ta Chen, *International Labor Review,* March, 1927. It is probable that the newspaper accounts exaggerated the strength of the Congress, and were later corrected by Liu Hsiao-ch'i. This frequently happens in China.

[2] P. Miff, in *Heroic China,* 1937, is vague on the point, saying only "July, 1921" (p. 15). In his autobiography Mao Tsê-tung says only that "In May of 1921, I went to Shanghai to attend the foundation meeting of the Communist Party." Nobody that I asked in Yenan could give me the exact date. Communist groups, however, had been organized in 1920, and a representative of the Comintern arrived in China that year to help form a national party. This was M. Marlin, and I believe it was during his visit to Shanghai that the Labor Secretariat was formed in 1920 or early 1921.

that it included himself, Chang Kuo-t'ao, Teng Chung-hsia, and Han Ying. These individuals traveled all over the country in 1922, teaching methods of labor organization and organizing the strike movement.

Some of these Secretariat members had eventful careers later. Liu Hsiao-ch'i (a student from Moscow) became Commissioner of Labor of the Soviet Government in China, and is today the leading labor expert of the Chinese Communists. Chang Kuo-t'ao (also a student from Moscow) became head of the Soviet government in Ouyüwan and Szechuan but resigned from the Communist Party about 1939. I do not know what happened to Teng Chung-hsia, except that he led the last big strike in Shanghai of 100,000 workers at the end of 1927 and was still active in the labor movement in 1930.

So far as I know, the only person of working-class origin on the Secretariat at that time was Han Ying, one of the most famous of all China's labor leaders. He became Vice-chairman of the Central Soviet government in 1931, and in 1938 formed the New Fourth Army in central China, which organized guerrilla acitivities against the Japanese in that area. In 1941 he was captured and killed when Chinese Government troops attacked the New Fourth Army and killed 4,000 of his men.

The Secretariat had mapped out a systematic program of labor activities, and immediately after the Labor Congress on May 1, operations began. At the end of May, 1922, a strike was organized among the Peking-Hankow (Pinhan) Railway workers on the northern section from Changhsintien to Chengchow. Within three days this was successful. Railway officials agreed to the demand for a wage increase of $1.00 a month and permission to form workers' clubs. (In October, 1921, a workers' school had been organized in Changhsintien, and, at the end of the year, a club was formed.)

This success electrified the workers along the whole railway system, which was owned by the government. Other railway strikes occurred in later months: at Chent'ai (on the section from Shihchiachuang to Taiyuan), on the Lunghai line, on the Chinpu line, on the Chiaochi, Canton-Hankow, and other railways. All were easily victorious.

The main demands of these railway strikes were for wage increases and regular payment, double wages at New Year time, and recognition of unions. They also demanded that the hiring and discharge of workmen must have the approval of the union.

The success of the railway strikes stimulated city workers, especially in Hankow and Changsha, where many factories went on strike. During 1922 and early 1923 there were over a hundred strikes throughout the country, and nearly all were successful. This was the height of the pre-1925 movement. There were now 91 unions in China, representing 150,000 organized workers, and the movement was unified and directed by the Secretariat, according to Liu Hsiao-ch'i.[3] He probably included locals under the general unions that had been formed, rather than listing them separately.

It is very difficult to secure useful figures on this early period, and none are comprehensive. One trouble is that careless writers include all kinds of guilds and clubs as "unions," so their figures are usually higher than those of Left-wing sources who place a stricter interpretation on the word "union." Chen Ta reported 80 unions in Canton in 1923. Another source[4] listed 50 unions in Shanghai at the end of 1923 with 84,000 members. In his autobiography Mao Tsê-tung said:[5]

"In May, 1922, the Hunan Party, of which I was then secretary, had already organized more than twenty trade-unions, among miners, railway workers, municipal employees, printers and workers in the Government Mint. A vigorous labor movement began that winter. The work of the Communist Party was then concentrated mainly on students and workers, and very little was done among the peasants. Most of the big mines were organized and virtually all the students. . . . That spring there were many strikes for better wages and better treatment and recognition of the labor unions. Most of these were successful. On May 1, a general strike was called in Hunan, and this marked the achievement of unprecedented strength in the labor movement of China."

One strike that occurred in Shanghai in 1922 was especially

[3] P. Miff says there were 230,000 workers organized in 1923.

[4] *Papers Respecting Labor Conditions in China,* China No. 1, 1925, Cmd 2442, London, H. M. Stationery Office.

[5] *Red Star Over China,* by Edgar Snow.

notable as it was one of the first important actions of women workers. Twenty thousand women workers of twenty-four silk filatures in Chapei, joined by workers in the International Settlement, went on strike demanding the ten-hour day (they were then working fourteen hours), and an increase of five cents a day in wages. For three days they demonstrated in the streets with banners. Five of the leaders were arrested, and, in fear that they would be executed, the strike was called off. Hours were reduced to eleven and a half temporarily, but were soon increased again to the old fourteen-hour schedule. The wage increase was not granted.

The center of labor activities in factories and plants, however, was Hupeh. Lowe Chuan-hua [6] quotes a statement that in 1922 the Hupeh Provincial Labor Federation had 24 unions with 400,000 members. He also states that the strike at the Ping-hsiang Colliery near Hankow, September 15-18, 1922, involved 20,000 workers, although I have not seen this figure elsewhere.

Next to the railway workers, the Hanyehp'ing Union, an industrial union, near Hankow (the Pittsburgh of China), was the most powerful in the country. It was organized before 1922 by Li Li-san, Han Ying, Tsai Shu-fan and others. Tsai Shu-fan told me the story of his experiences there when I talked with him. This included the Tayeh and Anyang iron mines and the Hanyang Works (collectively known as the "Hanyehp'ing Mines"), and had about "7,000 workers militantly organized," according to Han Ying, "led by the advanced steel workers of the Hanyang Works." The subsequent history of the Hanyehp'ing miners is interesting. When these mines closed down in 1925 (though they were partially reopened some time later), thousands of miners, iron and steel workers, machinists, etc. were thrown out of work. Many of them joined the revolutionary armies during 1925-1927, concentrated in the famous "Ironsides" Fourth Army, the best army of the Northern Expedition. Yeh T'ing's division of the Fourth Army was almost entirely composed of them. In 1927 this division formed the main force of the first Red Army, and scattered Hanyehp'ing workers gathered to reinforce the Red Troops. In 1938 Han Ying and Yeh T'ing organized the "New Fourth Army," named for the original "Ironsides" Fourth Army, to fight the Japanese, and led

[6] *Facing Labor Issues in China,* by Lowe Chuan-hua.

32

guerrilla warfare in central China. Some of the Hanyehp'ing workers carried on all through the civil war and are now fighting against the Japanese, although most of them were killed in 1927 and after.

Prior to 1925, workers' clubs were a very essential part of labor organization. These existed nominally for cultural and recreational purposes, but actually they were a center of labor activities and political education. The club was formed first and the union followed. Nearly all the early demands included the right to form clubs.

Of the many individual strikes little record remains. One article by T. Y. Chang [7] is interesting but of dubious accuracy. For example, he says the Hong Kong Seamen's strike of 1922 involved 2,500 workers, whereas the figure given elsewhere is from 30,000 to 65,000. For what it is worth, however, I shall summarize the information given:

T. Y. Chang says that in Shanghai, "laborers in this city called 152 strikes from 1920 to 1922. Three of these were important. On June 12, 1920, 1,000 Chinese carpenters struck for a week against the encroachment of other unions (?) into their trade jurisdictions." The second was a strike of 1,000 workers on the French tramways, March 3, 1921, tying up traffic four days. The third, involving "10,000 cotton mill and cigarette workers broke out in the middle of 1923." It was caused by the closing of the Pootung Weavers' Club. The strike resulted in forcing the reopening of the club.

As to central China, he says there were six important strikes from 1920 to 1924: (1) The Hankow Iron and Steel Company workers started to organize in July, 1922, and 72 workers were dismissed. A strike of 1,000 workers was called, resulting in securing union recognition and reinstatement of the 72 who had been dismissed. (2) In August, 1922, the Hanyang Arsenal workers went on strike demanding shorter hours. As they supplied a large part of the ammunition and military goods for use in North China, it was ended by bayonets; strikers were killed, and the plant damaged to the extent of $6,000,000. (3) The Ping-hsiang Colliery strike of 10,000 men in September, 1922, near Hankow,

[7] "Five Years of Significant Strikes," *Chinese Students' Monthly*, XXI, No. 8, June, 1926, 19.

33

was caused by low wages, flogging by the foremen, lack of an organ to voice the workers' grievances, and influence on the workers of other near-by strikes. The employers accepted all of the seventeen demands presented; increased wages from 25 per cent to 100 per cent; and the company provided $10,000 for a club building and a monthly subsidy of $200. (4) At the beginning of July, 1922, 1,500 weavers in small firms in Hunan carried out three strikes which failed, and the owners closed down the businesses. (5) In November, 1922, over 6,000 workers of the Watermouth Mining Company in Hunan walked out, making eighteen demands, including establishment of a clubhouse and wage increases. A deadlock ensued for twenty to twenty-five days, when the provincial government mediated in adjusting the demands and ordered the employers to build the clubhouse. (6) "The most notorious strike in the annals of the Chinese labor movement was the strike in the Anyuang Mine and Chuping Railroad in September (1922), involving an overwhelming body of 20,000 miners and 1,500 railway workers. Witnessing the victory won by the workers of the Hanyang Iron and Steel Company at a strike for establishing their union clubhouse, the workers in Anyuang and Chuping started to organize themselves and built a clubhouse which was only another name for the union." The superintendent tried to close the club by force, and a strike resulted making thirteen demands, including wage increases and union recognition. The work stoppage lasted four days and the union won.

T. Y. Chang also mentions the railway strikes. In October, 1921, 800 workers on a branch of the Canton-Hankow-Szechuan railways petitioned for wage increases which were refused. The resulting strike lasted a month, and in November their seventeen demands were granted in modified terms. The labor superintendent on the Canton-Hankow line was very "unreasonable," so 5,000 workers went on strike early in September, 1922. Their six demands included dismissal of the superintendent. After sixteen days of struggle the railway management "totally yielded." In the same year, the Chentai railway workers made nine demands on the management which were refused; 2,000 men then walked out with four additional demands. They received sympathetic support from the students and other unions. Through mediation of officials all the demands, in modified form, were granted after twelve days of

34

industrial war. Wage increases of from 7 per cent to 20 per cent were won.[8]

An important strike occurred in North China in 1922 at the Kailan mines. Chen Ta [9] gave the background on this situation as follows: Tongshan, near Tientsin, was the most important industrial district in north China, the principal industries being mining, railroad engineering works, cement, ceramics and rugs. The Tongshan mines were the first in China to use modern methods, having been instituted in 1878. According to Chen, workers' clubs were organized at the mines at the end of the Manchu dynasty, and there was a Kwangtung Guild for social purposes, created for the southern workers who had migrated to this region for employment. When the 1911 revolution was successful, the Kuomintang encouraged the workers (the Kwangtung Guild being a point of contact), and organized a Labor Party with headquarters in Shanghai, but its membership was in Tongshan (700 members). In 1912 the leaders were expelled and the Labor Party dissolved. In 1912 the name "Kailan Mining Administration" was taken for the mines, after a merger of Chinese and British ownership. The K.M.A. operated five mines along the Peiping-Mukden railway, with an annual output of 4,500,000 tons and a labor force of 20,000 men.

Around 1919 employees of the Peking-Mukden railway line and of the K.M.A. "began to organize along the lines of the modern labor union. A series of strikes followed. In 1920 the

[8] T. Y. Chang mentions the Peking-Hankow strike, saying that up to the beginning of 1923, all railway workers were organized by sections or shops, and the Peking-Hankow line was the longest, having 22 sections. At the meeting on February 1, 1923, 130 representatives were present from 35 local unions, 65 from unions of other railway lines, and 30 representatives from newspapers and students. Three were killed on the day of the meeting. Four days later the whole line was on strike involving 7,000 workers, and traffic was halted. All union offices along the lines were closed and "a thousand strikers were discharged in addition to many who were injured and killed during the strike." (There were 20,000 involved in this strike, according to all other authorities.—N.W.)

[9] "Labor in China During the Civil Wars," by Ta Chen, *Monthly Labor Review*, XXXI, July, 1930, 1. *See also Analysis of Strikes in China 1918-1926*, by Chen Ta. It may be noted that Mr. Chen is not always well informed on organizational and political facts, as most of his information was derived from newspaper reports.

employees of the Kailan Mining Administration struck and won a victory."

In 1922, from October 10 to November 16, a strike occurred at the Kailan mines. This began with a strike in the Shanhaikuan and Tongshan machine shops on October 10, supported by other workers in the Kailan Mining Administration. The demands were: (1) that the Administration recognize the workers' club being formed and (2) that no laborer could be dismissed without the approval of that club. By October 23, four mines were on strike and the Ma Chia Kow mine joined on October 26. About 20,000 workers were now on strike. Two hundred armed policemen were sent from Tientsin. On October 25 a clash occurred in which several workers were killed, wounded, and arrested. Then a regiment of troops arrived. Communist literature was found among the strikers, and the students of the universities near by supported the strike. Railway workers held meetings to raise funds for supporting the Kailan strikers. Chen Ta reported that $16,000 was received from sympathizers in Peking, Tientsin, and Tongshan, including some from merchants; $10,000 came from Canton; and $20,000 from Shanghai and Hong Kong.

The economic loss was heavy, but finally the strike was settled by a 10 per cent increase in wages and work was resumed November 16. Liu Hsiao-ch'i told me that the British refused to recognize the right to form clubs or unions.

Now we come to the February 7 affair. In 1922 and 1923, Marshal Wu Pei-fu dominated the Peking government and considered the railways part of his military machine. He and the railway management had been flabbergasted at the new labor phenomenon during the successful railway strikes of 1922, which had astounded the whole country. Taken by surprise at first, they had no method of handling labor. By early 1923, however, he was determined on strong measures.

All the different railways had local unions, but the Peking-Hankow Railway workers were the strongest. This was almost a complete industrial union,[10] except that white collar workers were not included. All the workshops, trainmen and apprentices

[10] Others were not so well organized. For example, the Peking-Suiyuan workers had three separate unions, dividing the men in the workshops, the locomotive drivers and stokers, and signalmen and shunters, etc.

were included in the unions. Dues were paid at the rate of one-half a day's wage monthly.

The Peking-Hankow railway workers decided to form a general union and called a conference of Peking-Hankow locals to meet in Chengchow, Honan, February 1, 1923. The workers did a good deal of publicity in the newspapers and invited other unions to send delegates to the conference for moral support.[11] They sent four delegates to Wu Pei-fu to talk over the situation, but he refused to recognize them. "His attitude was not very threatening, however," Liu Hsiao-ch'i told me, "though he demanded that further organizational activities be stopped."

By the end of January all the delegates had arrived for the conference. On January 30, Wu Pei-fu informed the Chengchow authorities that all meetings without permission should be prohibited. On orders from Wu Pei-fu, soldiers and police surrounded the hall on February 1 and refused to permit the delegates to enter. They pushed through, however, after a struggle, and the meeting began. Presently, soldiers and police entered and arrested several delegates, striking down those who resisted. The meeting grew very excited and voted a strike to oppose the action of the authorities. The General Union of Peking-Hankow Railway Workers was successfully formed nevertheless, though its existence was kept secret from the authorities.

That same night, the leaders went to Hankow to organize a general strike all along the Peking-Hankow line. The secretariat gave orders to all the railway locals throughout the country to strike in support of the Peking-Hankow action, such as those on the Lunghai, the Chinpu, the Canton-Hankow railways and others.

The general strike, supported by about 20,000 railway workers, began February 4 and lasted until the ninth or tenth, when the newly formed General Union of Peking-Hankow Workers ordered cessation.

On February 7, 1923, the militarists began breaking the strike by closing down the union offices, and by resorting to armed force,

[11] Chen Ta reported that the February 1 conference included 130 representatives of 35 Peking-Hankow locals, and 65 representatives of other railway unions, as well as 60 representatives of newspapers and schools in other cities.

resulting in "Wu Pei-fu's Massacre of Railway Workers," as the incident was called.

Workers were arrested and killed at several railway stations. One of the bloodiest incidents was at Chang-an station near Hankow. The organizing center was kept secret from the authorities, but Chang-an still had an open branch union, so they thought this was the center of the whole Peking-Hankow movement. The head of the Chang-an union was Ling Ch'ang-ch'in, a Communist party member. Governor Hsiao Yao-nien ordered him to stop the strike and, when he refused, had him executed. Some ten thousand railway workers gathered to prevent Hsiao Yao-nien's troops from closing down the Chang-an union headquarters. About forty were killed and one hundred wounded in the struggle, according to Liu Hsiao-ch'i. At the same time, Ssŭ Yang, the Communist lawyer of Hankow who had organized the Ricksha Pullers' Union in 1920, was executed. At Chengchow several were reported killed and many wounded, and so on along the line. The total number is unknown.

After February 7, many railway unions were disorganized and workers' clubs destroyed by the suppression of the militarists. Active unionists were discharged and the leaders were plunged into despair from their previous high pitch of enthusiasm. Several betrayed the movement and opposed the Communists. The activities of the Secretariat went underground.

"One cause of the failure of the strike was that the workers were too cocksure and emotional because of their previous successes, and did not take care of themselves," Liu Hsiao-ch'i told me, "and another was that the Chinese authorities were learning from the foreigners in China how to beat strikes and unions, whereas previously they had had no experience."

This series of strikes caused the Peking government to decide on some modern labor legislation for the first time. The Labor Secretariat drew up a draft of the laws it wanted proposed and sent them to a session of Parliament in Peking through some liberal members of Parliament. Other pressure was brought to bear, and on March 29, 1923, the Provisional Factory Regulations were promulgated, but no attempt to enforce them was made.

The Secretariat also published many articles on the labor question in the newspapers and through these created public interest in the subject.

38

"In this first stage of the Chinese labor movement," Liu Hsiao-ch'i explained, "many advances were made, such as organizing the workers for struggle, creating unions and raising the political level of the working class. It also had many weak points. The organization of the Communist Party among the workers was weak and we did not use the conflicts between the ruling class to advantage. There were few political leaders among the workers themselves and nearly all the Secretariat members were intellectuals. Quarrels occurred among the Secretariat members. One group felt that heads of unions could be chosen from intellectuals; others opposed this. In this stage, too, the unions made the mistake of opposing the staffs (clerks, white-collar employees, etc.) of the railways and factories."

The sudden rise of the labor movement in 1922 took everyone by surprise. Neither the government bureaucrats, the militarists, nor private management had had any experience in handling unions or strikes. The only answer they knew was to call out troops and police, which had the effect of infuriating labor and increasing its political consciousness. The railway strikes of 1922 were actually a kind of *coup d'etat*. It took some time for the Chinese to learn methods of handling *organized* labor. In fact, they have never actually learned this method, but only how to handle *unorganized* labor. Conservative unionism has been a lost cause, therefore, on the whole. The recent Nazi "labor front" idea adopted in Chungking is still experimental, though it is partly modeled on the Japanese system and has been quite successful there in controlling Japanese labor.

The foreigners in China have been more efficient in handling labor troubles, but their record is not one to be proud of. The British tended to give economic concessions and thereby prevent unionization. The Japanese dormitory system has been very effective, literally imprisoning the workers.

III. SECOND STAGE: THE UNDER-GROUND PERIOD FROM 1923 TO EARLY 1925

In its second stage the main stream of the Chinese labor movement went underground and was secret. This period dates from the suppression of the railway strikes on February 7, 1923, to the May 30 Incident in Shanghai in 1925.

Due to war-lord control in the interior provinces, little open activity was possible except in Shanghai and Kwangtung. Nevertheless, though railway activities were ineffectual, about February, 1924, the General Union of Railway Workers was secretly organized in Peking—the first national union in China.

In Hunan labor activities were semi-open and comparatively active, led by Mao Tsê-tung and others. This was a peculiar situation in which the militarist in control, Tsao Heng-t'i, was utilized by the labor leaders for, with his feudal psychology, he saw little to choose between the merchant employers of the workshops and the workers themselves.

Liu Hsiao-ch'i told me that some time earlier Mao Tsê-tung and a few labor delegates had gone to Governor Tsao Heng-t'i and requested him to give protection to a labor movement. They explained the purposes of their plan and told him they were Socialists. He had never heard the word before, so it meant nothing to him. He felt that labor was no threat to his sovereignty. His real enemies were only rival militarists, and he feared nobody who did not have a gun in his hands. The Governor was impressed with the students and as a result of the interview agreed not to oppose their activities.

Thus during and following 1922 Hunan was a little world of its own in labor activities. The most active center was the An-yuang Mines, on the Hunan-Kiangsi border, where 20,000 miners had won a big strike in 1922. Here the organization of workers was very strong. Schools were founded, even for the miners' children, and educational work at the mines was carried on all during the 1923-1925 period.

40

One notable strike occurred in Hankow on September 15, 1924, when 8,000 ricksha pullers went on strike against the inauguration of a bus service in the city, which they felt would destroy their means of livelihood. After property of the bus company had been damaged by the strikers, the bus service was prohibited by the authorities and the rickshamen won a victory.

In Shanghai many strikes were conducted in cotton mills and textile factories after 1923, and organizational work proceeded, directed by the Labor Secretariat. It was reported that at the end of 1923 there were 50 labor unions in Shanghai with 84,000 members, as compared with 24 unions and 40,000 members at the end of 1922. By 1925, 100 unions were reported with 80,000 members.

The years between 1923 and early 1925 were a preparatory period for the revolutionary movement which burst out on May 30, 1925, and continued gathering momentum until the split in 1927.

"The real reason why the revolutionary movement after May 30 could begin was that the basis for it was laid in the railway workers' movement," Liu Hsiao-ch'i told me. "The second tide of the labor movement began after the Second Labor Congress on May 1, 1925. The political reasons were (1) that the unification of the Kuomintang and the Communist Party was achieved; (2) the sovereignty of Wu Pei-fu and Tsao Kun was broken and the workers' emotion rose, as they had oppressed labor severely; and (3) Sun Yat-sen came from Canton to Peking to discuss public problems with Tuan Chi-jui and the Communist Party was able to use the meetings to welcome him in order to organize the mass movement and do propaganda."

No attempt to hold a national labor congress was made after the first meeting on May Day of 1922. The Second Labor Congress opened at Canton on May 1, 1925. After this congress the Labor Secretariat stopped its work, and the Communists operated largely through the elected leaders of unions, many of whom had now joined their party. The Second Congress was not called by the Secretariat but by the four big unions, the General Union of Railway Workers, the Chinese Seamen's Union, the Hanyehp'ing Labor Union, and the General Labor Union of Canton. According to Liu Hsiao-ch'i, the two hundred or so delegates represented 200,000 organized workers. Other sources report that 230 delegates attended, representing 570,000 workers. The Congress passed reso-

41

lutions to organize an All-China Labor Federation; to join the Red International of Trade Unions (Profintern), and to unite with the peasant movement.

The All-China Labor Federation was immediately formed and elected its committee of twenty-five members, with the seaman, Lin Wei-ming, as chairman. National headquarters were established at Canton, with branches in Shanghai and the northern provinces. At the time this was broken and forced underground in 1927, it represented about 2,800,000 organized workers.

After the Hong Kong Seamen's Strike in 1922, labor activities were fairly open in Canton and were not suppressed as in other provinces. In the meantime important political changes were coming about in the national picture. Early in 1923 Dr. Sun Yat-sen gained firm control of Kwangtung Province in the south and started his government in Canton in opposition to the Peking regime under the northern war lords.

On January 20, 1924, the First National Congress of the Kuomintang, the Nationalist party, was called, resulting in a radical reorganization upon the recommendation of Dr. Sun.

A united front was made with the Communists on a basis of common allegiance to the new Three People's Principles of Nationalism, Democracy and Improvement of the People's Livelihood, as interpreted by Dr. Sun in lectures in Canton from January to August of 1924. Dr. Sun and the Kuomintang also built up co-operation with the Soviet Union, and Michael Borodin and other Soviet advisors helped in organizing the new revolutionary movement. In 1924 Whampoa Academy was established in Canton to train military leaders for the Northern Expedition against the northern militarists. Before the expedition was organized, however, Sun Yat-sen died of cancer on March 12, 1925.

The two principal leaders of the Kuomintang at that time, Sun Yat-sen and Liao Chung-k'ai, the latter Sun's closest friend and leader of the Left-wing Kuomintang, were sympathetic with labor and co-operated with the Communists on this issue, in contrast with the recalcitrant Right-wing attitude. Lowe Chuan-hua comments that: "During the second period (1920-1925), Red Labor unions began to grow by leaps and bounds, particularly in Kwangtung Province. It is true that as early as May, 1919, Dr. Sun Yat-sen himself had encouraged the formation of labor unions in

China and had given an appropriation to the well-known Communist labor leader, Tan Ping-san, to conduct propaganda activities and to secure the support of the labor organizations in the Nationalist Revolution, but labor unions could not function freely and did not acquire any centralized leadership until the Communists were admitted into the Kuomintang." [1]

Dr. Sun himself is said to have been personally responsible for the inauguration of a few labor unions in Canton. Liao Chung-k'ai was made head of the Kuomintang Labor Department in 1924, as well as being Political Director of Whampoa Academy. It was Liao, a veteran Kuomintang man, who had greatly influenced Sun Yat-sen in causing him to shift his previous policies of depending upon uneasy military and political liaisons with various groups, to a dependence upon labor and other mass movements in attempting to achieve the national revolution.

Tension between the Right, Left and Middle in the Kuomintang existed all during the period of Sun's Canton Government, and in August, 1925, Liao Chung-k'ai was assassinated by the Rightists in an attempt to break the Leftist control of the party and to prevent him from assuming the mantle of Dr. Sun, who had died six months earlier. This was a blow to the labor unions, who thereby lost their two best friends in the Kuomintang leadership during 1925. Since then, however, Madame Sun Yat-sen and Madame Liao Chung-k'ai, both political leaders in their own right and always friends, have persistently defended the rights of labor. Liao's son, Liao Chin-chih, had an active and interesting career organizing among the 30,000 Chinese seamen in Europe, which he once told me in detail. From 1938 to the fall of Hong Kong to the Japanese in 1941 he was the Eighth Route Army representative in Hong Kong.

The Kuomintang Congress in 1924, which reorganized that party and its platform, "adopted a resolution to instruct the Nationalist Government to enact labor laws, to improve labor conditions and to protect labor organizations. Consequently in November of the

[1] *Facing Labor Issues in China.*

Lowe Chuan-hua divided the stages of the Chinese labor movement as follows (p. 38) : "The development of organized labor in China may be conveniently divided into four periods : the embryonic state from 1911-1920; the period of recognition from 1920-1925 ; the period of rapid expansion from 1925-1927, and the period of retrenchment and reorganization from 1927-1933."

same year, Dr. Sun promulgated the Trade Union Regulations, which included:

"1. Recognition that trade unions and employers' associations are on an equal footing;

"2. Recognition of the principle of freedom of speech on the part of the trade unions;

"3. Recognition that trade unions shall have the right to conclude collective agreements with the employers;

"4. Recognition that in case of disputes a union shall have the right to ask the employers to set up a joint arbitration committee, and the right to apply to the proper administrative authorities to conduct an inquiry or institute arbitration proceedings;

"5. Recognition of the right to declare strikes;

"6. Recognition that trade unions shall have the right to participate with employers in regulating hours of work, working conditions and factory hygiene;

"7. Recognition of the principle that in disputes in a private industry, the Government authorities shall only investigate or arbitrate but shall not enforce decisions by compulsion;

"8. Guarantees to trade unions for the security of their property and belongings;

"9. Provision that the prohibition of meetings and of association contained in the Provisional Penal Code of 1912 and the law relating to the Preservation of Public Order of 1914 shall not be applicable to trade unions;

"10. Encouragement of the principle of organization by industry." [2]

May Day of 1924 was celebrated by mass parades of about one hundred thousand workers in Shanghai and some two hundred thousand in Canton.

Lowe Chuan-hua comments on this 1924-1925 period: "It was also during this time that labor organizations in China, which so far had been merely piecemeal and disjointed agitations, became consolidated into a national movement, nominally under the leadership of the Kuomintang but actually under the direction of such radical leaders as Liao Chung-k'ai, head of the Kuomintang Labor Department, Su Chao-jen, head of the Chinese Seamen's Union, Tan Ping-san and Li Lih-san."

[2] This quotation is from Lowe Chuan-hua, *Facing Labor Issues in China*.

44

IV.   THIRD STAGE: THE 1925-1927 REVOLUTION

THE NEXT tide of the Chinese labor movement rose from 1925 to 1927, stimulated by the leftward swing of the nationalist movement.

The opening shot of the revolutionary upsurge of 1925 was fired by the British during the famous May 30 Incident in Shanghai. This is the background: In January, 1925, the Labor Secretariat organized a strike in a Japanese-owned textile factory which lasted over a month. As a result the owners increased wages one-tenth but refused to recognize the right of the workers to form a union. The partial success of this strike, however, according to Liu Hsiao-ch'i of the Secretariat, made possible the subsequent rapid organization of textile workers in Shanghai. In the attempt at organizing that ensued, labor organizers were beaten in several factories, and in April one factory dismissed a number of such workers. The movement centered in the Hsiao Sah Tou factory district, where there were ten or more cotton mills owned mostly by Japanese and British. Each little incident created more and more indignation among the workers. "These foreigners, however, had had much experience in handling labor," Liu Hsiao-ch'i told me. "They blockaded the news and kept it secret. Later when the news got out, the students heard of it and made speeches so the story became known to the public."

The leader of the workers in the Hsiao Sah Tou district, Ku Tsen-fung, was murdered by the Japanese foreman of one of the Nagai Wata Kaisha cotton mills. As he was popular and well known, this aroused great resentment, and a big protest strike was called in the mill, this being the main cause, although economic demands were also made. The strike occurred on May 4, and by May 15 five cotton mills had joined in a sympathetic strike movement. About ten workers were wounded in the violence that followed.

The Shanghai students now entered the fray, making speeches on the streets, organizing demonstrations and collecting funds for the strikers. On May 30, a demonstration, which was trying to secure the release of several who had been arrested, was fired on

45

by British police on Nanking Road and twelve students and workmen were killed. Next day the newspapers carried the story, and the whole country heard of it with great excitement.

This was the signal for a spontaneous national rise of revolutionary feeling. The shooting roused the students and urban middle class to join the nationalist movement in force. In Shanghai a Federation of Workers, Students, and Merchants was organized which formulated seventeen demands against the authorities. The Shanghai General Labor Union was created, which directed the strike movement in the city, and 72 new labor unions appeared within a few weeks. About 200,000 workers went on a general protest strike in Shanghai which lasted a month, according to Liu Hsiao-ch'i, who also told me that during that month the Communist Party membership in the city increased from about 200 to 800.

Altogether some 135 labor strikes throughout the country rose directly out of the May 30 Incident, of which 104 occurred in Shanghai. The number of workers reported in 94 cases totaled 381,387, and the average duration of the strikes was estimated at about 66 days.

During the whole year of 1925, there were 318 strikes in the whole country. In 198 cases for which figures were reported 784,821 workers were involved, and the average duration of the strikes was about 19 days.

The British foolishly persisted in their tactics. On June 12 they killed eight workers in Hankow and wounded twelve others. On June 18, Chinese seamen in Canton walked off British ships and were followed by a strike of most of the Chinese employed by foreign firms in Canton and Hong Kong. June 23 came the "Shakee Road Massacre," when British and French machine-gunners fired on a demonstration in Canton, in which 52 students and workers were reported killed and 117 wounded.

A general strike and boycott of British goods was declared and Hong Kong became a dead port. The Hong Kong-Canton Strike of about 160,000 workers, which is said to have involved from 200,000 to 250,000 at its height, lasted about fifteen months, from June, 1925, to October, 1926. A hundred thousand workmen evacuated Hong Kong and stayed in Canton for the duration, the Canton government providing $300,000 a month to support the strikers, while other funds were collected by union members and students. This general strike, one of the most remarkable in the history of labor in any country, was efficiently managed by a Workers' Delegates Council of 800 delegates, out of which a Strike Committee was chosen, Su Chao-jen being chairman. Public kitchens, schools, a hospital and 2,000 armed pickets were organized by the workers themselves, who showed extraordinary initiative and ability.

The Hong Kong-Canton Strike had great influence in encouraging the whole 1925-27 revolutionary movement. It demonstrated the power of labor and the effectiveness of the strike and boycott as political weapons and gave high prestige to the Left-wing program. The methods developed during the strike were later used in other situations. The strike was finally stopped by General Li Chi-sen of Canton, not by the action of the strikers, though many had returned to work before it was over.

When the All-China Labor Federation called the Third National Labor Congress on May 1, 1926, the 600 delegates represented 540,000 organized workers, according to Liu Hsiao-ch'i. Fang Fu-an, Lowe Chuan-hua and Chen Ta reported for this Congress 400 delegates, representing 400 unions in 19 provinces and 1,240,000 workers—a considerable discrepancy in the figures.

The Congress passed resolutions to request the Kuomintang armies to march forward in the Northern Expedition. The technique of strike struggle was discussed in much detail. Liu Hsiao-ch'i told me there was a sharp division of opinion on the issue of whether or not the interests of the workers should be subordinated to the Kuomintang.

On July 9, 1926, the Northern Expedition began for the purpose of destroying the war lords in other provinces and establishing the Kuomintang government over the whole country. It met with rapid success and reached the Yangtze Valley within six months. The Kuomintang government moved from Canton to Hankow in November.

The labor movement in south and central China developed with amazing rapidity and reached its height about February of 1927. Then the reaction began. The Chinese middle class, financial, and industrial interests became as frightened as the foreign and landlord elements against which the anti-imperialist, anti-feudal revolution was directed. In Hunan Province, for example, 80,000 union

47

members were reported in May, 1926, and 350,000 a year later. In Hupeh comparatively few unions existed in 1926 and I have no figure for that year, but in 1927 there were 450,000 organized workers. Han Ying, who was Organizing Secretary of the Hupeh Trades Unions and in command of the Hankow pickets, said there were 280,000 union members in Hankow alone in April, 1927. In 1926 Hankow had had only 42,000. In both Hunan and Hupeh, *hsien* districts had small local unions, all co-ordinated with the provincial General Labor Union, showing that the labor movement had deepened to include the workers in towns and villages. Labor in Kwangtung had reached its climax before the government moved to Hankow in 1926. In 1926, 207,000 organized workers were reported for Hong Kong, and 250,000 in 1927. At the end of 1926 Canton had 250 unions, of which Y. L. Lee [1] made a survey of 180 unions representing 290,620 members, commenting: "Although up to the present Canton has been essentially a city of home industries, its laborers are quite well organized, so much so that their organization can be favorably compared with that in some of the more industrially advanced countries. This was especially true between 1925-1926 when the city was dominated by the Communist Party." As of May, 1927, the total for Kwangtung province was given as 400,000. Shanghai had 149,000 union members in May, 1926, and 800,000 in May, 1927.

Several hundred strikes occurred during the Northern Expedition and early in 1927. Chen Ta reported 535 strikes in 1926, for which he secured figures on 313 strikes involving 539,585 workers. These figures are incomplete. No national figures are available for 1927, but 110 strikes were reported in Shanghai, involving 230,256 workers (not including the uprising and general strike in taking over the city).

"At first the strikes were very Leftist in tendency and later more Rightist," Liu Hsiao-ch'i told me. "This is an error of opportunism. All strikes were victorious because the tide of revolution was very high. Sometimes the workers' demands were too high. In general, the level of knowledge and experience of struggle improved but there was one weak point: the idea of the old guild became stronger among the workers. Labor union influence was very important.

[1] *Some Aspects of the Labour Situation in Canton,* Canton, January 10, 1928.

48

Wages had increased to a high point. Although at this time labor had great power, the workers never paid attention to the question of the seizure of power. The Communist Party made the same mistake. They thought the existing Kuomintang government was not reliable but failed to plan how to establish a new sovereignty. In Wuhan the labor unions always had conflict with the Kuomintang and the government, though the unions were very powerful and active in the government. Later on the Labor Federation and the Communist Party were directed by the Comintern to enter the Wuhan government and to form a Labor Department of the government. But the Communist Party still had not much sympathy and interest in this important work. This was a Leftist error.

"Later on the Party line was directed by Ch'ên Tu-hsiu and it was felt that the workers' movement was too high, so orders were given to restrict this movement. This was an error of Right opportunism and all the unions and the Communist Party took the opportunist line.

"During this period the labor movement was at a high point but the experience of the leaders was inadequate. For example, the labor leaders did not know that farm employes are also workers, so they did not permit farm laborers to join unions. Also the democratic spirit was not good enough and the movement was not led by leaders risen from the rank and file. This was a serious weakness. The education of the workers was also inadequate. In this period, too, the same mistake was made as earlier in opposing the staffs of the factories (clerical workers, etc.). The workers passed resolutions to prevent staff members from joining unions and also keeping out the foremen."

On January 4, 1927, the Hankow workers occupied the British Concession in Hankow and controlled it for one day before the Chinese troops took over. After negotiations the British agreed to return the Concession to Chinese sovereignty. H. Owen Chapman, who was an eyewitness at some of these events, told graphically of this incident: [2]

"Feeling had been rising among the crowds in the Chinese city which adjoins this Concession, until on the afternoon of the 3rd the storm broke, thousands of yelling Chinese—coolies with carry-

[2] *The Chinese Revolution 1926-27*, by H. Owen Chapman, 1928, Constable & Co., London.

ing poles and others of all sorts and conditions—worked up to a frenzy by the desperate efforts of the agitators among them, stood facing a thin line of British marines with fixed bayonets, drawn up across the end of the British Bund.

"On one side the mob, reinforced by the most turbulent spirits from the water-front of the native city, became more and more threatening. As the hours passed and the British withheld their fire, they not unnaturally concluded that their opponents feared to go to such a length; and the seething mass pressed ever forward with wild yells, fusillades of stones, and brandished poles, until they were actually engaged in places in hand-to-hand struggles with the marines and attempting to run through the gaps in the sparsely held line.

"On the other side of the string of bayonets, several score paces back, were machine-gun squads, and supporting them the warships in the stream with their guns trained on the scene of action."

Next day the same scene occurred again and the British withdrew. Chapman commented: "Surely a masterly handling, this, of an economic weapon tipped with steel. A dangerous weapon to use, horribly clumsy, and casual enough to curdle the blood of the onlookers: and yet—again not a life lost, civil or naval, and the coveted Concession occupied at the cost of a few bruises and scratches on either side, three British sailors felled to the ground, and two Chinese with bayonet wounds."

To the story of the historic incident Liu Hsiao-ch'i added this, which I believe is also an eyewitness account: "There were many British warships at Hankow who had defensive works on the river banks. The workers opposed this and destroyed these works. The British, however, had had the experience of May 30 and were afraid of the mass movement so the authorities of the Concession ordered that they could not fire but only use bayonets against the workers. Several were wounded by bayonets and all the workers became very excited and fought with the British who escaped to their ships. The workers remained in the Concession and for the length of one day the pickets maintained order and had full occupation. The wharf workers especially hated the Sikh policemen of the Concession and their pickets arrested them. The Wuhan government sent a delegate to the British authorities and negotiated for the recovery of the Concession. The soldiers then took over and maintained order."

All during the 1925-27 period the pickets, armed and unarmed, were an essential part of administrative apparatus. Chapman wrote: ". . . it early became necessary to provide special machinery in the form of a large army of pickets. They were dressed in a distinctive uniform not unlike that of the police, armed with wooden staves and a business-like air of authority, and soon became one of the most noticeable revolutionary features on the streets. They were not only used for rounding up attendances at meetings, but also for collecting members' dues, generally set at a very substantial figure, and for rigidly enforcing strike orders. . . . The influence of the pickets can be illustrated by the fact that when, at a later stage, the Government found it necessary to guard against excesses and violence by the populace in the streets, they frequently used pickets in preference to the police, whose power was of quite an inferior order. . . .

"The Executive Committees of large Labour Unions in Hankow, such as the Hupeh General Labour Union, were practically Government Departments with full administrative authority over their own people. They promulgated edicts and regulations, and used to arrest, try and punish their members. In Hankow they used pickets armed with staves to carry out their decisions: in Shanghai they were armed with rifles until Chiang Kai-shek disarmed them. In many of the country towns of Hupeh, as I myself saw in Teian and heard from Chinese and foreign colleagues and friends in other towns, the Governor of the town, holding his appointment direct from the Nationalist Government in Hankow, and having Nationalist troops quartered in the town, was yet unable to take any action contrary to the wishes of the two or three leading Labour Unions. . . .

"At the great Hanyang arsenal the shifts were double-banked, and thousands of workmen fed the machines and furnaces night and day without ceasing, current propaganda holding them up for public eulogy as, equally with the men at the front, helping to win the war. So hard pressed were the authorities that by 17th May a large number (said to be 80 per cent) of the Hankow pickets, a most essential factor in the industrial organization, had been enlisted for military service; and their police duties, in a way that could surely only occur in China, were largely taken over by boy scouts, who were at this time mobilized in large numbers for the purpose."

The greatest single achievement of labor during the 1925-27 revolution was the capture of the Chinese part of Shanghai by the labor unions before the Nationalist troops arrived. Two uprisings for this purpose failed, but the third was carefully prepared and so successful that it was called a "model uprising" by the Comintern, which held it up as a standard. The first attempt occurred when the Kuomintang armies were as far away as Hangchow, but the third was organized when the troops were nearing Shanghai.

One of the important leaders was Chou En-lai, now liaison officer in Chungking for the Eighteenth Group Army. Others were Chao Shih-yen, Ku Shun-chang and Lo Yi-ming, who were executed afterward along with Ch'ên Yen-nien (son of Ch'ên Tu-hsiu). Chou En-lai told the story to my husband, Edgar Snow, when he talked with him.[3] Military training was given secretly to 2,000 cadres in premises in the French Concession. Mausers were smuggled into the city to arm 300 marksmen picked as an "iron band," and 50,000 pickets were organized. On March 21, 1927, a general strike was called and the response closed down nearly all the industry in the city. The workers seized the police station first, then the arsenal and garrison. Sun Chuan-fang's troops were disarmed or defeated, and 3,000 guns were captured. Soon 5,000 workers were armed and six battalions created. A "people's government" was proclaimed which held power briefly, the Shanghai General Labor Union being the main administrative body. It is estimated that about 600,000 workmen participated in taking over Shanghai, their purpose being to establish Kuomintang sovereignty in the city.

Then came the day which marks the end of the 1925-27 "Great Revolution," April 12, 1927. By February the split between the Right and Left in the revolutionary movement and the suppression of labor had already begun. Unions were closed and workmen attacked in Kanchow, Nanchang, Kiukiang, Anking, Wuhu, and Hangchow. In Shanghai the Rightist Kuomintang plan to destroy the labor movement was carefully prepared. Merchants and bankers met with Chiang Kai-shek at the end of March to organize and finance the plan. On April 12, the attack began, and it is estimated that about 5,000 workmen were killed in the streets during the two days' fighting. Wong Son-hua, head of the Shanghai General Labor

[3] See *Red Star Over China*, by Edgar Snow.

52

Union, was killed and about three hundred Communists were executed by General Yang Hu at the Shanghai Garrison.

Chiang Kai-shek's army had only about 3,000 troops in Shanghai. The destruction of the unions and most of the killing was done by the gangsters of the Shanghai underworld, the secret Ch'ing and Hung *pongs*. These gangs controlled the opium racket of the lower Yangtze Valley. Thousands of *pong* gangsters were armed and organized to destroy the unions in the whole lower Yangtze region. In Shanghai they took over union headquarters and started the "Workers' Trade Alliance" in opposition to the real unions. This was managed chiefly by Chen Chuen, then secretary to the gangster chief, Chang Hsiao-ling, and temporarily head of the Political Department of the Kuomintang troops in Shanghai commanded by Pai Chung-hsi. Chen Chuen later became secretary to another chief. "Reorganization" and "Unification" committees for labor unions appeared, operated by the *pongs* chiefly, with co-operation from the Kuomintang. During the following years, the gangs were the chief anti-labor instrument in Shanghai. They sent armed gangsters to break strikes and subsidized individuals to control or destroy unions or organizations that might arise among the workers. They controlled the "labor racket" in Shanghai, as well as prostitution, kidnaping, child slavery, and other unsavory businesses.

Lowe Chuan-hua describes this period in 1927 as follows: "The golden age, however, was soon shortened through the adoption of a repressive policy toward labor by the conservative and, particularly, the military elements in the South China and the lower Yangtze regions. Alarmed at the excesses of the labor unions and at the conspiracies of the Communists in Central China, the authorities in Canton on April 14 raided all the Red unions in that city, including the Canton branch of the All-China Labor Federation, the Chinese Seamen's Union and the Kwangtung Provincial Peasants' Federation. More than 2,000 labor agitators were reported to have been arrested and many of the leaders killed as a result of the raid. Meanwhile, the garrison commander in Shanghai ordered an attack on the Red labor unions in Chapei. Fighting began on April 12 and lasted for two days. On April 15, the political department of General Bei Chung-hsi's army took over the Shanghai General Labor Union, and a committee for the unification of labor unions in Shanghai was immediately created. Later in the summer the military authorities in Wuhan (Hankow) copied the tactics of their partners in Canton and Shanghai. . . ."

The Rightists under Chiang Kai-shek formed the Nanking Government in opposition to the Leftist Kuomintang government already established at Hankow, and preparations were made for civil war between the two wings of the Kuomintang.

On May 20, 1927, the first Pan-Pacific Trade Union Congress was held in Hankow with about sixty delegates, including a number from foreign countries. Su Chao-jen was elected to head the Pan-Pacific Trade Union Committee, with Earl Browder of the United States as first secretary of the Secretariat. Other foreign delegates who attended were Tom Mann of the British Unions, Jacques Doriot of France, Sydor Stoler of the Soviet Union and others from oriental countries.

On June 23, 1927, the Fourth All-China Labor Congress was held in Hankow with 300 delegates representing 2,800,000 union members, according to Liu Hsiao-ch'i, although many unions were already driven underground and being smashed in various cities. At the Pan-Pacific Trade Union Congress a month earlier, Su Chao-jen had reported a total of 3,065,000 organized workers in all China, which included, interestingly, 6,000 in Honan, 4,000 in Shantung, 15,000 in Shensi, 10,000 in Tientsin, 45,000 in Szechuan, and 5,000 in Manchuria—places where the revolutionary movement had scarcely touched. Su Chao-jen's figures showed the largest classification of organized workers as 250,000 "employees," though I cannot make out what that figure means; 180,000 cotton mill workers, 160,000 seamen, 150,000 transport workers, 120,000 silk factory workers, 120,000 workers in "architecture," 80,000 policemen, etc.

On July 15, 1927, the Left Kuomintang split with the Communist Party, and soon afterward its government collapsed, and the leaders either went into exile or joined Chiang Kai-shek. Of all the important leaders of the Kuomintang only Madame Sun Yat-sen remained steadfastly in support of strong labor unions and the agrarian movement, in accordance with the original program of Sun Yat-sen and the reorganized Kuomintang from 1924 to 1927.

This was the beginning of the ten-year period of suppression of the labor movement and of civil war in China. Thousands of union leaders, Communists and progressives were killed or executed, and

54

no labor movement was able to rise again in the tense political atmosphere. Two of the most important union leaders, Hsiao Tzŭ-yu and Tai Tso-ming, were executed. Most of the principal labor leaders who were not killed, being either Leftists or Communists, went into the illegal underground Communist movement or joined the Red armies and fought in the civil war.

In March, 1928, the Pan-Pacific Trade Union Secretariat reported that during 1927, 32,316 persons were sent to prison, while 37,985 were killed and executed, of whom 25,000 died in open struggle, and 13,000 were "executed barbarously."

No figure is available on the labor leaders killed in this period, but it was sufficient to cripple the movement. In his "Report of the All-China Labor Federation," [4] before the second meeting of the Pan-Pacific Trade Union Secretariat in Shanghai held February 3-6, 1928, the chairman, Su Chao-jen, stated that in February, 1927, the Chairman of the Kiangsi Provincial General Labor Union was assassinated at Kanchow; that Li Chi-sen arrested 2,000 workers in one night in Canton and shot 100, including the Chairman of the "Canton Workers' Assembly," without announcing their names; in Hupeh the officers of the Textile Workers' Union and the Ricksha Coolies' Union were killed; in Honan 300 textile workers were killed by Feng Yu-hsiang for striking; the Honan General Labor Union was suppressed, etc.

On the policies of the employers in canceling previous collective agreements he said that in April, 1927:

"To this end they called a national meeting of local and provincial Chambers of Commerce in Shanghai, and formed a central association. The program of this body, which is being put into effect by the Kuomintang, has four main points: (1) The Government shall cancel all agreements made between employers and trade unions during the previous period; (2) all trade unions shall be suppressed; (3) the right of hiring and discharging workers shall belong completely to the employers without any limitation; (4) the merchants shall set up their own armed forces ('merchants volunteers'). At the same time they are forming special employers' associations for certain industries. British, American and Japanese textile companies recently formed an association to oppose strikes and suppress the workers."

[4] See *The China Outlook,* April 1, 1928, p. 12.

He also reported that the labor "Reorganization Committees" were forcibly collecting dues and were being opposed everywhere; that this committee in Canton had taken $43,000 of the previous Seamen's Union funds and spent it; that the Seamen's Union agreement won in the big strike had been canceled; that the Kwangtung Mechanics' Union which had 8 per cent to 10 per cent of the workers was now dominated by secret Communist unions.

At this meeting Su Chao-jen said no figures could be given on membership in the All-China Labor Federation which had had 2,800,000 members in June the year before. The Secretariat's manifesto, "The Workers' Viewpoint," reported that the average wage in Shanghai had been reduced to $11 ($5.50 U.S.) a month, and that working days were from twelve to sixteen hours long; "in spite of all strikes being outlawed, in Hankow strikes have been fought by ricksha coolies, railwaymen, textile workers, and arsenal workers. In Shanghai strikes have never ceased, there being 50 in December alone."

Labor did not go down in 1927 without a fight, though it made every concession to the Kuomintang to prevent the split. The labor movement was, of course, controlled by the Communists who were dominated by Professor Ch'ên Tu-hsiu.

"Just before the Kuomintang betrayed, the Communist Party adopted the policy of concession and gave orders to the unions to give up all arms, so many workers became passive and some wavered," Liu Hsiao-ch'i explained to me. "The leaders of the Wuhan labor movement left Wuhan, as the Kuomintang gave orders to stop all activities of the Communist Party and began arresting members. Using the anti-Communist slogan as an excuse, the Kuomintang destroyed the hidden power of the Wuhan workers. On August 7, 1927, the Communist Party Conference supported a manifesto to correct the error of Ch'ên Tu-hsiu's opportunism and after this meeting many uprisings took place in such cities as Hankow and Changsha. At this time the workers' unions still had much hidden power. But these uprisings all failed. After the Canton Commune the power of the workers' unions was completely destroyed. Only the Shanghai workers still had hidden power, so after this Shanghai was the center of the labor movement of China. During the period of Li Li-san's line the power of the Shanghai labor unions was also destroyed. The uprising policy decided by the August 7 meeting

56

was correct but before the uprisings they did not always have a correct estimation of the objective circumstances, so in the end every uprising failed.

"During the period of the Great Revolution the Communists showed great courage and their organization of the workers was very good. The peasant movement in Hunan, Hupeh, Kiangsi and Kwangtung was also excellent. But in the armies the Communist Party work was weak and insufficient. The Party had little influence and could not control the armies. This failure to work with the troops was a mistake and caused great loss to the revolutionary movement."

The tragic split and counter-revolution in 1927 has been the subject of much controversy. China, in 1944, is again confronted with a similar crisis, the outcome of which is not yet clear. Party labels and accusations only serve to confuse the issue. Perhaps the simplest statement of the case is a general one in terms of the social forces involved. Economically and politically the middle class in China is too weak to lead and control either a democratic or nationalist revolution in which the poor peasants and workers participate, yet without this participation no success can be achieved. This class, therefore, fears to co-operate with a democratic mass movement, and, as soon as such a movement rises in strength, joins forces with the reactionary feudal power and any other allies available to suppress it. This happened in 1927 and again during the war with Japan. On the other hand, the peasants and workers and revolutionary elements of the petty bourgeoisie have mobilized and organized themselves to overthrow feudal remnants and foreign domination, either with or without the support of the wavering middle class.

As China has been a weak, semi-colonial country, the foreign powers have been a strong influence in the course of development. If, for example, by a stretch of imagination, Britain and the United States as well as Russia had encouraged the 1925-1927 revolution in China, as a balance to the growing strength of Japan, and had a united democratic government similar to that in Canton and Hankow been maintained, China might now be well on the way to becoming a powerful stabilizing center for peace and prosperity in the East, although the war with Japan would probably not have been avoided. If, today, the three great powers of the United Nations support a unified democratic mobilization of the people and a constitutional liberal government representing the population, Japan could be swept out of China and Manchuria by an effective allied effort.

The political factor dominates the military situation. The same mobilization carried out in 1925-1927 could be repeated today, as demonstrated by what the Communists are now achieving independently in the guerrilla areas simply by a democratic, anti-Japanese program. In other words, if the people are given a stake in the war, they will rise to the occasion as they have done in the past. Poverty, suffering, disruption, and economic troubles will be factors for victory instead of defeat. The people will deliver themselves from bondage on the principle of dynamics that any motive power rises under pressure. This rise must occur, anyway, and it would serve a more useful purpose if it were now directed against the Japanese instead of exploding in all directions. One must not be deceived by the present lull before the storm in China.

This situation is not peculiar to China but in varying stages is common to other semi-feudal, semi-colonial countries where the middle class cannot develop the strength necessary to dominate the revolutionary movement, as in France, England, and other countries many generations ago. The question in China is not one of communism vs. capitalism but of democracy vs. feudalism and colonialism. Whether capitalism or socialism or an intermediary form develops out of this democratic revolution in China is a secondary question at present, as it was in 1927; whichever is the most workable will probably win out in the end. But Japan must be driven out of China and the feudal system destroyed before either form of society can be achieved. The new democracy in China may possibly be one similar to that in Hankow in 1927, in Republican Spain or Mexico, but it cannot be established without giving the farmers and workers a voice in government, as they constitute 90 per cent of the population of 450,000,000. Foreign influence is a powerful factor in pushing either to the Right or the Left, although one must bear in mind that pressure intended to help the Right may have the opposite effect, if it is for imperialist or non-progressive purposes. There can be no charge of imperialism in China, however, against any influence brought to bear for the purpose of strengthening China's sovereignty and mobilizing her people in their own interests.

The situation is complicated by the fact that the Communists in China have taken leadership of the democratic mass movement since 1927. If there were none, it would have been necessary to invent them. Had the Left Kuomintang carried out to conclusion the policies of 1925-1927, they would probably have been called "Communists" just as they were in that period or the name would have meant the same; so one is only quibbling with words. People who would be known in other countries as mild reformers are labeled Communists in China.

It is a peculiarity of the Chinese labor movement that since 1927 the only party which has been identified with the cause of labor has been the Communists, and this is the only labor party that has developed there. In fact, there have been only the two important parties in the country, and third party attempts have thus far failed to develop successfully. Since 1927 the Kuomintang has had a one-party dictatorship and no other party has legal standing, although in 1943 constitutional government was promised after the end of the war. There are several small parties in China struggling to rise, which in 1941 established the Federation of Chinese Democratic Parties. Their otherwise excellent ten-point program makes no mention of labor. None of these groups have worked in the industrial labor movement or done anything specifically to encourage it, which is one reason for their helplessness. However, had they done so, they would doubtless have come under the usual Communist ban. There are, of course, many progressive-minded individuals in China sympathetic with labor, but their contacts with the labor movement have been largely limited to outside observation, statistical surveys, and distant well-wishing. Organized labor has always been delicate ground except for those willing to risk their necks in the process. It is not difficult to see why an independent or conservative labor party or movement could not exist in a country as sharply divided politically as was China, where civil war raged from 1927 to 1936 and, afterwards, war with Japan.

Anarchists, Socialists, and Syndicalists have had little influence in China, though before 1924 there was some interest in these theories, and no social-democratic ideology has reached the working class in a form that could win its interest. The anti-labor policies of

59

the Kuomintang made it impossible for that party to win any following among the working class after 1927. The Kuomintang theory has been that labor will swing radically to the Left as soon as suppression is lifted, so it has never experimented by permitting any free labor movement to rise. In 1932 and 1933 Fascist ideas were brought into the Kuomintang program by two different cliques, and these have naturally had no appeal to labor. The recent attempt of the CC clique to regiment labor through compulsory joining of government-dominated unions is not likely to win the support of labor.

Though the Communist Party is the only workers' party in China, its contacts with industrial labor in the cities has been very limited since 1931. This party is remarkable for the influence it has had with so few members. It has functioned chiefly through its peripheral following and mass organizations. Beginning in 1920 with only a few scattered individuals having the general idea in mind, the party was officially founded in July, 1921, at the First Congress held in Shanghai with only thirteen delegates present. It probably had only a few score members that year and functioned chiefly through the Labor Secretariat in Shanghai. The Second Congress was held July, 1922, with twenty delegates. Though the Secretariat directed most of the labor union activities from 1921 to 1925, the Communist Party claimed a total membership of only 400 at its Third Congress held in Canton in June, 1923. At this Congress it was audaciously decided to join and work inside the Kuomintang in order to convert it into a revolutionary mass organization. The Fourth Congress held in January, 1925, reported only 994 members. By July of that year the membership in Shanghai had increased from 200 to 800, and the total membership at the end of 1925 was 3,500. Early in 1926 it had risen to 5,000. The Fifth Congress held in Shanghai April 27, 1927, reported 57,957 members, of whom 53.8 per cent were workers, nearly all leading the labor union movement. These 30,000 Communists dominated the 2,800,000 union members of the All-China Labor Federation. The remaining half were somehow able to dominate the nine or ten million organized peasants and also the student unions, though they did not have much voice in the nationalist armies. The circulation of the party organ increased from 7,000 at the time of the Fourth Congress to 50,000 at the time of the Fifth Congress, it was reported.

I have not seen any published figure on the number of Communists killed and executed in 1927. Miss Tsai Chang, one of the important women leaders, a member of both the Kuomintang and the Communist Party, and an organizer among women workers and students from 1925 to 1927, told me that they kept no statistics but estimated that: "In all China over 1,000 women leaders were killed in 1927. Some were bourgeois and many were students. Not all were Communist Party members but all were leaders. In all China over 10,000 responsible Communist Party members were killed in 1927. There were many incidents—April 12 in Shanghai, in Hunan, Wuhan and the north. About 120,000 were killed from April to the end of December, 1927. During this time the brutality was like nothing else in the world." She was present during the killings in Hankow but escaped.

As of June, 1929, the Communists claimed 133,365 members, 10 per cent being workers. The Kiangsu Committee (Shanghai) had 6,800 members, including 591 industrial workers. Chou En-lai reported in September, 1930, 120,000 members and 2,000 factory workers. In 1933 Wang Ming gave a figure of 410,000 members, 1.6 per cent being industrial workers. In 1934 the Long March began to the north and the membership declined. About 1938 the membership was probably some 200,000. In 1943 Chou En-lai reported that the Communist Party had 800,000 members, the peak in its history.

The majority of the Communists are young and belong to various youth organizations. Many of the labor organizers of 1925-27 were members of the Communist Youth League and not of the party. This antedates the founding of the party. Fang Wen-ping, Secretary of the Communist Youth when I talked with him in 1937, told me that the Socialist Youth was formed in 1918 and decided to join the Communist Youth International in May, 1920, the principal leader being Chang T'ai-lei, who later was a chief figure in the Canton Commune. At the First Congress of Youth Leagues convened in Canton in May, 1922, 4,000 members were reported. At the Third Congress in February, 1925, the C.Y.L. had 9,000 members, 30 per cent being workers. In April, 1927, the membership was 35,000, 41 per cent being workers, and the Young Pioneers numbered 120,000 members. During the Li Li-san period in 1930 the C. Y. was abolished and became a department of the C. P.

However, it was revived again in January, 1931. In 1933 the C. Y. had 60,000 members and in 1934, 100,000. During 1933 and 1934 the C. Y. recruited 130,000 soldiers for the Red armies, Fang Wenping told me, of whom about one-third were C. Y. members. A big Youth Congress was held in Yenan April 12, 1937, at which the name of the C. Y. was changed to the "Youth Union for National Salvation" and was broadened into a general organization. In 1942 the Communists claimed to have organized 1,024,814 youth and 2,203,136 children in guerrilla areas, under the general direction of the Youth Unions.

During 1925 and early 1927 industrial workers joined the Kuomintang, though since the 1927 reorganization few have done so and Kuomintang officers of unions are usually labor politicians placed over the organization from above for political purposes. At the Second Kuomintang Congress held in January, 1926, it was estimated that out of 278 delegates, 168 were Leftists, 45 Rightists and 65 Centrists. At the Third Congress held in February, 1927, it was estimated that out of a total number of 300,000 Kuomintang members, only 40,000 to 50,000 belonged to the Right Wing. The majority of the members were said to be peasants and the second largest classification industrial workers. Most of the 58,000 Communist members were likewise Kuomintang members. The Right wing was a minority at the time of the *coup d'état* in 1927, but it had control of the armies though these were not large. At the end of 1925 the Nationalist troops at Canton numbered about 40,000 men and in the middle of 1926, 100,000. About 50,000 to 60,000 troops embarked in the eight armies of the Northern Expedition. They were enlarged on the way and after the occupation of Hankow numbered 90,000 men and 14 armies. In early 1927 the total was about 150,000 soldiers.

For ten years the Kuomintang has claimed about 2,000,000 members, though how many pay dues and are active members is a question. It does not function as a mass party now but as a divided group of cliques and political machines.

V. FOURTH STAGE: THE CIVIL WAR PERIOD FROM 1927 TO 1937

THE CIVIL WAR between the Communists and the Nanking government lasted from the Nanchang uprising of August 1, 1927, to the final settlement of the Sian incident in the spring of 1937, a few months before Japan attacked on July 7. During these ten years the peasant movement was on the offensive and the labor movement on the defensive and the two forces were physically isolated from each other except in a few instances, the industrial cities being in government territory. The peasant unions with their nine or ten million members estimated to exist in 1927 were largely destroyed along with the labor unions, but this movement was quickly rebuilt under the soviet system. The 3,065,000 organized workers reported by Su Chao-jen in May, 1927, of whom 2,800,000 were represented by union delegates at the Fourth National Labor Congress, did not fare so well, though until 1931 organized labor fought back in a losing retreat. Since 1931 organized labor has been in a very low state, caused partly by the economic depression which crippled industrial activities. However, unorganized labor has never ceased its spontaneous economic struggle for existence, even though it has not been legally permitted to create permanent organs for independent action.

When the Communists decided upon armed resistance on August 7, 1927, the labor union leaders decided also upon a policy of uprisings against the Rightists, whom they considered counterrevolutionary against the original Kuomintang program formulated by Sun Yat-sen in 1924, though all these uprisings failed to succeed.

The Canton Commune uprising occurred on December 11, 1927, and the city was held three days by the workers and 2,000 cadets. Here there had been over 200,000 trade-unionists before the split with the Kuomintang. During the Commune, however, only 2,000 workers were armed. These disarmed the police and took over the city internally, while the cadets attacked the garrison troops. Kim San, an eyewitness,[1] told me that 30,000 workers and sympathizers

---

[1] A detailed story of the Canton Commune is told in *Song of Ariran*, by Kim San and Nym Wales, John Day Company, New York, 1941.

gathered at a mass meeting and elected Su Chao-jen (in northern spelling Hsü Chao-chêng) as chairman of the city soviet that was created. Su Chao-jen himself was not present, as he had gone to Tungkiang nearby to organize an army of farmers to hurry to the aid of the Canton workers. The Commune was destroyed by several divisions of Kuomintang troops and by a thousand or so armed gangsters inside the city, though the armed workmen fought back from telephone poles and street corners until they were surrounded. It is usually said that during the insurrection only about 200 persons had been killed, but when the Kuomintang recovered the city some 5,700 workers and others were dead on the streets. Kim San told me 7,000 were killed in the recovery of the city.

Liu Hsiao-ch'i described this period to me, saying: "After the August 7 Congress the power of labor in Wuhan, Changsha and Kwangtung was all lost. In Shanghai, however, labor still had some power. Just before the Canton Commune Teng Chung-hsia led a big strike in the Pootung factory district in Shanghai among the workers in textile mills owned by the Japanese and British. About a hundred thousand workers joined the strike. The main demands were economic but they were not granted and the strike failed completely. After the victory of the Canton Commune, the strike was suppressed in a few days. The Central Committee of the Communist Party had appointed Li Li-san to go to Kwangtung and point out to the leadership that they had committed the error of Right opportunism. When the National Labor Congress was held in Shanghai, one group held that we should prepare and could not sacrifice. Another group insisted on uprisings again. The uprisings policy was victorious.

"In conclusion, we may say that the weak points and causes of failure in this period were these: (1) The Communist Party was unable to retreat well in order to maintain its power; (2) because in the past we had worked openly, we lacked experience in secret work and could not do this well; (3) the Communist Party made Leftist errors; (4) the white terror was very strong. In this period the Kuomintang organized Yellow trade unions, and the Communists directed the Chinese workers not to join these Yellow unions. Later on part of the workers joined the Yellow unions by themselves. In 1929 there were seven big Yellow unions in Shanghai, such as those of the Commercial Press, the Post Office and others. At this time it was necessary to join the Yellow unions but the Communist Party did not adopt this policy and on the contrary opposed the Yellow unions. Because of this the Red labor unions not only could not co-operate with the Yellow unions but also came into conflict with them, and the Red labor unions could not win over part of the workers who were misled by their leaders into joining these unions. At the Fifth National Labor Congress, however, which had several tens of delegates though it was held secretly, it was decided to join the Yellow trade unions. After the Shanghai war in 1932, there was a strike in P'u Hsi in Shanghai which failed but because of this strike many workers joined the Red labor unions. In January, 1934, there was a big strike in Changsha which had a partial victory. Besides these there were many strikes led by the Yellow labor unions."

During the years from 1927 to 1931 the leadership of the Chinese labor movement was practically if not literally beheaded and the suppression and other difficulties were so great that it has thus far been unable to recover. Labor went into a period of depression though underground methods were improved. Prisons in China were constantly filled with accused Communists during the civil war and the charge carried the death penalty.

In the last half of 1928 a strike wave [2] began and labor began to show signs of recovery from the shock of 1927. This trend continued until the end of 1930. Regarding this as an upsurge of the revolutionary labor movement, the Communist Party, dominated by Li Li-san, decided to launch another series of labor uprisings known as the "Li Li-san period." This began in the summer of 1930 and lasted until January, 1931, when Li Li-san was dethroned

[2] In his pamphlet *Heroic China*, P. Miff says (p. 65): "About 50,000 Shanghai workers took part in the First of May demonstration in 1929; and over 100,000 workers in different parts of China responded to the appeal of the Communist Party to demonstrate on International Anti-War Day on August 1. In 1930 the strike movement continued to grow and assumed a more persistent and organized character." On p. 68 he reports: "Counting on the immediate victory of the revolution all over China, Li Li-san completely ignored the everyday struggle of the workers and peasants. He dissolved the Red trade unions on the ground that they were superfluous during an insurrection....Li Li-san's policy caused enormous damage to the Party...."

from the leadership and sent to Moscow for discipline and training and his policy changed.

All the Li Li-san labor uprisings failed and the policy brought down fresh reprisals from the anti-labor forces. In 1931 the secret Communist Central Committee moved from Shanghai to the soviet areas and the Soviet Republic was established November 7, 1931. Then the civil war began in earnest on a major scale, the government launching a series of campaigns against the Red armies and enforcing a blockade which finally succeeded in driving the Red armies out of the south at the end of 1934.

The years 1931 and 1932 were a period of political crisis in China in many fields, one cause being the Japanese occupation of Manchuria on September 18, 1931. The Kuomintang was at a low ebb and rent with internal strife: there was one movement to do away with it altogether, while, on the other hand, the Wang Ching-wei "Reorganizationists" were demanding its reorganization. It was partly this internal dissension that had given labor a breathing spell up to 1932. Under these circumstances, two different cliques, the Blue Shirts and the CC P'ai, turned to Japan, Italy and Germany for Fascist methods of "regeneration" and "unification." The Blue Shirts reorganized military affairs and the CC's took over control of the Kuomintang civilian political machine. Two separate networks of secret political police were created which became quite efficient in their methods, especially against the Communists and labor. The Wang Ching-wei Reorganizationists were given nominal posts without power, such as Ch'ên Kung-p'o, who was appointed Minister of Industries from 1932 to 1935, the government Labor department being under this Ministry, while the real power was *sub rosa* and control of labor in the hands of the CC's co-operating with the Ch'ing-Hung *pongs,* etc.

From the 1931-32 period to the present no organized labor movement can be said to have existed in China, except in Communist areas where political power was based upon the organization of peasants and workers. Or, to use Madame Sun Yat-sen's phrase describing conditions in 1944, one might say the situation was characterized "by the absence of a true labor movement in most of our territory." A favorable opportunity to revive the labor movement existed in the liberal period following 1937, but little was achieved.

66

Nevertheless, an "unorganized" labor movement has seethed constantly below the surface and burst out in sporadic and spontaneous strikes and disputes, in which Chinese labor has shown remarkable resourcefulness, tenacity and courage. There is no doubt in the minds of Chinese who have had experience in organizing Chinese labor that, given an opportunity, Chinese workers will demonstrate quickly enough that they have not lost the ability to organize themselves very effectively. Nor is there any doubt in the minds of those who have been obliged to spend a good deal of their time since 1927 in preventing this phenomenon from recurring. The so-called "backwardness" of Chinese labor is no item in considering its future potentialities, contrary to the opinion sometimes expressed by foreigners. Against its own historical background, it has been very forward indeed. China has gone through the phases of a strongly organized labor movement from 1922 to 1927; of a "reorganized" movement from 1927 to 1931; and of an "unorganized" movement since. But this movement has never died nor become stagnant from natural causes.

Figures on strikes and especially on the number of workers involved are not carefully collected in China and are always incomplete, but some idea of the labor situation may be judged from such as are available, which I have listed in a later section summarizing statistics on the labor movement, "Strikes and Unions." These activities are remarkable for the fact that they were ordinarily carried out without union organization. Most of the strikes and disputes occurred in Shanghai. In the last normal year, 1936, 278 labor disputes were reported for all China, resulting in 134 strikes. Partial figures showed that 215,490 workers were involved in 72 of the strikes.

On October 18, 1929, the Nanking Government promulgated the Labor Union Law, which was far different from the original Kuomintang regulations in the days of the Canton and Hankow governments. This placed such restrictions upon labor organization that no union could be legal which was disapproved of by the authorities and no agreements could be made other than those meeting with the approval of the authorities. In effect, independent labor unions could not be legally organized. In Shanghai and other cities directly under Nanking, the Kuomintang Bureau of Social Affairs has been designated as the supervisory authority over labor since 1933, becoming a government ministry after the removal to Chungking.

Following 1927 the Kuomintang "Reorganization" committees reorganized various labor unions, but that party was too frightened of labor to take leadership of a conservative labor movement and its policy soon stifled and destroyed all initiative. Only in cases where the unions could be used against foreign owners did the Kuomintang encourage comparatively strong unions, and even this policy lapsed after 1931. Subsequently a further reorganization policy came into effect under the Bureau of Social Affairs, controlled by the anti-labor CC clique, which successfully crippled what remained of labor strength in such organizations. Specific regulations permitted the existence of carefully-controlled "special unions" among workers in government-owned enterprises such as railway and postal workers, under which the right to strike was prohibited and only limited rights of collective bargaining enjoyed. The structure of these Kuomintang unions is such that they would hardly be called "unions" in the parlance of free trade unionists. The rank and file have thus far been unable to break through controls at the top, though there is always pressure from below for this purpose which will doubtless some day be successful.

Since 1927, and especially since 1931, one must be very chary of accepting official statistics on labor unions. Only the general figures on participation in strikes and disputes are of much value. The only way to judge the justification of the term is to examine each union individually. For this purpose, I have included in a separate section Lowe Chuan-hua's account of four labor unions. As Lowe Chuan-hua commented in 1933: ". . . the labor union is so widespread in China that its very name has already become a much over-worked term. It is freely used by a variety of workers' organizations, ranging from the Chinese guild of the medieval type to the trade union in the Western sense. . . .

"Speaking politically, we have the 'Red,' the 'Grey,' and the 'Yellow' labor unions. The 'Red' unions do not exist openly but are reported to be quite influential, especially in strategic industrial centers like Shanghai, Hankow, Canton and Tientsin. The 'Grey' unions refuse both the direction of the Kuomintang and of the Communists. The 'Yellow' or Fascist unions are openly organized and run by the appointees of the various Kuomintang branches in China, and have enjoyed a rapid growth since April, 1927.

"In order to gain public favor and the support of the workers, many guilds, pseudo-unions and 'company unions' also call themselves labor unions. Even workers' organizations of a recreational nature and bogus societies formed for exploiting the ignorant workers exist under the name of labor unions."

It is quite natural that in a stage of disruption where medieval practices co-existed with the most modern forms of organization, the nature of labor unions runs a gamut of the most diverse varieties. The unions organized from 1922 to 1927 were organized for the most part according to good labor practice, though the old guild tradition was never entirely eradicated in some places, notably Canton. Those created among unorganized workers in modern industries were very advanced, and one of the complaints against them in China by such writers as Chen Ta is that they were much too "foreign" in their methods and organization.

In 1936, the government reported that there were 872 labor unions in all China with 743,764 members. Hardly any of these, however, could be considered "unions" in the accepted sense of the term.

The viewpoint of Lowe Chuan-hua, a Y. M. C. A. secretary, whose book *Facing Labor Issues in China* has an introduction by Ch'ên Kung-p'o, then Minister of Industries, will doubtless be of interest to the reader on this difficult period in the history of Chinese labor. He says (p. 47): "With the fall of the Wuhan Government in the autmn of 1927 and the subsequent elimination of the Communists and the Leftists from the political arena, the labor movement dwindled into a stage of retrenchment and reorganization. As soon as the Kwangsi faction occupied the Central China provinces, it dissolved all the labor unions there. In Tientsin and Peiping, the laborers met with the same fate from the Shansi generals shortly after these two important cities were turned over to their control by the National Government in Nanking. With the establishment of the National Government in Nanking and the reorganization of the Central Kuomintang, a new policy was adopted toward all popular movements. At the Fourth Plenary Session of the Central Executive Committee of the Kuomintang held in February, 1928, it was resolved to abolish the Peasants, the

Workers', the Youth, and the Merchants' departments of the Central Party headquarters, and instead to establish a department for the organization and training of mass movements. Henceforth the promotion and training of peasant and labor organizations was to be under the sole direction of the Party organs. All peasant and labor unions of a questionable character were to be either abolished or reorganized in accordance with the proper procedure promulgated by the Kuomintang. All slogans used during the period of co-operation with the Communists were to be dropped, and all publicity of the peasant and labor unions was from then on to be of an economic or education nature. In short, the Kuomintang then commenced to enforce its policy of moderation and doctrine of Party government. It claims that since the masses are ignorant and are apt to become the victims of vicious propaganda, the Nationalist Party should perform the duty of organizing and training all the mass movements in China. As soon as the laborers are able to assume this important leadership, the Kuomintang will turn over to their hands the direction of China's labor movement.

"In conformity with this policy, the Kuomintang established in every one of the important industrial centers a so-called Labor Union Reorganization Committee, certain members of which are appointed by the Party organ in the locality concerned. On July 9, 1928, the National Government promulgated the Provisional Regulations for the Settlement of Disputes between Capital and Labor, thereby removing extreme labor agitations. . . .

"Since its split with the Communists, the Kuomintang has stood for a positive policy of promoting co-operation in industry. While the present regime in China does not acquiesce in unwarranted labor agitations, it claims that it has done its utmost to carry out its determination of affording legal protection to labor's legitimate interests. The National Government has also shown a great interest in the international aspects of China's labor problems. . . ."

Mr. Lowe continues on p. 50: "Since the emergence of the Nationalist Revolution in China, no other social organization has aroused as much anxiety, disturbance and heated discussion among industrial and business circles as the labor union. How many labor unions there are in China today and how large their membership is are questions which no one can answer definitely, since these numbers fluctuate widely with the ups and downs of the domestic political situation. However, a few official estimates may be reviewed here. In a survey made in the latter part of 1928, the Ministry of Industry of the National Government found that there were altogether 1,117 labor unions in China [3] with a total of 1,773,998 members (*Chinese Labor Year Book,* Second Edition, Institute of Social Research, Peiping, Part II, pp. 15-16), which was a little more than one-half of the number of organized workers reported at the Pan-Pacific Trade Union Conference in 1927. A second investigation was made by the Ministry of Industry in the spring of 1930 and covered 27 important cities, representing nine provinces of China. In this study, the Ministry of Industry found that there were only 741 labor unions, with a total of 576,250 members. The big difference between the total number of organized workers for 1928 and that for 1930 is due partly to the efforts of the Kuomintang to reorganize labor unions in various parts of China and to the occurrence of civil war, which prevented the second investigation from reaching quite a few important sections of the country. In both the 1928 and the 1930 studies, Kwangtung province had the largest number of labor unions while Kiangsu province came second. Of the various industries, cotton weaving and spinning, transportation and communications, and the machine industry were the three most extensively unionized. In April, 1932, the Ministry of Industry gave out a report which showed that there were only 621 labor unions in China, although it did not give the exact number of union members."

Until 1931 the All-China Labor Federation still existed actively, though it was underground and directed by the Communists as previously. The last National Labor Congress was called by this Federation in November, 1929, claiming to represent 64,381 (or 70,000) union members, of which three-fifths were in the soviet regions. Of these, 5,748 Red trade-union members were specified as in the cities of Shanghai, Hong Kong, Hankow, Tientsin, Wusih, and Amoy. From 1932 to 1937, the Communists continued to or-

[3] Such figures are very questionable, as they were put out by the Government for propaganda purposes to answer criticism of the destruction of the unions; and also the Government had no means of getting in touch with the underground union leaders. Another reason was that various cities were under control of different militarists, some hostile to Nanking, and there was too much disruption to collect statistics.

ganize certain labor activities in the cities and to have small "secret unions," the others being known as "open sign-board unions," instead of the previous terms "Red" and "Yellow" unions. They worked chiefly as individuals and in small groups, however, as the extermination campaign against Communists was highly effective, especially in the labor movement.

The situation of the Red trade unions in 1928 was indicated in a report [4] at the third plenum of the All-China Labor Federation held October 27, 1928, in Shanghai:

"All the advances gained by the workers during 1925-1927 ... have now been abolished. ...

"In the period from January to August, 1928, according to our statistics more than 100,000 workers and peasants have been slaughtered, of whom 27,699 were executed by formal processes of the Kuomintang Government. At present 17,200 are in prison.

"Within the factories, if one worker is caught in connection with our Red trade union work, then five or ten other workers in the same factory, picked at random, are also punished publicly to terrify the whole body of workers and make them afraid of any contact with us."

Su Chao-jen reported at the second meeting of the Pan-Pacific Trade Union Secretariat on February 4, 1928, that "The old Shanghai General Labor Federation, the Canton Workers' Assembly, the Hankow General Labor Union, all the industrial unions; and the assemblies in the big cities all still exist and function, but now in secret."

Though the labor movement as a movement was too crippled and bound with restrictions to rise again, the pressure from the overworked and underpaid workers was so constant as to make necessary the employment of many and varied devices to demoralize labor and prevent the existence of independent unions, aside from using the Communist charge to arrest the leaders.

One measure was to dismiss wholesale former active union members and to bring in raw workers from the provinces and women and children who could be more easily handled than men.[5]

---

[4] "The Chinese Trade Union Movement in 1928," by Lo Chao-lung, *China Tomorrow*, February 20, 1929.

[5] Lowe Chuan-hua reported in 1933: "Excepting the mechanics and foremen who receive relatively good remuneration, the average monthly wage

In Shanghai, the "labor racket" became highly profitable. Here labor activity was greatest after 1927, due in part to the fact that modern influences were not quite so unfavorable as the feudal reaction which engulfed the rest of the country in ruthless and arbitrary military control. Yet even in Shanghai the most effective method of labor control was essentially feudal in character—through the gangsters and spies of the Ch'ing and Hung *pongs,* which were the chief strikebreaking organizations in Shanghai and vicinity. These usually made short work of any serious labor threat and were well paid for their efforts; they blackmailed both the owners and the workers. These *pongs* co-operated with the Kuomintang and police agents, many of whom were members of the *pongs.* Labor leaders were kidnaped and disappeared, aside from quasi-legal arrests on the charge of Communism, usually without evidence. Armed thugs, sometimes with sub-machine guns, were rushed to the scene of strikes.

Shanghai was divided into the industrial areas in foreign concessions and those under Chinese control. The International Settlement workers were fortunate in the existence of the Industrial Section of the foreign-controlled Shanghai Municipal Council, headed by Eleanor M. Hinder, and with Rewi Alley as Factory Inspector, which made a brave attempt to safeguard the welfare of the Settlement workers, though having no power of legal compulsion. As Miss Hinder said : [6]

"The Council's Industrial Section worked steadily at improving health and safety in the Settlement's industrial enterprises. In its desire that nothing should interfere with a possible agreement with the Chinese authorities, it did not, prior to 1937, compete in the mediation of disputes but remained in the less controversial field of

---

for a female worker in the modern industries in China is not more than $15, and that of a male worker is about $20. At the same time thousands of workers receive wages below these figures.... Since wages for women and child workers are usually lower than those demanded by men and since the former group of people are much easier to control than the latter, there is a strong tendency among employers to hire women and children. This results in a number of evil practices among the foremen and the factory authorities. Gradually the women and the minors replace the adult workers, as shown in several industries in Shanghai."

[6] *Life and Labour in Shanghai,* by Eleanor M. Hinder, International Secretariat, Institute of Pacific Relations, New York, 1944, p. 12.

hygiene and safety promotion.... Relying only on the general authority of the Council and on reason and good will, the Industrial Section used educational means to induce employers to take steps toward factory improvement. The Court could not be invoked, but considerable success was nonetheless achieved."

Rewi Alley, who was Factory Inspector for the Shanghai Municipal Council from 1933 to 1938, and who had previously held the same post for the Fire Department, is one of the few foreigners who ever penetrated into the depths of China's labor problems. His unbounded admiration and respect for the working men and women of China is a testimony of what he found, and the stories I have heard him tell of the labor struggle in Shanghai during those dark years would provide a dramatic if depressing chapter in the history of the world's labor movement. Since 1938 he has devoted himself to the Chinese industrial co-operative movement in the interior. Altogether he has spent seventeen years of his life in China with a constant personal concern and sympathy for Chinese labor. A Chinese engineer once said to me: "Rewi Alley is the best foreign friend labor in China has ever had."

The use of secret societies, gangsters, and terrorism was not confined to Shanghai; in fact the world of labor became an underworld for the most part, and it is a story only for those with very strong stomachs. The situation is almost inconceivable to the average union organizer in America or England, for such medieval conditions and subterranean networks of secret gangster organizations are beyond his imagination. Out of this dismal swamp, the courage and heroism of Chinese labor in its bitter fight for human rights stands out in bright relief. When a Chinese worker goes on strike he is likely to be hungry for the duration and often has to pawn everything but his clothes to survive. Strike leaders usually had to hide after the strike was settled to prevent kidnaping or arrest as "Communists," and to find other jobs, where they might be discovered by the network of spies and organized gangsters permeating the ranks of labor in the factories.

Lowe Chuan-hua put the situation mildly when he said in 1933 (p. 49) : "As indicated elsewhere in this volume, the overwhelming majority of the labor organizations are controlled by a limited number of petty politicians, professional union officials and gangsters." On page 72 he continues: "Another problem in the field of labor

74

organization is the domineering influence which numerous labor bosses and gang leaders exert over the labor unions in China. Some unions are entirely run by individuals or small groups of individuals, such as the 'Green' (Ch'ing *pong*) and 'Red' (Hung *pong*) gangs in Shanghai. The grip which these mercenary elements have over the workers is so strong that nothing short of drastic legal action and a widespread educational program among the men can remove this bondage.... Simultaneously, the employers should be brought to realize that it would be beneficial to their own interests if they would voluntarily recognize trade unionism, try to meet its legitimate aspirations and cooperate with it in developing a genuine leadership amongst the workers, and in helping to remove the parasitical elements that stand between them and their employees. Unless this barrier is wiped out, the labor unions in China will not have any great improvement in their programs or activities."

It is important to note that factory owners suffered from racketeering methods as well as labor, having to pay tribute to the gangsters for protection. An interesting study could be made of the losses they suffered, as compared with the gains they might have made in efficiency and actual money if the contact had been direct between a union and the employer, without the middleman labor-racketeer. For example, in 1936 there was a strike in the Chinese-owned Hua Cheng Tobacco Company in Shanghai. The labor-racketeers in control of the so-called "union" who negotiated with the owners raised the actual demands of the workers as a bargaining point, so that they could secure a higher bribe from the owners for "settling" the strike. The workers were furious, but they were successfully kept from any contact with the owners. Finally, several delegates from the workers secretly asked an outsider to call at the company office to explain the situation, which resulted in a direct hearing between the owners and the workers.

The situation of Chinese labor after 1927 cannot be understood without knowledge of the *pongs* and their methods, though little has been printed on the subject. One reference may be found in the chapter "Gang Rule in Shanghai" in a booklet, *Five Years of Kuomintang Reaction,* printed in Shanghai in 1932 by the *China Forum.* A few excerpts may give the reader part of the picture.

"Prior to 1927 the gangs of Shanghai generally confined their activities to opium and slave traffic, working in conjunction with the then-overlord, Sun Chuang-fang, a feudal militarist of the old type. It was not until the Reaction set in against the rising Revolution in April, 1927, that the gangs emerged as a political instrument of the first order. . . .

"From 1927 onwards the gangs became increasingly an important arm of the Kuomintang, used chiefly to keep the lid down on the workers' mass movement, to smash strike actions through intimidation and control of all so-called labor organizations. With the smashing of the revolutionary labor unions and the establishment of 'respectable' trade unions, the gangs assumed full leadership and have functioned in that capacity ever since. . . .

"The Kuomintang-controlled trade unions are placed entirely in the hands of the gangsters, who as officials can act in labor disputes independent of the rank and file. . . .

"They get a rake-off from workers' wages, from every job given a worker, from the 'squeeze' manipulated by foremen and contractors, from direct subsidies provided by grateful factory-owners, from selling opium to workers and from buying their children as slaves. . . .

"In addition to sending spies and *provocateurs* into the ranks of the working class and in addition to controlling the labor market and the trade unions, the big gang leaders enter the repressive machinery in person as 'arbiters' of labor disputes and strikes."

The first Peasants' and Workers' Red Army was formed during the Nanchang Uprising on August 1, 1927. A large proportion of this army was made up of workers and labor union men, such as railway workers and the Hanyehp'ing miners. Most of them came from the areas around Hankow, Changsha and Nanchang.

The Red Army increased in size and by 1930 claimed to have 62,000 soldiers. By the end of 1931 this had developed to about 150,000 soldiers, aside from self-defense units of workers and peasants in the Red Guards and other semi-military forces.

At the end of 1931, the Congress of Chinese Soviets was held, and the Provisional central Soviet government was elected with Mao Tse-tung as chairman, and Han Ying, the labor leader, as one of the Vice-chairmen. A population of about nine million was then included in the several Soviet regions. A constitution and laws were adopted, which provided for the eight-hour day for labor, equal pay for men and women workers, protection of trade unions, a minimum wage, social insurance for workers, protection and fair wages for apprentices, etc.[7] All these measures were enforced and labor had a strong voice in government, in spite of the fact that few modern industries existed in the Soviet regions. This is shown by the composition of the 821 delegates attending the Second Congress of Soviets on January 22, 1934; eight were industrial workers, 244 artisans, 53 coolies, two shop assistants, 122 agricultural laborers, 303 peasants, 25 middle peasants and 64 small shop-keepers, students, professionals, etc.[8]

In 1934 there were about 300,000 men in the trade unions in the Central Soviet districts and 10,000 women. When the Red Army retreated on the Long March to the north in that year, twenty per cent of the trade unionists were mobilized to guard the rear, under command of Han Ying. The Nanking government soon afterward recovered Kiangsi and all unions were destroyed, most of the members being either killed or driven into the hills, where they fought guerrilla warfare or hid during the next two years. After the war with Japan began in 1937, Han Ying called all these refugees together and started the New 4th Army to fight the Japanese. These guerrillas penetrated to the outskirts of Shanghai and were joined by many workers from occupied cities.

There were also labor unions in the other Soviet regions up to the time the Red armies left these areas, but I have no figures on the membership.

After the Long March the Soviet headquarters was set up in North Shensi, in 1935. At the time I visited Yenan in 1937 there were 13,000 members of unions in the regions under the government. This figure, however, included farm laborers. Only a minor percentage were industrial and handicraft workers, as the principal industries were salt mining, coal mining, garment making, leather tanning, etc. In Yenan town I visited the various union headquarters of the bricklayers, barbers, shoemakers, tailors, blacksmiths, printers, etc. There were 600 women and 400 men in factories making uniforms, bedding, etc., for the army. Wages had been increased 50 per cent in the region, and the average working

[7] See *Fundamental Laws of the Chinese Soviet Republic,* Martin Lawrence, London, 1934.
[8] P. Miff, *Heroic China,* p. 75.

77

time was eight hours on a six-day week. Eighty per cent of the workers had learned to read and write, and each union had its own night school, recreation center, political discussion group, etc. Wages were determined by the Wage Committee of the Union and increased according to output. The unions controlled the hiring and discharge of workmen. Collective bargaining was enforced for private owners and also for government-owned enterprises, conducted by the unions. The unions, in fact, were responsible for the whole system of production, such as it was in this very poor and backward region. They had competitions and one-year and two-year plans, etc., modeled after Russia.

In September, 1937, the Soviet Government was changed and the Soviets were given up in favor of a democratic system with universal suffrage for landlords and owners, as well as workers and poor peasants, who had previously voted through their Soviets and unions. The Communist movement expanded rapidly into new territories and organized new labor unions wherever it went.

The emancipation of village workers from medieval conditions carried out under the Communists has been an important step in the progress of China, even though much of it was not permanent, as they were driven out of one province after another. Among their most devoted supporters, for example, are such miners as these described by H. D. Fong in *Industrial Organization in China,* p. 40:

"There are miners in the coal mines of Shansi who have for fifteen and twenty years been working twelve hours a day underground for a wage of ten cents a day: 'How did they get recruited in the first place for such a living hell, and how does it come they are still there?' They were recruited just as are the young cotton mill workers and apprentices for the multitude of small industries, by contract between some boss and the parents. There was some debt to be paid, or there simply was not enough to eat to support the whole family. So one boy or two went to the mine. There was no escape afterwards because the contractor controls the workers' expenses and never permits him to get out of debt."

These conditions remind one of those in the mines of south Wales a century ago at the time of the famous Tredegar strike, when some 20,000 desperate miners marched across the Glamorganshire mountains in 1816 rallying the men from every mine and ironworks as they passed. Their children went to work at the age of six or seven, and families were so indebted that they hardly ever touched a coin of money from one month to another. In China, it frequently happened that as soon as the Red Armies approached, the miners ran out, received arms, then marched over hills and valleys to rescue the workers in other mines and formulate new labor unions for self-protection.

VI. FIFTH STAGE: THE WAR WITH JAPAN FROM 1937 TO THE PRESENT

DURING the first two or three years of the war with Japan the high state of patriotic feeling and the continued pressure of Japanese attack created a unified resistance that promised to be very effective in maintaining unity and mobilizing the population for a strong people's war. This national movement gained ground until the fall of Hankow and Canton at the end of 1938, after which it slackened. The political situation deteriorated to the point where civil war has threatened since 1943, and occasional clashes between Government and Communist troops have occurred since 1941. After 1941 the guerrilla areas of north China were under a complete blockade by Central Government troops along the border of the two territories.

The industrial workers of China are divided into three distinct areas of control, geographically and politically: (1) the large cities and coastal region controlled by Japanese and puppet authorities; (2) the guerrilla areas in or near Japanese-occupied regions dominated by the Communists, and the unoccupied Shensi-Kansu-Ninghsia Border Government area in the northwest with its capital at Yenan; (3) the region under the Chungking Government in interior China. The problem before China and before the allied strategists is how to reunite the two latter areas in a common struggle to drive the Japanese out of their stronghold. This requires a common democratic program in order to release the energies of all troops and conflicting groups for the war against Japan, as such energies are now becoming paralyzed by internal political tension. It is impossible to see how any real labor unions can exist in Government areas until a general democratic upsurge begins again, for Chungking fears any kind of spontaneous mass movement and has swung further and further into an anti-democratic position, due largely to its increasing weakness and economic and financial difficulties.

1. LABOR IN THE JAPANESE-OCCUPIED CITIES

The main body of employed industrial workers is in the Japanese-controlled cities, where nearly all the important factories were located prior to 1937. In all China there were not more than about 2,000,000 industrial workers before the war, of whom less than half were employed in industrial establishments using machines driven by motor power or regularly employing thirty or more workers. About 70 per cent of modern industry was concentrated in the Shanghai-Wusih area. By the time Japan had occupied Hankow and Canton in 1938, the invaders had taken over or destroyed nearly 90 per cent of China's modern industrial plant. Until Pearl Harbor there were still independent British, American and Chinese-owned plants in the foreign concessions, but the Japanese have taken over most of these. Attempts at Sino-Japanese co-operative ownership and management have not been too successful. The Japanese are now operating a number of factories and plants of various kinds, with Chinese labor, but it is difficult to obtain accurate information about them.

A peculiar development in labor organization seems to be taking place in Shanghai and Nanking under the aegis of Wang Ching-wei and his two chief lieutenants Ch'ên Kung-p'o and Chou Fu-hai. All three of these have had a special kind of interest in labor during their checkered careers. Wang and Ch'ên were originally leaders of the Left-wing Kuomintang, after which they headed the "Reorganizationists" and tried to utilize labor unions for their political purposes occasionally. These elements in the Kuomintang were briefly responsible for reorganizing the guilds in Peking and Tientsin into unions in 1928. From 1932 to 1935 Ch'ên Kung-p'o was Minister of Industries and the Labor Department of the Nanking government was under his Ministry. While Minister he wrote the introduction to Lowe Chuan-hua's book *Facing Labor Issues in China,* which is not uncritical of Kuomintang labor policies. Chou Fu-hai and Ch'ên Kung-p'o were two of the seven original founders of the Communist Party. Both, however, were expelled soon afterward and Chou Fu-hai became secretary to Chiang Kai-shek. This background is interesting, as it corresponds somewhat to that of people like Jacques Doriot in France and similar traitors to their people in time of foreign conquest. Chou Fu-hai is considered the brains of the Nanking puppet government today. He was educated in Japan, where he was the founder of the Communist movement there among Chinese students. As soon as Wang Ching-wei and his clique set up their government in 1939, they proceeded, with Japanese co-operation, to organize labor activities in foreign-owned plants for the purpose of embarrassing foreign interests and of consolidating their own power.

Early in 1939 the Japanese-sponsored "Chinese Republic Workers' League" appeared in Shanghai and was used to stir up labor disputes in two foreign-owned enterprises during the summer. This disappeared and its place was taken by the "Chinese Workers' Welfare Association," which was much more active and created strikes in several British and American-owned industrial establishments. This Association collected fees from the workers, but after October, 1939, was inactive in labor disputes. At this time the Wang Ching-wei group began its usual "reorganizing" and this type of labor organization became more successful.

"After June 1939 the influence of labour organizations under several names grew steadily," wrote Eleanor M. Hinder, in *Life and Labour in Shanghai.* "In November 1939 there arose the 'China Labour Movement Association,' which for a time confined its activities largely to enterprises in the western district Extra-Settlement area. The first significant dispute with which the Association was involved at this period was a strike among mechanics, conductors and chauffeurs of the China General Omnibus Company, one of the public transportation companies in the Settlement. The success made it more influential. In June 1939 a first reorganization took place, after which the 'Shanghai General Labour Union' emerged, frankly under the direction of the Shanghai Branch of the Social Movement Direction Committee of the Ministry of Social Affairs of the Nanking authorities. Under this master union, the organization of unions in various trades proceeded. In December 1940 this General Labour Union, together with a body with headquarters in another part of the city and a Workers' Welfare Association, merged in the Shanghai Municipality Labour Movement Adjustment Committee, directed by the Social Movement Direction Committee of the Nanking Ministry of Social Affairs. During the first half of 1941 this Adjustment Committee busied itself with the organization of labour unions in various industries. These organizations were stimulated by the Nanking Chinese authorities with the dual purpose of increasing their own power and troubling the peace.

"It is interesting to note that the new Nanking authorities pursued a course not unlike that of the Kuomintang Government a decade earlier. Labour was regarded by the new regime as a factor in the political movement. Once organized it had to act if the organization were to retain the interest of the workers. Hence newly formed groups were encouraged by their organizers to initiate a positive programme, in short to present demands. If increased earnings were secured through such united action, the workers would then be bound in gratitude to the group which organized the struggle. The political hold of the responsible party increased over that section of the community which the workers represented.

"Thus twice in the space of fourteen years, labour in Shanghai was wooed by a political party. There is no denying the existence of generally unsatisfactory working conditions and inadequate earnings. From this point of view labour should in any case press for improved conditions. Yet the interest of a political party in the welfare of the working class has had in part a political, not wholly a humanitarian inspiration. A spontaneous self-directed labour movement like that in many western countries did not exist in Shanghai.

"The diminution of industrial activity following the outbreak of Pacific hostilities lessened also labour union activity, but it was not eliminated. The Social Movement Direction Committee of the Nanking authorities continued its work and stimulated workers in such trades as continued to flourish, as for example in the leather shoe trade. Here a strong union representation of workers was able to obtain through the Division's mediation in August 1942, a collective agreement embodying a minimum monthly pay of CRB$200 whether employees worked or not during slack months when otherwise they would not be able to earn this amount. Unions, too, were active in claiming on behalf of their members adequate discharge allowances.

"It can thus be seen that labour was by no means inarticulate, nor did it necessarily await the stimulation of political groups to lend it cohesion and the power to act in concert. When impelled by a sense of economic needs, workers formulated demands which they pressed

83

upon employers. Leaders emerged to conduct negotiations, often with considerable astuteness, and though in many cases they were almost illiterate, they were often keenly intelligent."

Miss Hinder also tells briefly of the work of the Industrial Relations Section of the Shanghai Municipal Council, created in 1940, in mediating disputes and serving in a consultative capacity for the factories of the International Settlement.

At the end of 1937, only 21,500 workers were employed in the Settlement, due to hostilities. A year later 178,000 were back at work and early in 1941 the figure had increased to 257,000, of whom 138,000 were employed in textiles. The Settlement was the principal manufacturing center after 1937. The increase in its importance is shown by the fact that in 1934-35 only 170,704 persons were employed in 3,421 factories and workshops, 75,000 being in textiles. From 1938 to the end of 1940 the Settlement experienced an industrial boom, as it was the only important place on the coast where Chinese capital could be employed with comparative safety and without Japanese control.

The rising cost of living caused labor unrest in Shanghai as soon as more normal industrial conditions were resumed in 1938, and at the end of 1940 the economic situation began to deteriorate, causing great hardship to workers and widespread labor troubles. After Pearl Harbor, Shanghai industry faced great difficulties. Miss Hinder reported: "Checks made by the Division in the spring of 1942 indicated that only 55 per cent of former plants carried on, and these with only some 50 per cent of the former working force. Approximately 100 American and British-owned plants, the most significant enterprises in the city with the exception of the textile mills, came under Japanese control. These were variously dealt with. Some continued operations fulfilling orders for military purposes. These included breweries, bakeries, cigarette plants and rubber shoe factories, as well as machine shops making subsidiary munition parts. Others produced goods for civilian use. Some were operated under direct Japanese control. Others continued to be operated by former foreign staffs under Japanese supervision and instruction.

"Industry in Shanghai began to conform to the pattern laid down for it by the Asia Development Board, the instrument of the Japanese military forces of occupation in the economic field. . . .

84

"Thus very soon after the commencement of the Pacific hostilities, the former bustling industrial Shanghai died."

Statistics on strikes and disputes for all Shanghai are not available. During 1940, however, the Industrial Division in the Settlement mediated 111 disputes, in which 431 establishments and 35,000 workers were involved. In 1941, 138 cases were mediated, including 57 strikes and 81 cases of unrest in which strikes were avoided; these involved 245 establishments and 45,000 workers.

Little other information is available about recent labor activities in Japanese-occupied cities, but these could be a key factor when the time comes to drive the invaders out. A general strike in all Japanese industrial establishments would be of major strategic value when allied troops approach the cities either by land or sea, These workers, however, are living in conditions of slavery and martial law, and probably a good deal of underground organizing work would be necessary to make their activities effective and co-ordinated properly with the allied attack, and also to counteract the Wang Ching-wei influence. One difficulty is that only the Communists seem capable of doing this type of organizing and of winning the confidence and support of the workers for such dangerous activities—and the old problem comes up again that the cliques controlling Chungking labor policies are opposed to this even in Japanese territory. Measures against such Communist influence are already in operation through the agents of the CC clique, Tai Li and the old Ch'ing and Hung *pongs*. The active workers who might be willing to take great risks against the Japanese, are demoralized by fear of these secret agents who might betray them as "Communists," even though there were no justification for such a charge. In the past, this has been the practice for many years in destroying independent labor leadership. It is asking a great deal of a worker to take leadership in carrying out the extremely dangerous task against the Japanese when he fears that even if he is successful, he may be kidnaped and shot by his own countrymen as a "Communist" shortly afterward. Therefore, one of the prerequisites for an effective anti-Japanese movement among these workers would seem to be guaranteeing legal rights for labor leaders and unions and protection against the anti-labor cliques and arrest by secret police who have taken the law into their own hands. This means instituting constitutional government and civil liberties under the

85

Chungking government so that the workers everywhere can have trust in the government and its representatives and a stake in making sacrifices to win the war.

In the north the Communists have had some success in making contact with the workers in Japanese plants and also in Hong Kong. The Shanghai situation is very complicated. This strategic point is now a center of activity for the various Chungking cliques. In the city and surrounding area are the agents of Tai Li and the Chen brothers, who work with the network of Ch'ing and Hung *pongs,* though all three distrust each other and form liaisons for or against the other.

An attempt is now being made to organize in a manner similar to 1927 for the purpose of taking over power when the Japanese are driven out, preventing any Communist influence, controlling labor, etc. Some of these agents have connections with the Japanese and Wang Ching-wei puppets; others are actively anti-Japanese. Tai Li has his own guerrilla units, who have fought against those controlled by the Communists, as well as carrying out anti-Japanese work. Secret agents have penetrated into guerrilla ranks as spies and betrayed their Leftist leaders to the Japanese. There are thousands of members of the *pongs,* mostly opium runners, riffraff, criminal elements, etc., but also including ordinary workers, especially those engaged in transportation and the carrying trade with Japanese. Tu Yueh-sen, however, did not sell out to the Japanese, and his organization is probably the key contact which the Chungking cliques have with Shanghai and that vicinity. It will be recalled that in 1932 his armed members did a great deal of the fighting against the Japanese in Chapei. His large economic interests to Shanghai give him a stake in recovering the city and he is one of the powerful financial figures. For example, in 1938, during a banking panic he prevented a run on the Chinese banks by a curious method; all that was necessary was for the banks to add his name to the board of directors and advertise this fact in the newpapers and the run ceased. Bank after bank did this and he became a member of nearly every important bank board in Shanghai.

When the New Fourth Army established guerrilla units on the outskirts of Shanghai early in 1938, a great many factory workers joined these forces, including girls as well as men. There were some girls of the Hua Cheng Tobacco factory in Shanghai whom I knew.

When the Japanese took over their factory, nearly a thousand of them fled to the International Settlement and set up a refugee center in an old warehouse, where they had the most extreme difficulty keeping alive, with little food and no medicines. Cholera and other diseases broke out and many of them died. The Japanese made them a good offer to return to their jobs, but the girls were well-organized and voted to refuse. In the refugee camp they formed a "union" with definite rules and regulations to govern the camp, though I believe their factory had had no union just before this. This union kept up morale and its leaders tried in every way to obtain employment for its members.

Several of the leaders came to see me one day, having heard of a plan to organize industrial co-operatives in which I was interested, the purpose of which was to evacuate such workers and help them to start production in the interior. They wanted to learn about it and offered to go to the interior to make cigarettes for the soldiers. I could not raise any money to help them, and the Indusco movement had not yet been started. The only thing I was able to do was to get the American Red Cross to give them some medical supplies. That and one other small contribution: an American aviator who had fought with the Loyalists in Spain had just come to me asking help to get some articles published about his experiences, as he was without funds, and also he wanted to join the New Fourth guerrillas as a machine-gunner. I told him that I would help on condition that he go down to the refugee camp of these girls and teach them some modern sanitation, the lack of which was a reason for the cholera epidemic. He collected some funds from the American Marines stationed in Shanghai, bought a few bags of lime and other equipment, and started operations, to the great delight of the tobacco workers.

A number of these girls, including the leaders, secretly escaped from Shanghai and joined the New Fourth guerrillas just outside the city, and I have no doubt that they are today doing very effective work, as they were extremely competent and intelligent. The leader was a tiny, pretty girl of eighteen, named Li Mei-chen, whose father had been foreman of the factory. She had led a big strike in the factory some months before the war, and neither her father nor all the gangsters brought in to break it, were able to daunt her. She had become quite famous during the negotiations.

Rewi Alley, who was then Shanghai Factory Inspector and who knew a great many of the Shanghai workers by their first names, told me about this later. He had been greatly impressed by the incident. When the strike was over, she had been obliged to go into hiding to prevent being kidnaped by the strike-breaking gangster organization, but had appeared again on the scene as soon as the Japanese occupied the factory.

Li Mei-chen was one of the first to join the New Fourth Army guerrillas outside the city, and she kept in contact with the other girls and with other workers in Shanghai, influencing quite a number of them to escape from the city and join the guerrillas. These girls were well informed on the war and on what was going on in the world. They held discussion groups and read the newspapers with great interest. The workers in any country will do well to match the eager spirit, initiative, heroism and union solidarity of such girls as these, and they were only a small group among many. At that time there were about 600,000 idle workers in Shanghai, many dying of hunger and cold in the streets. It is not surprising that so many had to take employment under the Japanese. They had no alternative.

I always remember these girls and similar incidents, when I think of the fact that the Allied War Relief Committees of the C.I.O., A.F.L., and Railway Brotherhoods of this country have failed to send any of their China Relief Funds either to the industrial co-operatives in China, to the unions in the guerrilla areas, or to the workers who joined the guerrillas as fighters and have fought the Japanese relentlessly so many years with no outside help of any kind. I am astounded to hear American union leaders say that because China is a semi-feudal, backward country, of course the unions are weak and nothing better than those represented by the Chinese Association of Labor in Chungking is to be expected. The long history of the Chinese labor movement seems to have escaped their attention.

The New Fourth Army was driven out of the Shanghai area after 1941, by the combined opposition of the Japanese and Tai Li, and has moved its base farther north.

Other workers, however, joined the guerrilla forces near Hong Kong, Peking and in Shantung. Until 1942 guerrillas were active in the Hong Kong and Canton region, and so well organized that a number of foreigners as well as Chinese were able to escape with their aid. Skilled workers joined and built up a whole network of mobile arsenals. These guerrillas, however, being considered under Communist influence, were attacked by Chungking's troops in the rear and many of them were killed and driven out. How strong they are now is a question, but some escaped to join the New Fourth Army and other guerrilla forces farther to the north.

An important element in the south are the workers in the nine Hong Kong shipyards. These shipyards were not properly destroyed by the British, and were used by the Japanese, supplied mainly with Chinese labor. It was reported, however, that there was a continual go-slow strike among the workers and that efficiency was about 25 per cent of normal. Recently the docks were damaged by American bombing.

2. LABOR UNIONS AND LABOR ACTIVITIES IN THE GUERRILLA AREAS

The term "guerrilla areas" in China is used specifically to describe the regions under Communist influence and protected by the Eighteenth Group Army, made up of the Eighth Route Army and the New Fourth Army. Nearly all of these areas are in the north and northwest above the Yangtze River, though there are a few scattered forces in the south. The Central Government Armies have not encouraged guerrilla activity to any extent and in the few instances where this was attempted the forces sometimes deserted to the Communists. The main guerrilla area of the Central Government armies is a little pocket near Shanghai under control of Tai Li's group, though there are a few others under Admiral Shen Hung-lieh in Shantung and elsewhere.

As Japan has control of most of the large cities in the guerrilla areas, there are few factories or industrial plants in the hands of the Eighteenth Group Army. Most of the workers in their regions are handicraft artisans, miners, railway workers, arsenal workers, printers, textile workers, carpenters, bricklayers, etc.

The Communists have had remarkable success in building up popular resistance against the Japanese in the occupied areas, besides which they have a base in the northwest unoccupied by the

Japanese. There are six areas, four of which have well-organized regional governments.

To indicate the extent of their activities the following figures are taken from a booklet "North China Unconquered," published in China by the Communists in June, 1943, and from other sources:

Region	Population	Name of Labor Unions	Membership of Labor Unions
(1) Shensi-Kansu-Ninghsia Border Region (Lin Pei-ch'u, chairman)	2,000,000	General Labor Union of the Shansi-Kansu-Ninghsia Border Region	55,694 (in 1940)
(2) Hopei-Shansi-Chahar Border Region (under General Nieh Jung-chen)	8,600,000	A. Hopei-Shansi-Chahar Labor Federation B. Southeastern Shansi Federation of Unions C. Federation of Tahang Range Unions D. Labor Federation of the Chengting-Taiyuan and Tatung-Puchow Railways E. Central Hopei Labor Federation Total of Five Unions	600,000 (in 1943)
(3) Shansi-Suiyuan Border Region (under General Ho Lung)	1,750,000	No detailed report available	?
(4) Shansi-Hopei-Shantung-Honan Border Region (under Generals P'eng Teh-huai and Liu Peh-ch'en)	13,470,000	" " " "	?
(5) Guerrilla Bases in Shantung (under General Lin Piao)	10,700,000	" " " "	?
(6) Other Regions	?		
	36,520,000	Total Membership of the North China Federation of Trade Unions	1,000,000 (1943)

This population figure includes primarily only the *hsiens,* or counties, where local administrations of democratic self-government are functioning. The figure usually estimated by outsiders is that fifty or sixty million people comprise these "guerrilla areas." In 1944 Chou En-lai made a public statement that the Communist Party had 800,000 members.

It is very difficult to obtain detailed information from the guerrilla areas, as a blockade has been enforced against the Communists since 1941. The Communists, however, claim there are a million members of labor unions in all their areas. In 1943 all unions were organized into one central North China Federation of Trade Unions.

The first general union was created in 1940 when the General Labor Union of the Shensi-Kansu-Ninghsia Border Region was organized, which then had 55,694 members, of whom 63 per cent were farm laborers, 22 per cent handicraft workers and 15 per cent industrial workers. I have not been able to secure exact figures for 1944, but a 1943 report from the *Allied Labor News* stated that "As a result of the drive to industrialize the Border Region, the number of machine-shop workers has since increased (since 1940) by 41%, textile workers by 25%, needle trades workers by 6%, paper workers by 8%, printers by 5% and other industrial workers by 17%. The size of the union has increased proportionately."

The Shensi-Kansu-Ninghsia region has fewer industries than the other areas, so the proportion of industrial workers would be higher elsewhere. As 15 per cent is the figure given for industrial workers in the Shensi-Kansu-Ninghsia Unions, I think the total percentage for the million members of the North China Trade Union Federation might be estimated at 20 per cent to 25 per cent, or perhaps about 250,000 industrial workers.

In Shansi and Hopei there are coal and iron mines and iron foundries in the villages, as well as other types of industry. Shansi has been a center of native small-scale iron mining and smelting for generations. In the Shensi-Kansu-Ninghsia Border Region 78 per cent of industry is government-owned. However, in other guerrilla regions most of the industry is privately owned.

Wage laborers on the farms are included in the one million members of the North China Trade Union Federation, so possibly over half the membership is made up of this type of workers, the others being handicraft and industrial workers.

In labor unions, as in other controlling organs, the Communists are enforcing the "one-third system," which means that no more than one-third of the membership of elected organizations should be Communist Party members. This is for the purpose of encouraging a broader democracy and full representation of all groups.

The figures for the guerrilla areas are probably fairly accurate, for it is the policy of the Communists to organize every man, woman and child into his proper grouping as quickly as possible—into labor unions, peasant unions, youth societies, co-operatives, people's defense corps, etc. It is upon such that the political power of the Communists rests. Every available worker is undoubtedly organized into a union as quickly as possible.

A report written by Michael Lindsay, a British professor who escaped from Peking through guerrilla lines in 1942 and has been in the guerrilla regions since that time, quotes figures dated July, 1942, showing that in the provinces of Shansi, Chahar, Hopei, Honan and Shantung ten and a half million were organized into civil organizations and eight million in military services (self-defense corps' militia, etc.). These figures included 513,308 workers, 4,722,760 farmers, 1,024,814 youth, 2,124,208 women, 2,203,136 children, 6,956,983 in self-defense units and 967,179 in the militia. The figures overlap, however, as a man in the militia might also be a member of a labor or farmers' union.

The booklet *North China Unconquered,* published in June, 1943, gives the following table of figures, and states that the people organized in the various associations total over twelve million and the armed self-defense corps six million.

	Peasant Associations	Workers	Youth	Women
Shansi-Hopei-Chahar	875,761	234,682	280,954	710,535
Shansi-Hopei-Shantung-Honan	1,670,000	123,625	273,990	834,673
NW Shansi	125,000	55,000	70,000	87,000
Shantung	1,070,000	200,000	400,000	400,000
Central China	1,200,000	150,000	350,000	500,000
	4,940,761	763,307	1,374,944	2,532,208

	Children's Associations	Self-Defense Corps	Militia
Shansi-Hopei-Chahar	628,871	3,812,991	619,691
Shansi-Hopei-Shantung-Honan	1,070,000	1,087,510	356,318
NW Shansi	25,264	200,000	
Shantung	358,567	1,356,982	
Central China		620,797	
	2,082,702	7,078,280	976,009

This booklet has a section on "The Workers," which tells of some of their activities. The following quotation refers to the Japanese-operated Kailan coal mines at Kuyeh, Hopei, which is near Tientsin on the coast, and which was bombed by the American air force in 1942. In the spring of 1938, these "miners went out on a strike which lasted over a month. Altogether sixty thousand from five different mines walked out for higher wages. During the strike, they kept in close touch with the 18th GA guerrillas, who were already within the territory of the bogus 'autonomous zone' of East Hopei (established by the Japanese as early as 1935). They were close to the outskirts of Tangshan where the main mines are situated. As a result five or six new guerrilla detachments including five thousand miners were formed spontaneously. Their leaders were also coal miners. These worker guerrillas cooperated closely with the local peasant guerrilla groups which sprang up sporadically as a result of Japanese oppression. The worker guerrillas served as intelligence workers inside the city, as messengers, and as active fighters in the field. They contributed very much to the military activities of the Chinese troops by their intimacy with the locality, their engineering skill, their courage and experience of disciplined life. When the strike was over, two thousand men left their work and remained with the guerrillas."

Another paragraph is interesting: "In the autumn of 1940, when the 'hundred regiments' battle gave the 18th GA possession of the biggest coal mine in North China, the Tsingching mine on the Ch'eng-tai Railway, the workers strongly supported and cooperated with the troops. The 18th GA did not plan to occupy the mine permanently, but to destroy it so as to handicap the Japanese production. For three days, the miners used the tools with which they had formerly been forced to work for the Japanese oppressors, to damage the equipment of vital importance. It rained heavily during these three days. Water coming down from the hills flooded the damaged mine so thoroughly, that it took the Japanese half a year to start work again. Many of the miners joined the guerrillas, taking their families. Many workers with these guerrilla units were formed under the auspices of the Workers' National Salvation Association. This was especially true among the railway workers who had a tradition of fighting against their oppressors, long before this present war. It began to be common to find highly skilled

93

workers speaking perfect Peiping dialect in the remotest villages of Shansi, working in some small foundry, paper manufactory, or hand grenade plant.

"Like other groups of the population in the guerrilla areas, the workers have been completely mobilized to contribute the best of their ability to war against the Japanese."

In guerrilla areas Chinese industrial workers have carried out many important activities against the Japanese, especially in interrupting lines of communication. I have no detailed report on this, but these workers include detachments of railway workers from the Peking-Hankow, Peking-Mukden, Tientsin-Pukow, Shansi and Shantung railway lines; workers from the Kailan and Tsingching coal mines near Tientsin, and steel and arsenal workers from Hankow. It was reported in 1943 that there were 27 guerrilla units fighting against the Japanese in north China composed principally of railway workers from Hopei, Shantung, Shansi and Honan, but also including miners, cotton mill operatives and former longshoremen. Workers who volunteered in the guerrilla regions have created a network of small arsenals, kept some of the coal and iron mines of Shansi going, and they supply the needs of the armies and population, for the Communist areas are under complete blockade of Chungking troops and have had to build up self-sufficiency and to make their own arms and ammunition or capture it from the Japanese and Wang Ching-wei puppet troops.

An *Allied Labor News* dispatch from Chungking dated July 8, 1943, states the following:

"Unions in the guerrilla areas of North China differ from those in Free China in one important respect: they are controlled by the workers themselves rather than by the government. Whereas the officers of the Chinese Association of Labor—only labor organization in Free China recognized by the government—are appointed by the Ministry of Social Welfare in Chungking, officers of the North China unions are elected by the membership and are subject to recall. The National Mobilization Law, passed by the Chungking government last year, made membership in CAL unions compulsory; membership in North China unions is voluntary, and workers are free to withdraw at any time they wish.

"According to the constitution of the General Labor Union of the Shensi-Kansu-Ninghsia Border Region, promulgated in 1940, all

94

workers are free to join the union 'regardless of age, sex, nationality, political affiliation or religion.' The only qualification for membership is that a worker 'must abide by the union rules and pay dues.' The officers of the union, who must be members in good standing, are elected by referendum vote and 'if found unworthy of the confidence placed in them, they can be recalled immediately and others elected in their place.' All workers have the right to express themselves freely at membership meetings.

"Despite the fact that seventy-eight per cent of the industry in the Border Region is owned by the government, the General Labor Union is an independent organization. The labor policy of the Border government, drawn up at a joint conference of representatives of the union and government and announced by Border government chairman Lin Pei-ch'u in May 1941, is designed 'to safeguard and improve the workers' livelihood, increase production, and strengthen the workers' organizations so that they may become the backbone and mainstay of the anti-Japanese democratic political structure.' Newly chartered union locals are aided by the government in the following way: the enterprise concerned, whether owned by the government or private individuals, is taxed to the amount of 6% of the total wages it pays to its workers. This amount is handed over to the local, for use in developing educational and cultural projects and defraying initial administrative expenses.

"Other points in the Border government's labor policy are: 1) 'To increase the number of workers in the area by intensifying industrialization.' 2) 'To establish a floor as well as a ceiling for wages—on the one hand, exploitation of the workers by the employers is not permitted, on the other hand, the employers must not be deprived of their normal profits.' 3) 'While the 8-hour day is the ideal for the future, in the present war situation the 10-hour day is admissible.' 4) 'Through self-imposed discipline, the workers are expected to respect their contracts and do everything in their power to increase production.'

"In a message to all its locals, the General Labor Union called for full support of this policy 'as representing the best interests of the workers in our fight against the Japanese invaders.' The provision regarding the 10-hour day, first proposed by members of the Printing Workers Union employed in the Eighth Route Army print shop in Yenan, has been endorsed by all locals in the area. To carry out its main task—'to organize all the workers of the Border Region for active participation in the war of resistance'—the GLU is divided into the following sections:

"The Secretariat, which carries on correspondence and keeps the union's accounts; the Organization Department, which registers members, carries out inspections and organizes new locals; the Department of Culture and Education, which operates classes and study groups, has charge of libraries and social clubs, and publishes the union newspaper; the Production Department, charged with enforcement of labor discipline, organization of volunteer work-brigades and study of means of improving production techniques; the Labor Protection Department, which concludes collective bargaining contracts; the Youth Department, which organizes the education of young workers and takes care of their health; the Women's Department, which concerns itself with the working and living conditions of women workers. The General Labor Union has 30 *hsien* (district), 198 *chu* (section), and 1,223 *hsiang* (village) branches. These branches are grouped into four regional councils."

Many industrial co-operatives have been formed by the workers in the guerrilla areas, and the booklet "North China Unconquered" describes part of their activities. The Japanese had planned to make a vast cotton plantation out of southern Hopei, which intention was defeated by the action of the people who refused to plant except for the use of their own industries in the villages: "Cotton textile co-operatives have been organized throughout the area, under the leadership of the Regional Women's Association. Every village has several small cooperative units forming one or two cooperatives. Sometimes a cooperative unit is based on the family unit. In this way it is much easier to get common implements and better cooperation. Experience brought out one important fact. Units that are more or less family units, and the units that are scattered fit the objective situation better than others. Weaving and spinning are done by the women at home. When the Japanese come, they do not realize that these women are working for cooperatives under an anti-Japanese organization.

"The Cooperatives were first sponsored by the local governments which loaned the local Worker Association certain sums of money. The Worker Association bought a large quantity of raw cotton and

96

distributed it to their members to be spun and woven. When the cloth was sold, the women got half the price. . . . Before 1939 most of the cloth for this region had to be imported from the occupied cities. But by the autumn of 1940, the local product became sufficient to meet the demand. The regional government adopted a protective tariff for the homespun cloth as against the imported, which encouraged its development very much. In 1941, the cooperatives in South Hopei had surplus products to export to guerrilla areas which were not producing cotton. Now in the Border Region comprising South Hopei-Southeastern Shansi-Northern Honan, the soldiers and the peasants (are) wearing clothing of cloth produced by their proud sisters in South Hopei."

I have been unable to secure a good recent report on the development of industrial co-operatives in the Chinese guerrilla areas, but these have become an important form of production. As they are self-managing, such co-operatives can be mobile and easily set up by any small group of workers of a given industry. My book on the industrial co-operative movement, *China Builds for Democracy*, published in 1941, includes an account of the early attempt to create these guerrilla industries in the New Fourth and Eighth Route regions.

The original industrial Co-operatives in the New Fourth Army region in the south had a tragic history. By November, 1939, ten co-operatives were functioning under the New Fourth Army, capitalized with money raised for this purpose in the Philippines. Three of these made pulp and finished paper for the New Fourth printing shop; another made alkali and chemicals for the paper co-operatives. The women's spinning unit furnished yarn to a towel-weaving co-operative composed of New Fourth crippled soldiers. A cigarette-making unit provided twenty other disabled New Fourth soldiers with jobs. Another co-operative made sandbags for defense purposes. A transport co-operative of thirty carriers transported goods to and from the front lines. This Indusco center set up literacy classes and classes in co-operative management and accountancy, and printed a weekly bulletin. When last heard from directly, in 1940, seventeen new units were in process of being organized. Since that time, with interruptions, the New Fourth has continued to encourage this form of production, though no information is available on the present extent of the work.

The political situation in this region was very difficult as early as 1938 and 1939, and this crippled the development of co-operatives. Early in 1941 the New Fourth Army was obliged to leave the region under orders from the Central Armies. Industries and workers were evacuated with the army. As the long column was marching to its new base, it was ambushed by Central Government troops and 4,000 of the rearguard were killed. In this rear were the industrial co-operative workers, carrying their machinery and equipment, as well as the hospital workers, women and other civilians. A great many were killed or captured along with the New Fourth soldiers and most of the industrial co-operatives' equipment was destroyed or captured.

The Yenan Depot of Indusco, in North Shensi, was started in the spring of 1939 and by September had fifteen co-operative factories. The largest of these made uniforms for the soldiers and at that time was turning out every month 9,000 plain uniforms, 4,500 cotton-padded uniforms and 1,580 military caps. A chemical goods co-operative had a monthly production of 4,000 bars of soap, 3,000 packages of tooth powder, 50,000 sticks of chalk, 800 bottles of ink, and varying quantities of medicines, alcohol and soda. Other co-operatives made pottery, stockings, shoes, hemp paper, cotton gauze for the hospital, cotton cloth, yarn, knitted cloth, overcoats, leggings. Still others did spinning and weaving and tailoring. Capital invested in these co-operatives was $55,000 (Chinese currency), and merchandise valued at $117,625 was being produced *monthly*. Edgar Snow, who wrote a report on these co-operatives when he visited them at that time, stated: "Monthly production value appears to be more than two times greater than capital investment. Figured annually, the value of production would be over 25 times the size of the capital."

In 1939 the whole Shensi-Kansu-Ninghsia Region had 137 industrial co-operative societies with 28,326 members, and 104 consumers' co-operatives with 73,693 members. Of these producers' societies, 114 were engaged in cotton spinning, nine in oil-pressing, three in salt production, six in weaving, and one each in transport, flour-milling, charcoal-burning, bean-curd making, and porcelain and pottery work. Many villages possessed but one or two spinning wheels, sharing them co-operatively from house to house.

The guerrilla authorities were anxious to develop Indusco and also to co-operate with the Central Indusco organization in Chungking, but Central Government interference and political tension made such co-operation impossible after 1940. A fund of over Ch. $250,000 was raised in the Philippines to finance Indusco work in the guerrilla areas, but since then practically no outside help has been sent for this purpose.

A report dated 1943 concerning one regional Indusco undertaking illustrates the local situation: [1]

"Until May, 1941, the Southeast Shansi cooperatives worked as a part of the Northern Front Headquarters area whose center is Loyang, on the south bank of the Yellow River in Honan province. At that time, however, the Japanese pushed southward to the north bank of the Yellow River and the co-ops found themselves cut off from headquarters by a line of Japanese garrisons and defenses. At first the co-ops decided to stand their ground. They buried their machines in the earth and themselves took to the neighboring mountains. They expected that after a short period of 'mopping up' the enemy would retire and they would be able to resume business.

"This was not to be the case. No news came of the retaking of the lost territory, traitors were working actively, and bandits and hungry stragglers ravaged the countryside. Since measures had to be taken for self-protection, the cooperatives armed themselves with whatever weapons they could find, and organized a Kung Ho Self-Defence Corps. Soon realizing they would be annihilated unless they took more positive steps, they decided to move north to work under the protection of the Eighth Route Army. Discarding extra clothes, cutting down food to a minimum and traveling only by night they reached the Shansi-Honan-Hopei Border Region after ten days. On the road, one of the Depot Staff was killed by the enemy and the manager of the Marketing and Supply Store was wounded and captured while trying to save him. The manager later escaped and made his way to the Chinese Industrial Cooperatives.

"Immediately on their arrival the Eighth Route Army authorities loaned them Ch. $200,000 as an initial fund to get the cooperatives started. Moreover, they gave another loan for a Chinese Industrial Cooperatives store from the profits of which the Depot was to maintain itself. . . .

[1] Taken from *In Guerrilla China,* Report of the China Defence League, September 15, 1943.

"After completion of these preparations, and up to August, 1942, 51 cooperatives with 357 members had started work. They were engaged in shoemaking, paper making, leather tanning, rope-making, weaving, flour milling, coal mining, printing and the manufacture of agricultural implements. At one point conditions again became dangerous as a result of a new Japanese 'mopping up' campaign, but the cooperatives suffered no loss. They were now well organized and able to quickly hide their property. An economic trial came when the store suffered a business loss of Ch. $100,000 because of its efforts to speed up turnover in producing war goods. The loss was weathered, however, and the cooperatives continued their high productive level."

3. LABOR UNDER THE CENTRAL GOVERNMENT

Japan attacked at the Marco Polo Bridge near Peking on July 7, 1937, and soon occupied Peking, Tientsin, Tsingtao, Tsinan and other cities of north China. By the end of December, Shanghai, Wusih, Hangchow and Nanking were also lost in central China and the government moved from Nanking to Hankow on the Yangtze River. During 1938 the Japanese took other cities in the southern coastal region and in October both Hankow and Canton fell to the invaders, representing the last of the important industrial cities. Thus only in the foreign concessions in Shanghai, Tientsin and Hong Kong were there important industrial establishments not destroyed or under control of the Japanese, though attempts were made at Sino-Japanese management and ownership.

In October, 1938, the government moved to Chungking in the far west, having lost its modern industrial base to the enemy. The Japanese continued to advance during 1939, but since then military lines have not shown any great territorial changes and the war entered a more static phase, except for periodical engagements.

The problem of building a new industrial base in the backward interior was a difficult one, with the Japanese blockading the coast and only Burma and Indo-China open as a line of supply, aside from Russian aid that came in from the northwest. Soon after Pearl Harbor the Japanese took over the foreign concessions on the China coast and captured Hong Kong. Burma and Indo-China fell early in 1942, and air transportation from India was the only remaining line of supply from Britain and the United States.

The situation of labor under the Chungking Government may be judged by reviewing the limited industrial scene. Little machinery was salvaged from the cities until 1938. Altogether from 1937 to 1940, 117,375 tons of industrial equipment and material and 12,164 skilled workers were evacuated to the western provinces, in several stages. Of privately-owned factories 639 were removed, 70 per cent being in operation by 1940. Of these 254 were established in Szechuan, 121 in Hunan, 23 in Kwangsi, 27 in Shensi and 214 in other provinces.

The following table [2] shows these refugee factories operating in the interior:

THE INCREASE AND DISTRIBUTION OF SKILLED WORKERS IN THE 639 REMOVED FACTORIES

Kinds of Workers	1938	1939	1940	No. of Factories Operating 1940
Machine Making	797	5,588	5,968	230
Chemical	126	1,376	1,408	62
Iron and Steel	313	860	360	2
Electrical Manufacturing	161	684	744	41
Textile	135	1,603	1,688	115
Food	12	549	580	46
Educational supplies	184	606	635	81
Other Industries	50	270	404	54
Mining	15	377	377	8
Total	1,793	11,913	12,164	639

The *China Handbook* states: "The area which is known as Free China today was mainly agricultural, where very few factories were established. There was not a single blast furnace and not a single coal mine which annually produced more than 100,000 tons of coal. Of more than 5,000,000 spindles which China possessed before the war, only 17,000 were in the interior."

[2] Taken from the latest available Chinese Government figures in the *China Handbook*, 1937-1943, compiled by the Chinese Ministry of Information, by permission of The Macmillan Company, publishers, New York, 1943.

The refugee factories were removed with the aid of Government loans and supervision, and Government policy is to subsidize private industry while also building up state industry.

In 1942 Free China had a total of 1,915 privately owned factories registered with the government, each said to use mechanical power for production. Their distribution may be seen as follows:

DISTRIBUTION OF PRIVATELY-OWNED FACTORIES IN FREE CHINA

(Registered with the Ministry of Economic Affairs up to May, 1942)

Geographical Distribution by Province or Municipality	No. of Factories		Percentage Distribution by Industries
Chungking	584	Metallurgical	7.10
Szechwan	352	Machinery	28.55
Kweichow	49	Electrical Appliance	3.15
Yünnan	49	Chemical	27.24
Kwangsi	173	Textile & Clothing	22.72
Kwangtung	13	Food	5.15
Hunan	368	Printing	2.85
Hupeh	9	Others	3.24
Fukien	23		
Kiangsi	55		
Shensi	170		
Kansu	63		
Sikang	7		
Total	1,915	Total	100.00

In addition to the above, there were, in 1942, 110 factories established by provincial governments and 98 industrial plants owned by the state, which are under control of the National Resources Commission. The five principal industries in this latter category are these: (1) twenty electric power stations, 14 in operation; (2) eight iron and steel plants (about 40,000 tons of machinery was taken from the Hanyang Iron Works in Hankow and installed in Chungking), of which, however, several were not yet in operation, including the Wei Yuan Iron Works, the Tze Ho Iron Works, the Tzu Yu Steel Foundry, and the Ling Kiang Iron Foundry; (3) machine-making plants, total number not given, the largest being the Central Machine Works in Kunming, several others not yet in

102

operation; (4) electrical manufacturing, including the four plants of the Central Electrical Manufacturing Works in Kunming and Kweilin, with branch factories in Chungking and Lanchow, and the Central Radio Manufacturing Works and Central Insulator Works with their branch factories; and (5) chemical plants, including ten alcohol plants, the Tung Li Oil Works, a coal distillation plant, the Chemical Supplies Plant in Kunming, and the Kiangsi Acid Manufacturing Plant. The exact number of plants or workers in each category is not indicated in the government report.

There were 16 cotton mills in Free China, with 167,600 spindles. Four are government-owned and all but five are concentrated in Szechwan and Shensi. In these factories is the largest concentration of labor, though no figure on the number of workers is given.

No figure is given on the number of workers employed in the 1,915 privately-owned factories or in the 98 government-owned plants, except the statement that 12,164 skilled workers are employed in the 639 factories evacuated to the interior. I have been unable to get an estimate of the total number of industrial workers in Free China, except a general guess of from 100,000 to 200,000. It may be judged roughly, perhaps, from the total claimed as having membership under the Chinese Association of Labor. As all workers are now being forced to join "unions," the union members doubtless include all industrial workers available. In 1943 the C.A.L. claimed to have 138,583 industrial workers (including textile workers, miners, 12,245 cabinet makers, machine shop workers, printers and power plant workers) and 158,140 members of "special unions" (including 35,496 postal workers, 89,109 seamen and 5,565 railwaymen). Some of these, however, are in Japanese-occupied territory, and the seamen are mostly on foreign ships. It may be estimated, perhaps, that there are not more than from 150,000 to 200,000 workers employed in modern or semi-modern industrial enterprises in Free China.

Now we come to the complicated question of labor organization under the Chungking Government, which is a form of labor union conscription and regimentation. The situation may be judged by the official statements in the *China Handbook*:

"China had 4,033 registered labor unions with a total membership of 1,053,656 at the end of 1942. Of them 3,905 were ordinary unions with 942,243 members, and 122 special unions with 114,414 members. Of the ordinary unions, occupational unions numbered 3,492 while industrial unions numbered only 129. (See table, p. 106.) China has about 3,000,000 workers. Before the outbreak of the present war, there were 872 registered labor unions with a total membership of 743,764. Most of them were in big cities.

"Several sets of regulations have been promulgated for the control of labor unions in wartime. Among them are the *Regulations Governing the Organization of Public Bodies in Time of Emergency,* and the *Provisional Regulations Governing the Control of Labor Unions in Time of Emergency.* The *National General Mobilization Act* is applicable whenever provisions in it are involved.

"*The Provisional Regulations Governing the Control of Labor Unions in Time of Emergency* were promulgated by the Executive Yuan on August 21, 1941. The main points are:

"(1) The control of labor unions should be first applied to occupational unions and then extended to industrial unions.

"(2) The control covers the following matters: (A) Compulsory participation in the unions by qualified workers, (B) Strengthening of the organization of basic units of the unions, (C) Training of officers and members of the unions, (D) Dispatch of government officials to direct and supervise the work of the unions, and (E) Readjustment of the work and personnel of the unions whenever necessary.

"(3) Labor Unions should take the following as the center of activities: (A) Assisting the Government in the stabilization of wages, (B) Assisting the Government in the investigation of the workers' cost of living, (C) Directing their respective members in technical improvement and in the increase of production, (D) Promoting labor welfare projects, (E) Initiating wartime services, (F) Assisting the Government in the requisition of labor.

"(4) The Government may subsidize labor unions for the prosecution of work, or order the related entrepreneurs to make appropriations.

"(5) Unions of workers of state-owned, educational, communication, and public utility enterprises are not subject to the control of these regulations.

"(6) Any one violating these regulations is subject to punishment.

"Places where the control has already been enforced include 26 municipalities and *hsien* in Szechwan, 17 municipalities and *hsien* in Kwangtung, 14 municipalities and *hsien* in Hunan, five municipalities and *hsien* in Honan, four municipalities and *hsien* in Shensi, two municipalities and *hsien* in Kwangsi, and one each in Kweichow, Yünnan, and Chinghai."

The table compiled by the Ministry of Social Affairs is reproduced here. Such figures are highly confusing and impossible to analyze. They are useless to the student of labor affairs. The table includes eighteen provinces, part of these areas being under Japanese occupation, and the cities of Hankow, Canton and Peiping (Peking), as well as Chungking. Hankow (63,398 union members listed), Canton (73,194) and Peking (4,537) are occupied by the Japanese, so such figures must include the unions under the Japanese-Wang Ching-wei regime. Yet Kiangsu has only 184 members listed, and none for Shanghai in that province. The largest number of members in any province is 168 unions in Hopei (excluding Peking) with 201,284 members. These must be either Japanese-controlled or Communist-controlled unions. Yet apparently the Communist unions, claiming about a million members, are not included, for Shensi, Chahar and Shantung are not listed, though it seems curious if Japanese-controlled labor unions are listed and not those under the Communists. The compilers may have merely based their estimate on pre-war figures.

In the areas under Chungking's administration, as all workers are under law forced to join so-called "unions," they are *ipso facto* listed as members, whether or not actual organization has taken place, with or without the consent of the workers themselves. The table shows that only seven ordinary unions, with 2,964 members, and 19 special unions, with 32,425 members, or a total of 26 unions and 35,389 members, are "directly registered with Central Government." The only ones specified are six railway unions and thirteen seamen's unions. Most of the Chinese seamen are on foreign ships, and one can only speculate whether the railway workers include those on Japanese-operated railways, as only 2,725 kilometers of line were in Chinese hands.

In order to understand the status of labor under the Chungking Government and the nature of the "labor unions" being created, it is essential to note carefully not only the surface regulations but the general political situation.

105

REGISTERED LABOR UNIONS IN CHINA

(December, 1942)

	Grand Total		Ordinary Unions								Special Unions					
	Unions	Members	Provincial Unions	Municipal or Hsien Unions	Industrial Unions	Occupational Unions	Union of Various Kinds of Workers	Others	Total	Members	Railway	Highway	Seamen's	Junk	Total	Members
Hunan	733	194,030		27	34	640	2		703	174,908				30	30	19,122
Fukien	230	49,681		12	4	195			211	43,111		1		18	19	6,550
Szechwan	993	86,163	2	82	39	845	14	3	983	85,817				10	10	646
Chekiang	447	69,274		17	5	405			429	54,826				12	12	14,448
Honan	133	36,059		3	4	125			132	34,819				1	1	1,240
Kwangsi	125	40,919		10	6	101			117	37,074				8	8	3,845
Sikang	82	5,120				73	1		82	5,120						
Kweichow	145	11,058		9	1	135	1		143	10,517				2	2	541
Kiangsi	192	27,010		7	7	167	1		189	21,360		1		2	3	5,650
Shensi	65	14,827		20		53	1		65	14,827						
Kiangsu	2	184				1			1					1	1	184
Anhwei	173	41,103		4	1	161			172	41,037				1	1	66
Hopei	168	201,284		11		160	2	2	165	199,602				3	3	1,682
Kwangtung	60	30,795		4		51	7		54	22,682				6	6	8,113
Yünnan	95	27,880		1	9	77	1		92	23,104				3	3	4,776
Kansu	130	11,220		4	11	101	2	2	130	11,220						
Ninghsia	30	1,635		9		23			30	1,635						
Chinghai	11	2,239		6				9	11	2,239						
Hankow	57	63,398			3	52			55	51,782				2	2	11,616
Canton	64	73,179				63			63	72,669				1	1	510
Peiping	8	4,537			2	6			8	4,537						
Chungking	64	26,672			3	58		1	63	26,672				1	1	
Directly registered with Central Government	26	35,389						7	7	2,964	6		13		19	32,425
Grand Total	4,033	1,053,656	2	226	129	3,492	31	24	3,905	942,243	6	2	13	101	122	111,414

SOURCE: THE MINISTRY OF SOCIAL AFFAIRS

In 1942 a National Mobilization Act was enforced by the Chungking Government. This Act was ostensibly for the purpose of mobilization for the war effort against Japan. However, its chief purpose was to intensify Government and Kuomintang dictatorship and to prevent any democratic changes that might occur. It was not a war policy, in effect, but a *postwar* policy—i.e., it was intended to strengthen dictatorship over internal affairs in preparation for postwar problems. It was also preparation for a possible civil war. This can only be understood in its context in the general political situation in China. To put it frankly, after Pearl Harbor the reactionary elements in the Government and armies passively adopted a policy of not prosecuting the war against Japan if avoidable, but leaving this to Britain and the United States, while turning their attention to consolidating power over internal affairs and preparing for a showdown with the Communists.

To quote an article in *Amerasia,* "Organized Labor in Asia," May 12, 1944: "On May 5, 1942, the Government adopted the National General Mobilization Act, which is almost identical in its provisions with the General Mobilization Act adopted in Japan, and which gave the Government power to outlaw strikes and conscript labor. . . . These provisions are generally regarded as paving the way for continued government control over labor unions in the post-war period."

The type of "mobilization" and increased dictatorship enforced under the Act is opposed by all progressive forces in China, who feel that instead a democratic mobilization must be carried out to strengthen the war effort by improving unity and morale, thereby solving internal problems by democratic compromise instead of force. The increased dictatorship and accompanying policies have already had the effect of further paralyzing the war effort; putting the Communists and others on the defensive against the threat of extermination or civil war; creating dissension inside the government, the Kuomintang and the armies; and alienating the people from the government. In 1943 the Kuomintang promised to "institute constitutional government" a year after the war ends. This, however, does not help the war effort and the promise has been made many times before. It seems impossible to unify China either now or after the war except by democratic means, as China is in a stage of history where such democracy is an essential development.

107

The situation is entirely different from other countries where certain democratic forms have been temporarily suspended during the war and where no civil war threatens. China has not yet achieved democracy and her only strength today lies in giving the people a stake in their own liberation and progress—a progress denied them under the Japanese-Wang Ching-wei regime. As one illustration, one may compare the efforts of Mikhailovich in Yugoslavia with those of Tito, or similar situations in Greece, Bulgaria, etc. The Chinese Government is too weak and its economic and financial structure too far deteriorated to fight both Japan and its own people at the same time. Already peasant revolts have occurred in Kansu, Kweichow and several other places, caused largely by oppressive labor conscription.

Under the policies of the National General Mobilization Act, the Regulations Governing Labor Policy in Time of Emergency of October, 1942, provided the following in relation to labor unions:

"I. The strengthening of labor organizations shall be based on the *Law Governing the Organization of Public Bodies in Time of Emergency* and other related laws and regulations. (1) The basic units of various labor unions shall be strengthened. (2) All workers shall join labor unions. (3) Competent authorities shall appoint qualified persons to be secretaries of labor unions.

"II. Members of both ordinary and special labor unions may not declare strikes."

Other measures provided for restriction and investigation of wages and partial payment in kind; a maximum twelve-hour day and one day's rest in two weeks; welfare measures; and finally, Article VII: "To promote international labor cooperation, workers, with the permission of competent authorities may set up an organization in order to participate in the international labor movement prior to the formation of a national labor union and to make necessary associations with labor organizations in the democratic countries such as Great Britain, the United States, and the U.S.S.R."

The *China Handbook* continues: "The highest administrative organ of social affairs in China, including labor affairs, is the Ministry of Social Affairs. Specially created for the mobilization of manpower, as required in the National General Mobilization Act, is the Labor Bureau of the Ministry."

Following these emergency regulations, a new National Labor

108

Union Code was promulgated at the end of 1943. This is summarized by Israel Epstein in an *Allied Labor News* dispatch dated December 2, 1943:

"The Chinese government on November 20th promulgated the new National Labor Union Code, which was worked out by the Ministry of Social Affairs last February and now becomes law following its approval by the Executive and Legislative Yuans. The Code has thirteen chapters governing respectively general principles, organization, membership, administration, sources of funds, control provisions, legal guarantees, dissolution and liquidation, general unions, unification of unions, rights of unions to impose fines and penalties and 'special' labor unions.

"The main changes in relation to the old code are as follows: Where the old code states that industrial unions must have at least 100 members and craft unions at least 50, the new one reduces the required number to 50 and 30 respectively. Members must be over 16 years of age and officials over 25. Where membership in unions used to be voluntary, the new Code makes it compulsory for all workers. Moreover, there are no provisions for withdrawal from unions. Initiation fees must not exceed one day's wage and membership three per cent of monthly earnings.

"The functions of unions are given in the following order: raising the level of skill; raising productivity; improvement of working conditions; assistance to the government in strengthening national defense. 'Supervision and control' of unions are vested in national and local organs of the Ministry of Social Affairs, in conjunction with other bodies dealing with the regulation of production. These supervisory organs may dissolve any union and thereby render it illegal for 'serious violations,' which are not specified. Dissolved unions may appeal such decisions.

"As distinct from ordinary unions, workers in government and defense enterprises may belong only to 'special unions'—with no right to strike and limited rights of collective bargaining. Ordinary unions are in some cases permitted to strike, but only after arbitration has failed and after the supervisory organs are convinced that the majority of the members have voted by ballot in favor of a walkout. The unions are held responsible, moreover, for 'refraining from actions disturbing social tranquillity.' Strikes are not allowed in 'periods of emergency.'

109

"Employers may not prevent workers from joining unions (which workers are compelled to do by law), neither are they permitted to discharge workers during arbitration of disputes. At the present time only a small proportion of Chinese workers are members of unions. A semi-official summary of the law states that much work must be done to put it into effect. It states further that organizing work will be in the hands of graduates of the special training classes being operated by the Ministries of Social Affairs and Economics."

A further quotation may be given from the *China Handbook:*

"The Ministry of Social Affairs has selected 11 districts as centers for the establishment of model labor unions. Special attention is being paid to the organization and training of the members of these unions, welfare projects, and wartime services.

"These model labor unions are distributed in Chungking, Chengtu, Wanhsien, Niekiang, Loshan, Kweilin, Kukong, Kweiyang, Kunming, Sian and Hengyang.

"The organization of model labor unions has achieved encouraging results. Most of the 64,055 members of the 19 unions have completed training courses. Labor welfare projects include the establishment of 12 clinics, eight vocational guidance institutes, 47 workers' clubs, cooperatives, dramatic clubs, and reading rooms, six schools for the workers and their families, and measures for the settlement of industrial disputes. Workers' service corps have been organized by all the unions, including 23 air-raid service corps. The model unions also help in raising funds for different purposes and in enforcing laws and regulations relating to the stabilization of wages and the mobilization of manpower."

Another interesting *Allied Labor News* dispatch from Israel Epstein in Chungking may be quoted. It is dated April 22, 1943:

"The central characteristic of Chinese labor—strict control by government—stems from the nature and basic conceptions of China's government and her main party, the Kuomintang. An accurate statement of those conceptions, as regards relations between workers and employers, is given by Chao Pan-fu, government labor expert, in the June 1942 *Economic Bulletin* of the Central Bank of China.

" 'China's industrial development assumed a distorted character as a result of our economic dependence on foreign countries and of the unequal treaties,' says Chao. 'Our industry had no solid basis, but on the other hand there did not appear among us a so-called capitalist class in the full sense of the word. Chinese workers sold their labor for low wages to foreign industrialists and their lackeys, the *compradores*. Our labor problems grew up not on the basis of the development of native industry but as a result of the unfavorable conditions to which it was subject. The opponents of the Chinese workers were not their own capitalists but the carriers of foreign aggression.'

"Going on from this definition to the development of Kuomintang and government policy on labor, Chao divides this historically into periods. The first period, he states, was inaugurated in 1924 when the national revolutionary forces were preparing to push north from Canton, and the Hongkong general strike paralyzed their enemies in the British colony. The Canton government at that time abolished the sections of the Chinese Law Code making strikes a punishable offense, and the first national congress of the Kuomintang proclaimed its support for the unionization of all workers. Chao calls this 'the period of free organization,' and sees the sole explanation of the policy of that period in the fact that the strikes then were mainly against imperialist enterprises and waged for nationalist ends.

"During the 10 years between 1927 and the outbreak of the Sino-Japanese war, Chao says, 'government policy toward labor was fundamentally revised and passed from the system of free development of the labor movement to the principle of regulated development.' (The Labor Union Law of December, 1929, decreed: the right of local government to dissolve a union or change its leadership; compulsory semi-annual reports to the government on membership and finances; obligation of unions to accept or refuse membership according to government directions; government sanction required to form a union or undertake international affiliations; government office workers and workers in military establishments barred from forming unions; government sanction required for all collective bargaining agreements; prohibition of the closed shop. The All-China Labor Federation was dissolved soon after.)

"The third period, according to Chao Pan-fu, began in 1937 with the outbreak of the war. Trade union activity was at a low

111

ebb, he says, and the government wished to organize workers for participation in the war effort. The 'program of Armed Resistance and National Reconstruction' passed by the Kuomintang and approved by all parties in 1938 called for the formation and strengthening of labor unions. In that year the Chinese Association of Labor was set up under official auspices. In 1939 the Department of Social Affairs of the Kuomintang Party was changed without any appreciable change of personnel into the Ministry of Social Welfare of the government, and the following year this new government ministry was ordered to institute control of all labor. The National Mobilization Law of 1942, which prohibited strikes and picketing, made it obligatory for workers to join unions. 'Thus in the interests of victory and reconstruction the government passed from the policy of partial control which characterized the second period to a policy of active control,' Chao concludes.

"Almost one third of the CAL'S membership of 422,652 is today in Szechwan province. Yünnan, despite its substantial industries, has only 5,385 organized workers, and Kweichow where many new factories are located, has 4,753. On the other hand the province of Kiangsu, which is largely under enemy occupation, is listed as having 96,280 workers in CAL unions—this figure probably includes workers in the Shanghai Settlement. Apart from Szechwan, the unoccupied provinces with most CAL workers are Hunan, with 50,348, Kwangtung, with 33,296, Fukien, Shensi, Hupeh and Kwangsi. All the rest have less than 10,000 apiece."

The above quotations are self-explanatory to those who understand the principles of *bona fide* labor organization. More important, however, is a knowledge of the character of the underlying political power in control of labor affairs in China. It is a great tragedy that the democratic changes hoped for in China have not yet materialized and an embarrassment to have to expose the facts before the outside public. Yet this is now necessary in order to support the democratic movement in China, which is fighting against the forces that are trying to destroy it. Labor is only one phase in a large picture and its future lies with the success or failure of other democratic forces. The situation is not at all peculiar to China. It exists in other countries in varying degrees. The people of China, including labor, have struggled many long years for democracy and a free nation, and there are indications that success

112

cannot be long in the future. The transitory present may be looked at as the darkness before the dawn.

Several points must be clarified. First of all, the labor question is very clear-cut in Chungking today. It is simply this: whether or not labor is to have the elementary right to organize in defense of its own interests. At present it is stifled by a network of control by the most anti-labor and reactionary elements in Chungking. The Communists do not enter this picture. They are isolated in their own regions and have their own system of labor unions. Neither do Socialists, Social-Democrats or other pro-labor ideologists. No such groups have any organization among Chinese labor. There is no question of Right or Left; therefore it is impossible to support one such wing against another. The question is whether labor unions shall exist which represent the workers and serve their interests, or whether organizations using that name shall instead serve the purposes of the anti-labor forces.

On the surface it may appear that "government-controlled" unions are no menace to labor in China, and the case of the unions in Russia is cited. China, however, is in a different period of development and presents an exact opposite. The problem is not so much whether or not there is government control as whether or not that control is pro- or anti-labor. If the Ministry of Social Affairs were pro-labor in its policies as the Hankow Government was in 1927, the situation would be entirely different.

It seems ridiculous to bring up the question of Fascism in China [3] today, where economic conditions for such a movement are lacking, yet this is the only parallel to cite in understanding the status of Chinese labor. The Ministry of Social Affairs is attempting to create a "labor front" copied after that in Japan and Nazi Germany. As Madame Sun Yat-sen stated in her "Message to American Workers" in 1944: "The Chinese people are strong in defense of their own soil as proved by their resistance through seven years.

[3] The epithets being exchanged in China are illustrated by the controversy over Chiang Kai-shek's recent book *China's Destiny*. In this Chiang refers to the Communists as "new style feudal war lords." Chen Pei-ta replied by saying: "Out of the 213 pages of the book, only twelve and a half deal with the war problem, while the bulk of it is on internal problems—opposition to liberalism and communism and advocacy of compradore-feudalist Fascism of the New Absolutism (formally still wearing the mask of the Three People's Principles)."

113

But reaction and Fascism in China are strong also. This is proved by . . . and by the absence of a true labor movement in most of our territory."

Labor is not the only field in which these Nazi forms are being attempted. The secret police, which have terrorized labor for several years, were trained in Himmler's methods with the aid of German advisors. The recently-organized San Min Chu Yi Youth Corps is modeled on Hitler Youth. There are several other phases also.

Let me recapitulate the political background briefly in order to clarify the picture. Since 1927 the Kuomintang has had a one-party dictatorship in China and has tried to control labor organization completely. From 1927 to 1932 the Kuomintang was in a state of disorganization, and control over labor was comparatively loose and poorly organized. Labor still had considerable passive power which it continuously lost, reaching a low in 1935-1936, due in part to the economic depression and unemployment.

Following the political crisis of 1931-1932, caused partly by Japan's occupation of Manchuria and by the intensification of civil war, the Kuomintang organization was tightened up and the party machine came under control of the most flatly anti-labor elements in the Kuomintang; its policy was dominated by this attitude. The bitter internal strife and class hatred colored the Kuomintang's attitude toward labor a very dark and reactionary shade, with or without reference to the Communist question. By 1933 the Communists were practically isolated from labor in the industrial cities and they are today isolated from labor in Chungking's areas. In general, the Kuomintang elements in control of labor were too opposed and distrustful of it even to permit their own "Kuomintang unions" to survive in a form recognizable as a semblance of labor organization. The party machine, however, was not so strong that it could have a hand in labor activities at all times and places and it never succeeded in destroying the spontaneous struggle of labor fighting desperately for sheer economic survival as it was more and more pushed to the wall. Even the ostensible forms of labor union methods practically disappeared and mediation method reverted more and more to old feudal forms.

Following 1932 and 1933 the Kuomintang party machine came more and more under control of the CC clique headed by the Chen brothers. Other cliques were formed which alternately opposed or

114

co-operated with the CC's. One of these which is today very powerful was a rival clique started in 1932 which at first had ideas of doing away with the Kuomintang altogether, but afterward decided to work within the one-party dictatorship. These Blue Shirts or Fu Hsin Shê (meaning Regenerationists) gained a dominant control of Kuomintang military affairs through co-operation with the Whampoa P'ai, while the CC clique represented a civilian power. Both cliques built up separate systems of secret police modeled after the Gestapo and became quite efficient.

An article in *Life* magazine published May 1, 1944, says:

"Today the Nationalist Party is dominated by a corrupt political clique that combines some of the worst features of Tammany Hall and the Spanish Inquisition. Two silent and mysterious brothers, Ch'en Li-fu and Ch'en Kuo-fu, known to all the foreigners of Chungking as the 'CC clique' (from the initial of their family name) practically control the thought of the nation through a combination of patronage, secret police, espionage and administrative authority. . . .

"The CC clique maintains its control over the party by a series of devices. The ruling group in the Kuomintang is the Central Executive Committee which is the closest approach in China to a decision-making body. This committee is chosen from the delegates elected by all the party cells to the Party Congress. There has been no election to a Party Congress since 1935. Hence, for the past nine years the Central Executive Committee has been the creation of a group of men elected in the most reactionary period of modern Chinese history. Some of the delegates elected then have since gone over to the Japs with Wang Ching-wei.

". . . Within the Nationalist Party itself there is a seething hate of the rule of the CC clique, its dispensal of patronage, its stupid refusal to treat any of China's major problems realistically.

". . . Through his control over the Ministry of Education, Ch'en Li-fu has inaugurated a state of intellectual terrorism that exists only in the other great dictatorships." [4]

[4] Another comment on this clique appears in *War-Time China*, by Maxwell S. Stewart, a pamphlet of the Institute of Pacific Relations, 1944, p. 37. "The C.C. P'ai has often been accused by democratic groups within China of Fascist, and even pro-Japanese, sympathies. Charges of this kind cannot easily be proved or disproved. But the CC group has invited it by adopting many

115

In the same issue of *Life,* an editorial "News from China" comments: "...the U. S. cannot ignore the fact that if China's government should become a fascistic, power-hungry, repressive, landlords'-and-usurers' government, it is all too likely to get into trouble with Russia; whereas a government which stands for freedom, reform and international cooperation is not. Under no circumstances would the American people ever wish to be embroiled with the Soviet Union in a struggle in which they would feel politically on the wrong side. But the freedom-loving, progressive China which some of her leaders are still trying to bring to birth would merit our support against the world."

One arm of the CC's power has been its control of the Kuomintang Bureau of Social Affairs, which in 1939 became an official government Ministry of Social Affairs, all labor matters being now under its strict control. In 1933 the Bureau of Social Affairs was given official authority over labor unions and mediation of disputes in cities under Nanking's direct administration. Since 1927 the CC's have considered labor their special province, though until 1933 they did not have full control. They are reported to have always had connections with the Ch'ing-Hung *pongs* and the regions around Shanghai and Nanking have been their special field of activities, with their long-time affiliations there above ground and in the underworld. The Chen brothers' uncle, on whom their fortunes were founded, was Ch'en Ch'i-mei, the powerful *tutuh* of Shanghai.

In general, since 1933, no individual could hold a position as a labor union official in any city under Kuomintang control without the authorization of the CC's, unless he had other protection such as from the Ch'ing-Hung *pongs*.

The CC machine represents to a certain extent a protection of industry against wage increases and labor demands. Its control was facilitated by the fact that a large percentage of Chinese industry was government-owned, hence it had a direct and legal responsibility for interfering in labor matters in such enterprises. Practically the only unions that survived the 1933 debacle were the

of the trimmings of Nazism and Fascism in its methods of party organization. Its secret police, for example, and its methods for control of labor and the cooperatives, were consciously patterned after German and Italian models."

116

"special unions" having no right to strike and only limited rights of collective bargaining, such as postal workers, seamen, railwaymen and miners. These were strictly controlled by the Kuomintang. However, the Chen brothers also represent a semi-feudal reaction back to the old guilds and secret societies; their philosophy is based on going back to the old social system while adopting modern techniques. They are not spokesmen for capitalism but rather for a confused and curious compromise between modern China and the old system. In fact, they are political enemies of the more progressive bankers, industrialists and economic experts of China, who want to see their country emerge as a modern economic state.

The policy of forcing workers to join "unions," inaugurated under the National Mobilization Act of 1942 and made law under the new Labor Union Code of 1943, is a new departure and still experimental. The so-called unions were organized by the Ministry of Social Affairs and the CC party machine; if figures can be believed, they did a very rapid job of it in a few months.

It is interesting, if fruitless, to speculate on whether or not the new regimentation policy will make it more or less difficult for real labor unions to be organized later on. Any labor union should be better than none in China; as unions representing the workers are impossible at present, the compulsory government-controlled organizations are the only alternative. However, when an anti-labor political organization uses the name "union" to designate a labor set-up designed for the purpose of preventing a real union from being formed and for the purpose of keeping wages down, and collects fees from the workers to perpetuate its control, thereby preventing free action by the workers to defend their interests, this cannot aid the cause of labor in China. On the other hand, if the workers are strong enough to utilize any permissible form of organization for their own purposes, in spite of the control by anti-labor forces, such "unions" may serve a useful function in the end. If labor is weak, the new "unions" will serve only as an additional burden of exploitation and suppression on their shoulders.

The underlying purposes of the new unionization program are quite clear: (1) to utilize the "unions" in order to help "stabilize" wages and also to enforce the "requisition" of labor (conscription); (2) to extend control of the Kuomintang party machine over labor

117

for political purposes as part of the general drive in this direction in all fields; (3) to institute a policy of "education" of workers in the ideas being promoted by the Ministry of Social Affairs; (4) to introduce welfare and recreational measures, largely for the purpose of preventing labor unrest; and (5) to provide a system of "unions" to answer criticism of anti-labor policies and to secure approval abroad—this latter strengthens the position of a Chinese clique at home; (6) possibly to forestall organizing action by the workers themselves, though it is difficult to judge how strong the pressure of labor may have been, and doubtless the network of secret police could quickly strangle any independent movement that might arise.

The Minister of Social Affairs, Ku Cheng-kang, seems to be quite efficient in his field. It may be noted, however, that his brother, the Governor of Kansu, Ku Cheng-lun, provoked widespread peasant revolts against his "efficient" labor conscription policy in that province. Another efficient brother, an expert in "labor camps," was recently mentioned in a *New York Times* dispatch of May 20, 1944, from Sian, concerning a visit to one of these labor camps where "political malcontents are 'rehabilitated' to fit them for a return to a law-abiding existence in accordance with the somewhat rigorous local standards. The camp is headed by the director of the Kuomintang Shensi headquarters, Ku Chengting, a German-educated brother of Ku Cheng-kang."

The cost of living in China has risen fabulously; factories are closing down; the general economic situation is very difficult. Hence the wage problem is a serious one. In this connection, it is essential to note that the free and independent occupational workers in China are able to obtain higher wages by individual methods than the more skilled industrial workers, who are concentrated together. According to the *China Handbook:* "The differences between the wage rates of industrial and occupational workers in Chungking is great. It was only 1.0 in 1937,[5] but rose to 13.0 in 1938, 126.3 in 1939, 550.2 in 1940 and 1367.5 in 1941. The wage rates of occupational workers are, therefore, three times those of industrial workers. The difference was still increasing in 1942. In July, 1942, it was 2809.6. . . .

"The following facts may summarize the wage situation of both occupational and industrial workers. First, wages did not increase

[5] Base period: January-June, 1937.

118

much before April, 1940, as commodity prices rose only slightly. Second, the increase of wages became rapid after April, 1940, when commodity prices began to soar with unabated speed. The year 1941 clearly demonstrated this. Third, the difference between the wage changes of occupational and industrial workers is chiefly due to the difference of their forms of labor. The change of the wages of occupational workers is greater because they are loosely organized and are not as easily controlled as industrial workers.

". . . Before March, 1940, index numbers of real wages of industrial workers were above 100. Since April, 1940, they have been declining and have been fluctuating around 50 since 1941, indicating that the standard has dropped by 50 per cent as compared with the prewar period. Index numbers of real wages of occupational workers were still above 100 by September, 1940, but slumped somewhat in 1941. Since January, 1942, they have been fluctuating between 70 and 80.

"The Ministry of Social Affairs began to regulate wages in December, 1940. On January 15, 1941, the Executive Yuan promulgated *Regulations Governing the Stabilization of Wages,* to be enforced first in Chungking and extended to other cities. . . .

"The regulation of wages was extended to the entire nation on January 15, 1943, following the adoption of the *Program for Strengthening Price Control.* . . .

"The Ministry of Social Affairs on December 19, 1942, sent a circular telegram to provincial and municipal governments in relation to the stabilization of wages. The main points of this telegram are: (1) Wages prevailing on November 30, 1942, should be taken as the highest rate for the fixing of wages. (2) Areas for the restriction of wages are to be the same with those for price control. (3) The restriction of wages are to be extended to the following occupations: salt, cooking oil, textile, machinery, fuel, paper, printing, flour, sugar, barber, knitting, rickshaw and sedan chair, junk transportation, carpentry, masonry, and stone work. (4) A committee should be organized in each locality to decide wage rates. It is to be composed of representatives of local Party headquarters, local government, local *San Min Chu I* Youth Corps, the chamber of commerce, the labor union, and other related organs. The local competent administrative organs are the final authority in deciding the rates. Such organs are the reconstruction department or the social affairs bureau of the provincial governments, and the *hsien* governments. . . ."

From the above it is to be noted that real wages remained above 100 (based on 1937) until 1940, when the Ministry of Social Affairs took over all labor control. In the decline that followed, industrial workers' wages dropped to 50, occupational workers' wages to 70 or 80, a slump occurring in 1941. Around this time, machinists and college professors began to consider pulling rickshas. Measures were taken to "freeze" industrial workers in their jobs. The first step of the compulsory "unionization" policy was to force occupational workers into "unions"—this was decided upon August 21, 1941. This was to keep their wages from rising further above the level of industrial workers. The natural law of supply and demand should have operated to increase industrial wages, as there has been a scarcity of skilled labor; however, recently factories have been closing down, so such labor is not in a good bargaining position. Yet scarcity of goods and inflation would have naturally increased the wages of productive workers, had not repressive measures been taken through the "unionization" and wage control schemes.

The need of the workers for real unions as a bargaining apparatus, and the opposition necessity felt by the Ministry of Social Affairs for a network of control through Kuomintang-managed "unions" to weaken labor's bargaining position, has greatly increased since 1942, due to rise in the cost of living. An article by Eric Sevareid in the *Reader's Digest*, February, 1944, "China's Skyrocketing Inflation," says: "In some provinces overall prices have multiplied by 250 since 1937—25,000%." And again: ". . . around Chungking, rice tripled in price between March and September of last year, rising from $500 to $1500 (Chinese) a picul (110 pounds)."

The *China Handbook* shows that wholesale prices in Chungking increased 95.6 per cent from October, 1939, to June, 1940, and 142.6 per cent from June, 1940, to May, 1941, the last figure given.

Finally, we come to the Chinese Association of Labor, which is of special interest abroad, as it is the present contact between China and international labor organizations, receiving nearly all relief funds sent to China by American labor unions. Because of this it is an embarrassing subject to treat frankly, and the best suggestion I can make is for American and British labor unions to make their own thorough investigation of the subject by sending a delegation to China to show their good-will and interest in the problems of the Chinese workingman. Suffice it to say that it has today no independence of the general labor setup under the Ministry of Social Affairs and is one of the instruments of its policies. Otherwise it would not be permitted to exist. The chief function delegated to it by the Ministry is to represent Chinese "unions" at I.L.O. conferences and in other international labor contacts. In this capacity it is expected to carry out that part of the Labor Policy formulated in October, 1942: "The Three People's Principles shall be publicized among international workers to enable them to understand the spirit of China's national reconstruction." At home it is expected likewise to assist in explaining this to China's puzzled workers and "to raise the cultural level of Chinese laborers." The principal job it has done so far in China is to help dispense some $600,000 of American labor's relief funds, used chiefly to establish recreation centers for workers, to evacuate skilled workers from the coast, and to provide supplementary feeding for soldiers in base hospitals. Its officers spend most of their time abroad. The C.A.L. as such did not organize the half-million members of unions which it now claims. Such organizing as was done was carried out by the Ministry of Social Affairs and the CC party machine and certain categories of workers and "unions" were arbitrarily placed under C.A.L. affiliation.

The *China Handbook* describes the C.A.L. as follows:

"Among the unions registered with the Ministry of Social Affairs is the Chinese Seamen's Union, which has its headquarters in Chungking and 12 branch unions, 154 sub-branch unions, and 437 small units, with a total membership of 37,667. This union is constantly fighting for the better treatment of Chinese seamen, especially those on foreign ships. Another organization is the Chinese Association of Labor, composed of 52 group members and 225 members, totalling more than 350,000 persons. It acts unofficially as the national organization for workers, as the National Labor Union is not yet established. Its chief purpose is to raise the cultural level of Chinese laborers in China and to promote labor welfare."

The C.A.L. is not a federation or council of trade unions, even if the unions affiliated with it could be considered authentic unions;

121

it performs none of the functions of such an organization. In the past a national or even an interprovincial federation was illegal, though national organizations were made permissible in 1942. Hence only a kind of welfare agency was permitted. Actually from 1938 to 1942 the C.A.L. was little more than a name under which its head was authorized to attend I.L.O. conferences.

When the C.A.L. was established in Hankow in 1938 under government auspices, it consisted of 31 persons, including, it is reported, a Communist woman named Liao Lu-kwan. Its president was Chu Hsueh-fan,[6] formerly an official in the Postal Employees' Union, who had been workers' delegate at the I.L.O. conference the previous year and has served as I.L.O. delegate since then. The C.A.L. became vaguely affiliated with the International Federation of Trade Unions.

Until compulsory membership in unions was instituted under the Mobilization Act of 1942, the C.A.L. claimed only to represent a few "special unions"—the Seamen's Union, the Postal Employees' Union and several railwaymen's unions. These "special unions," organized by the Kuomintang and under strict government control, were practically the only survivals of any kind in 1937, after which they were disorganized and could hardly be said to exist until the new "unionization" began several years later. They survived because they were in easily-controlled government-owned industries (except the seamen), and were covered by special legislation forbidding the right to strike and limiting the right of collective bargaining, and were therefore considered innocuous. Such "special unions" are still the basis of the C.A.L., though others have since been added. As restated in the labor policy formulated under the National Mobilization Act: "Workers in military industries do not possess the right of organizing unions. Special unions of public enterprises do not possess the right of striking and collective bargaining. Special unions of privately-owned public utility and com-

[6] It is of little importance to discuss the personal or political background of any individual in the C.A.L., as with the best of intentions no one could individually affect the present labor setup, which is controlled by the Ministry of Social Affairs and the anti-labor political cliques in Chungking. Chu Hsueh-fan is only a minor instrument of this policy, having no freedom of action. An interesting account of his connection with Tu Yueh-sen and the Ch'ing-Hung *pongs* is given in the book *Shark's Fins and Millet*, by Illona Ralf Suess, who formerly worked in Geneva on opium matters.

munication enterprises possess the right of collective bargaining but not the right of striking."

At the labor conference called by the Chinese Association of Labor in Chungking in April, 1943, membership was reported as follows: 138,583 industrial workers, 78,229 being textile workers; 14,532 miners (this referred to miners in Japanese-occupied areas as well as Free China); 12,245 cabinet makers, 5,070 machine shop workers, 5,881 printers and 1,956 power plant workers. In addition to these were included 158,140 members in "special unions," mostly state and public utility workers who do not enjoy the right to strike or in some cases to bargain collectively. Of these, postal workers numbered 35,496, seamen 89,109 and railwaymen 5,565. The rest of the membership was reported as 125,929 manual workers in small enterprises, such as 15,464 tailors, 24,272 construction workers, and 43,858 transport workers. The rest are small groups down to 367 fishermen. The total membership claimed was 422,652 workers. Of the total, 26,610 were women, of whom 21,415 were in textiles.

No independent investigation has been made as to how many of these unions and workers have actually been organized, and probably it would be impossible to conduct one under present restrictions in China. The question is a little academic anyway, as the method is that of the "labor front," under which all workers in a particular factory or category are considered union members *ipso facto*. Also the figures claimed are curious and confusing, as they include workers in Japanese-occupied cities and districts, such as 96,280 in Kiangsu. If such labor organizations exist in occupied cities like Shanghai, they can only be secret societies of the Ch'ing-Hung *pongs* possibly mixed up with the CC's and Tai Li. No other mechanism exists except the Wang Ching-wei—Japanese setup. Preparations for controlling labor when the Japanese evacuate such cities in the lower Yangtze Valley would naturally utilize the old *pongs*.

All this must make very depressing reading to the average labor union member. It need not, however, for it is only a brief ebb in the tide of China's modern history. Although real labor unions cannot be hoped for under Chungking until the present anti-labor and anti-democratic policies of the Kuomintang and the cliques controlling the government are changed, the change is already evident in stormy clouds on the horizon.

In the meantime, China's labor movement has been too long isolated from international interest and support. Below all these repressive government measures are the ordinary working men and women of China struggling for the elementary democratic right to organize in their own interests. The essential thing is only that every contact with China should be accompanied by a knowledge of the problems of Chinese labor, so that there will be no misunderstanding. And the way to learn is to jump into the water. American and British labor can make no mistake if they clearly indicate their impartial support for democracy and unity generally in China, and every avenue of reaching Chinese labor should be utilized. And they need not carry partisan quarrels to China, for there is no division inside the ranks of Chinese labor today: every worker in China, whether in Chungking, Yenan or Shanghai, has only one elementary demand: the right to organize unions as part of a new democratic system. When that system is achieved and when Japan is driven out of China will be time enough to argue over the future type of society.

4. THE CHINESE INDUSTRIAL CO-OPERATIVE MOVEMENT

The one important democratic people's organization existing in areas directly under control of the Chungking government is the Chinese Industrial Co-operative movement. How it has thus far been able to survive the general reactionary trend seems rather a mystery, though it can be explained. It constitutes the only independent labor organization and is the creation of China's common working men and women, a product of their initiative, ingenuity and organizational ability. In China today it is a very precious thing, and a symbol of the hope that democracy can develop without the overthrow of the present type of government and the usual civil war. Had other supporting people's organizations, such as labor unions, been created on a mass basis during the liberal Hankow period in 1938 and the months of indecision and disruption that followed, they might also have survived and turned the tide in favor of more democracy, which would have meant keeping up morale and improving the war effort.

Indusco, however, has had a very tortuous and difficult career.

How long it can continue to beat off its enemies is a question. Its future, like that of labor unions, is bound up with the general political situation.

I have little space here to review the interesting history of this successful Chinese experiment in democratic organization.[7] The idea originated in the Shanghai International Settlement early in 1938. On April 3, 1938, eleven persons, Chinese, British, and American, met to constitute themselves a Preparatory Committee for the Promotion of Industrial Cooperatives in China. Hsu Sing-loh, a liberal banker, later killed in a plane by the Japanese, was elected Chairman. John Alexander, a young British consul and co-operative enthusiast, served incognito as Secretary. The technical plan was drawn up by a labor expert, Rewi Alley, Factory Inspector of the Shanghai Municipal Council, and two of his close friends, Frank Lem and C. F. Wu, Chinese engineers of the Shanghai Power Company, with advice from others.

Various attempts were made to secure financial support from the League of Nations, from Chinese bankers, from relief organizations, from the Chinese government and elsewhere. The only result was a grant of $10,000 Chinese from the Paris trade unions, secured by Rewi Alley.

Finally the British Ambassador, Sir Archibald Clarke-Kerr, was interested in the idea. He took the plan to Hankow and presented it, with the result that it was adopted by the Chinese government and an appropriation of Ch. $5,000,000 was made. On August 5, 1938, the "Chinese Industrial Cooperative Movement" was inaugurated in Hankow, informally under the Executive Yuan. The administration was set up with Dr. H. H. Kung as Chairman; K. P. Liu, Secretary-General; Frank Lem, head of the Technical Section, and C. F. Wu as assistant. Rewi Alley served as Chief Advisor and Lu Kuang-mien was appointed Director of the North-west Headquarters. All of the above were later driven out of their positions by political pressure, except Dr. Kung and Lu Kuang-mien, who still retain their original status.

Field organization was begun immediately by Rewi Alley, Frank Lem, C. F. Wu, and Lu Kuang-mien, who were soon joined by half a dozen other Chinese engineers. This handful of organizers

[7] For reference on the Chinese Industrial Cooperatives see *China Builds For Democracy,* by Nym Wales, Modern Age Books, New York, 1941.

created 69 co-operative societies by December, 1938. By June, 1939, there were 724 registered societies. By December, 1939, a little over a year from the inauguration of the idea, there were 1,284 registered societies with 15,625 members and approximately 15,000 extra workers and apprentices. Loan capital invested was Ch. $2,607,302 and *monthly* production was valued at Ch. $3,000,-000, or a capital turnover of about twelve times a year.

All this was a very extraordinary and inspiring development which created much enthusiasm in some quarters and alarm in others. The experiment was proven a great success with immense potentialities on the horizon. As it is easy to see from the facts, the movement was actually the spontaneous creation of the Chinese workers themselves. The handful of initial organizers merely supplied the idea and the workers organized themselves into co-operative production. In the beginning there was no trained staff available and the organizers themselves had had no experience in industrial co-operatives. By 1939 a staff of 500 technicians and organizers had been more or less trained, for which the government provided a monthly salary allowance of Ch. $40,000.

This was the period of rapid growth, from August, 1938, to the end of 1939. During following months production and efficiency was improved, and schools for technical training, accountancy and organizational methods were started. As of June, 1940, there were 1,612 registered societies, with 21,330 members, about 30,000 extra workers and apprentices, 30,000 women spinners supplying yarn, and a technical and organizing staff of 1,000. At this time about Ch. $1,890,000 in Special Funds had been received from contributors abroad and in China, of which some $450,000 had been used for social services, education, etc.

By 1940 Indusco was engaged in fifty different types of industry in 16 provinces, the products of which were exhibited in Chungking. As of June, 1942, the 1,590 Indusco factories and workshops were divided as follows: Textiles 584 (36.7 per cent), chemicals 322 (20.2 per cent), tailoring 159, mining 111, carpentry and masonry 106, foodstuffs 70, machine and metal works 57, stationery supplies 43, transportation 7 and miscellaneous 131.

There are today 86 depots, under 7 headquarters, scattered through 18 provinces.

The following table shows the development of the Chinese Industrial Cooperatives from December, 1938 to June 1942:[8]

Year	No. of Societies	No. of Members	Share Capital Subscribed $	Paid-up $	Loans Outstanding $	Monthly Production $
1938 (Dec.)	69	1,149	16,292	10,206		
1939 (June)	724	9,534	163,188	91,842		
1939 (Dec.)	1,284	15,625	416,108	236,122	2,607,302	
1940 (June)	1,612	21,330	714,996	488,214	5,469,862	5,783,450
1940 (Dec.)	1.789	25,682	1,219,347	843,245	6,000,850	9,392,154
1941 (June)	1,867	29,284	1,835,793	1,357,858	12,520,365	14,246,595
1941 (Dec.)	1,737	23,088	2,348,084	1,972,204	13,893,045	14,478,892
1942 (June)	1,590	22,680	5,645,558	4,553,392	15,727,857	24,022,944

It will be observed that the movement reached its height in June, 1941, and has not since then showed much development. One reason for this is that co-operative societies were consolidated and the work was intensified internally rather than expanded. Another is that at present conditions for any kind of industrial production are very unfavorable due to inflation and high and fluctuating costs of raw materials and it is difficult to secure capital for industry. An important reason is the unfavorable political climate since 1941.

Indusco operations are divided into seven geographical regions, and Industrial Cooperative Unions are being created to strengthen the movement. As of December, 1942, the division was as follows:

Region	No. of Societies	No. of Members	No. of Industrial Cooperative Unions	Loans Outstanding $	Monthly Production $
Northwest (Shensi, Kansu, Ninghsia and Chinghai)	325	4,019	8	3,618,041	5,774,845
Southwest (Hunan and Kwangsi)	246	3,485	5	2,155,441	9,471,517
Szechuan and Sikang	247	4,800	9	3,152,112	4,411,285
Southeast (Kiangsi, Fukien and Kwangtung)	433	5,395	5	3,519,715	1,774,616
Yünnan and Kweichow	158	2,497	3	2,082,444	2,027,765
Shansi, Honan and Hupeh	118	1,610	3	616,597	327,052
Chekiang and Anhui	63	874	0	583,507	235,864
Total	1,590	22,680	33	15,727,857	24,022,944

[8] This table and other information are available in the booklet "A Nation Rebuilds," printed by the American Committee in Aid of Chinese Industrial Cooperatives at 425 Fourth Avenue, New York City, which provides such information from material received from China.

127

Indusco has tried not quite successfully to follow the original plan of having roughly three zones of industry:

(1) Larger units and heavier industry in the safe interior provinces (such as the 325 Indusco factories in the northwestern provinces, Shensi, Kansu, Ninghsia and Chinghai; the 247 in Szechuan and Sikang in the far west; and 158 in Yünnan and Kweichow);

(2) A middle zone extending across China in the rear of the fighting front (which now includes the 433 co-operatives in the Southeast—Kiangsi, Fukien and Kwangtung; the 246 in the Southwest—Hunan and Kwangsi); and

(3) Front-line and "mobile guerrilla units" to aid the fighting in active combat areas. The front-line co-operatives now include 118 in Shansi, Honan and Hupeh, and 63 in Chekiang and Anhui. The plan for guerrilla industries, however, was more or less nipped in the bud, due to political troubles, though a brave attempt was made before 1941. In 1941, Government troops completed a blockade around the guerrilla areas, which are under the Communists, and there was no hope of co-operation between Indusco and the guerrilla areas. Nevertheless, guerrilla co-operatives and other industries have developed in those areas independently of the main movement. I have been unable to obtain much recent information on these isolated co-operatives, and the subject is discussed in the section on "Labor Unions and Labor Activities in the Guerrilla Areas."

Indusco could have been most effective in the front-line and guerrilla areas, for which its organization is admirably adapted. However, it was impossible to obtain sufficient capital for these dangerous regions, as well as being confronted with the insuperable political obstacles placed in the way.

The total capitalization of the Industrial Cooperatives was estimated at Ch. $25,000,000 in June, 1942, of which 35 per cent was supplied by the Government, 20 per cent by paid-up capital from the members, and the rest largely from the banks. Interest rates vary, but in the beginning the usual rate for government loans was 6 per cent to 8 per cent.

One of the most important features of Indusco work is the new social consciousness it brings to the Chinese village. It is, in fact, bringing the Industrial Revolution to these interior villages and in a few cases transforming them into modern co-operative communities. Indusco now has five hospitals, 23 medical clinics, five nurseries, ten consumers' co-operatives, 8 hostels, 7 cafeterias, thirty clubs and 14 primary schools. It has also regular literacy classes for workers, technical training classes and apprentice schools. From 1939 to 1942, 3,962 individuals received training in management and technical subjects. Among the most useful projects are the nine Bailie Technical Training Schools for boys from the ages of 12 to 18, in which the students learn mechanics, chemical and industrial engineering and various kinds of modern industrial processes.

Indusco has made a good start in organizing its own marketing and transportation system, and the forming of Industrial Cooperative Unions is for the purpose of improving these facilities and of standardizing products. Regional federations are encouraged, and as soon as these are well established a National Federation will be formed, which, it is hoped, will be able to take over the present functions of the C.I.C. Central Headquarters, thus completing the apparatus of democratic self-government from the bottom to the top.

Each individual co-operative is democratically organized and self-managing as soon as the members learn the principles of co-operation with the aid of the trained staff. Membership is open to all qualified workers, the minimum number of each society being seven and the maximum limited only by the nature of production. Each member has only one vote, irrespective of the number of shares he may hold, and liability for loans in ratio to the share capital must not exceed twenty to one. Supreme authority in each co-operative is vested in the Central Meeting, which elects a Board of Directors and a Supervisory Committee. At the end of the year the net profit, after reduction of a maximum of 10 per cent for depreciation and interest on share capital, is divided as follows: 20-30 per cent for reserve funds; 10 per cent for emergency uses or contribution to C.I.C.; 10 per cent to the staff as bonus; 10 per cent to the Common Welfare Fund; and 40-50 per cent to members and workers as bonus. Distribution of net earnings is made on the basis of a bonus on wages.

Indusco has paid much attention to making war supplies and helping the war effort. It has manufactured 2,500,000 woolen blankets for the government armies, and regularly supplies such items as uniforms, shoes, harnesses, charcoal engines, paint, cartridge belts, thermos bottles, gunpowder, arms repairs, tarpaulins, flashlights, helmets, etc.

Special co-operatives are formed for disabled soldiers and also for the families of men at the front to guarantee them a living at home. There are now 51 societies of disabled soldiers, numbering 1,300 members.

The Indusco movement grew rapidly from 1938 to the end of 1939, and continued development until 1941, after which it was only able to hold its own, while improving techniques and internal organization. In this year political opposition to the movement crystallized and also economic conditions hampered its development. The movement was never able to secure sufficient capital for its use, and from the beginning it suffered from opposition, threading its way painfully between the various cliques that tried to secure control of it or to strangle it, and fighting constantly against bureaucratic controls at the top. In 1941 and 1942 it was in grave danger. The deteriorating situation, however, was improved in June, 1943, by a reorganization in Chungking upon the recommendation of Mackenzie Stevens and John Lyman, sent to China through the Cultural Relations Division of the State Department. Its position under the government was always ambiguous, being independent of the government apparatus as a special new organization formed under the Executive Yuan. Its status has now been fixed as a social organization under the Executive Yuan and it is still headed by Dr. Kung.

Rewi Alley, C. F. Wu, Frank Lem, and others of the original organizers, were driven out of their positions due to political pressure before the reorganization. A number of the Indusco leaders have been arrested. Some have been released, others are still imprisoned. A few "disappeared" after being taken by the secret police, accused as Communists. One of these was named Li, head of the Hanchung Indusco depot in Shensi, whom I knew when he was a student in Peking. He was simply kidnaped by the secret police in 1941 and buried alive on the outskirts of Hanchung, no questions asked. Thousands of such people, accused only of having "dangerous thoughts" are now in prisons or concentration camps in China, as part of the general drive to destroy the democratic opposition.

Rewi Alley, the New Zealander, loved and respected by the whole

130

Indusco movement, was dismissed from his government position as advisor, but permitted to remain quietly and unofficially with the Industrial Cooperatives in the field with salary paid by the American committee. He is suspected in certain quarters of being in sympathy with "Communist" ideas. The real reason is that he was a strong champion of the independence and democratic integrity of the Indusco movement and his ideas had too much influence to be countenanced by certain powerful elements opposed to such ideas.

It is interesting to analyze why the Indusco movement has survived as an uncorrupted democratic institution in its difficult middle position between the Right and Left in China. This was possible only because it had a policy from the start of remaining strictly non-political and non-partisan, refusing to come under any existing government economic department or to permit any political clique to get control of its organization. Had it fallen under the Ministry of Social Affairs, for example, it might have gone the way of other co-operatives in China and other labor organizations. It succeeded in remaining independent of all government departments and cliques, largely because of the jealousy and rivalry of these cliques, none being anxious to let the plum fall to the share of its rival. Its existence did not, therefore disturb the delicate balance of power. Also it was a small, bitter, green plum, burdened with debt and endless economic troubles, and its structure did not permit graft or lucrative practices, so it was not considered a very desirable plum, especially in the early years. The effort required to take it over was probably considered greater than the result would warrant. It grew up like a strange new weed in an otherwise strictly regulated garden.

Another reason is that Indusco was under the patronage of the Soong family, and particularly of Dr. Kung. In varying degrees it was given support by the three sisters, Madame H. H. Kung, Madame Chiang Kai-shek, Madame Sun Yat-sen, and also by Dr. T. V. Soong and some of his supporters. These were content that Indusco should remain independent of other government departments and retain its own identity and special organization, staying away from the powerful political cliques in control of other government bureaus.

A further important reason is the international support and enthusiasm for the Indusco movement that existed from the beginning. This began with the small promotion committee in Shanghai and sponsorship of Sir Archibald Clarke-Kerr. Overseas Chinese in the Philippines, Java and elsewhere supported it as soon as they learned of the movement in 1938. Promotion committees were started in Hong Kong, Chengtu, Manila and elsewhere, made up of Chinese, British, and Americans. In July, 1939, the International Committee for Chinese Industrial Cooperatives Productive Relief Fund was organized in Hong Kong, as trustees responsible for all outside contributions. After the fall of Hong Kong, this moved to Chengtu in 1942, where it is now functioning under difficulties, headed as formerly by the Right Reverend R. O. Hall, Bishop of Hong Kong.

In London the Anglo-Chinese Cooperative Development Society, Limited, was organized on June 5, 1939, including four M. P.'s in its membership—Alfred Barnes, President, Sir Stafford Cripps, John Jagger and G. S. Wood. Miss Dorothy Woodman was Secretary. Contributions came in also from Australia, New Zealand and Hawaii.

The American Committee in Aid of Chinese Industrial Cooperatives was organized in 1940 in New York by Miss Ida Pruitt, sent from China by the International Committee for this purpose. Its chairman in 1944 was Robert M. Field, and the sponsors include Mrs. Franklin D. Roosevelt, Lauchlin Currie, Admiral Harry E. Yarnell, Lieutenant Colonel Evans F. Carlson, Dr. Walter H. Judd, Mrs. Paul V. McNutt, Mrs. Wayne Coy, Mrs. Francis B. Sayre, Hon. Gifford Pinchot, Pearl Buck, The Reverend Bishop Herbert Welch, Msgr. L. G. Ligutti, Henry R. Luce, Philip Murray and many others.

The Indusco movement will doubtless continue to go through periodic crises, as is to be expected in any attempt to maintain a democratic productive apparatus in China today. In 1942 it was in process of being strangled, but the reorganization effected on June 3, 1943, gave it a draught of fresh air. The heavy bureaucracy, characteristic of all Chungking agencies, that had been built up at the central headquarters in Chungking was swept away. In place of this an Association for the Advancement of Chinese Industrial Cooperatives, with Dr. H. H. Kung as President, was set up as a promotional agency, with a three-man committee in charge—

132

J. M. Tan, William Hsu and Meng Yung-chien. The principle of democratic control and decentralized operation, for which the co-operators in the field had been constantly fighting since the inception of the movement, was reaffirmed.

The movement is at present suffering from the general economic and political decline in China as well as from its own peculiar difficulties. It failed to secure the capital and support necessary to weather heavy storms. Even so it is the healthiest productive apparatus in government areas today. It has not been corrupted and its enemies have thus far been successfully kept out of the organization.

A report from Miss Elsie Fairfax-Cholmeley, secretary in the A. A. C.I.C., shows the situation as of December 9, 1943:

"There are now 1,350 industrial cooperatives registered in China with about 25,000 cooperative members and a capitalization of around $150,000,000. (This represents government loans and loans from the four government banks.) . . .

"Many more than 25,000 people, however, are dependent for their livelihood on the cooperative industry. In addition to hired workers and preparatory members working in the cooperatives, there are many thousands of refugees, women workers, and family members who engage in such processes as spinning of cotton and wool for which they are paid by piecework.

"In spite of government backing, the C.I.C. is a private organization. It is listed as a social organization under the Executive Yuan. Both Chinese and foreigners are engaged in promotion of the movement; and the missionaries are in close touch and cooperation with it.

"There are two distinct facets: (1) The Chinese Industrial Cooperatives, embracing the small industrial units, their local, regional and national federations (the last named not yet organized); and the Association for the Advancement of Chinese Industrial Cooperatives, which is a purely promotional agency. . . .

"Work is at present being done for the Chinese and Allied Armies as follows:

"During October and the first two weeks in November contracts totalling $6,209,579.60 were signed with the American Army in Southeast China. They covered the building of 15 buildings and warehouses, 3 roads, 2,159 pieces of furniture (beds, bunks, clothes closets, chairs, desks, filing cabinets, writing tables, mess tables and window screens) ; 300 pairs of shoes, 200 heating stoves, 1,600 lbs. of jam and peanut butter, etc. . . .

"The main work for the Chinese Army is the supply of blankets. Up to September, 1943, over 2,500,000 had been delivered by C.I.C. to the Ministry of War, Bureau of Supplies. In addition C.I.C. has filled Chinese Army orders for leather goods (belts, revolver cases, etc.) tin hats, and straw sandals.

"Work has also been done in the disabled soldiers camps to train and set up disabled soldiers in cooperatives. At Chuanhsien (Hunan) there is a disabled soldiers' co-op which makes 1,000,000 cigarettes a month, and 75% of the flour-milling of that city is also done by C.I.C. One of the flour mills is run by disabled soldiers. . . .

"Libraries and the distribution of reading material are also an important branch of education and welfare work. C.I.C. work is difficult. It needs untiring patience, initiative, drive, and a broad understanding and human sympathy. Many staff members are highly educated and technically expert men and women. They have lived abroad and in big cities, and when sent to small country towns and villages often feel that they are in an intellectual desert. It is very important, therefore, to find ways to keep them in touch with national, international and general economic affairs and modern technical progress. At present the C.I.C. has a monthly in Chinese called *Chinese Industry* and a semi-monthly news-letter issued by the National Coordinating Committee. The Regional Offices also put out their own local newsletters."

The most recent information is a Chungking cable from Miss Cholmeley dated March 23, 1944:[9]

"Latest figures show that units of the Chinese Industrial Cooperatives now working full or part-time have approximately 18,000 members. In considering the number of people for whom C.I.C. provides a living, however, it is necessary to include workers and apprentices as well as outside people who contract to process raw materials for co-ops in home industries. Outside spinners dependent on the co-ops number 10,000 in Paochi, Shensi, alone and the total number of such outside dependents is certainly considerably in excess of the total numbers of members.

"The last survey, made in Chengtu in October 1942, put the

[9] *Allied Labor News,* Chungking, March 23, 1944.

134

number of C.I.C. members at 23,481, so a decline has taken place. The chief reason for this is capital famine. Already in August, 1943, John L. Lyman, U.S. State Department advisor to the C.I.C., estimated that Ch. $300,000,000 ($15,750,000 U.S.) in loan funds were needed to put the cooperatives on a sound financial footing. Since then the government has paid out Ch. $40,000,000, and an additional Ch. $25,000,000 in bank loans is under negotiation. It cannot therefore be said that the problem is near solution.

"Apart from the decrease in the number of cooperatives, the effect of the capital famine may be seen in the number that are partially paralyzed. A survey made in November 1943 showed that about one-third of all units were working only part-time. In every case, these gave as the reason the fact that they did not have enough operating capital to keep supplied with raw materials or found it difficult to obtain raw materials under Government monopoly.

"In recent months some co-ops have also been compelled to suspend operations because of difficulty in marketing their products. In places accessible from the coast, it is becoming more profitable to import goods than to make them locally. Difficulty in obtaining raw materials has hampered the development of the co-ops in yet another way. In order to prepare for competition with post-war factory production, the C.I.C. must produce more economically and standardize output. This can only be done by mechanization. The co-ops need machinery. But machinery means increased production, which in turn requires more raw materials and more operating capital.

"When the C.I.C. was first organized, most members were refugee workers. At present the great majority are natives of the places where they work, with only 16 per cent of all members refugees and five per cent disabled soldiers. Another tendency is away from specialization. A great variety of goods of prime necessity are produced in each place, with the greatest emphasis on textiles. Specialization must have advantages under other conditions, but it is not practicable under present day Chinese conditions. Each little town and each village in China tends to rely increasingly on local production. That is why, despite all difficulties, the C.I.C.—which is capable of creating small producing units wherever raw materials are available—continues to provide the best answer to China's production problem."

135

VII. LABOR LEGISLATION AND WELFARE WORK

Protective labor legislation in China is largely a subject of discussion rather than of practical application, as it has been on the whole unenforced and unenforceable, except during the brief days of the liberal Canton and Hankow governments. The only solution to the problem is the establishment of democratic controls in government, so that organized labor itself can assert its rights and claim legal protection. This would require a change in the Labor Union Law, permitting independent trade unions to be organized as an effective instrument for collective bargaining. No amount of progressive legislation on hours, child labor, factory inspection, etc., can be successful unless labor has the strength and legal right to fight for its own interests. Independent labor unions are the only instrument through which progressive laws can be enforced in China in the present stage of development. Again, however, the whole economic system has to be improved and Chinese industry organized on a more efficient basis before modern labor standards can be achieved.

The original laws promulgated by the Peking government in March, 1912, forbade the right to strike under Article 224 of the Provisional Penal Code. After the railway strikes of early 1923, the Peking government, under pressure, promulgated the Provisional Factory Regulations by Presidential decree, but they remained a dead letter.

During 1924 to 1927 the revolutionary governments in Canton and later in Hankow more or less enforced the progressive labor regulations adopted in 1924, in territory under their control, through the instrument of strong labor unions organized by the workers themselves.

After the Nanking government was set up in 1927, a period of lawlessness and chaos ensued. On June 9, 1928, Nanking promulgated regulations governing labor conciliation and arbitration which I shall discuss in a separate section on labor union law. It was not until December 30, 1929, that the Factory Act was promulgated, to come into effect February 1, 1931, a date postponed to

August 1. This was amended December 30, 1932, and again March 27, 1935.[1]

The important reforms indicated in the Factory Act were these: prohibition of the employment of children under the age of fourteen; prohibition of the employment of women and children in certain dangerous industrial processes and in night work; limitation of hours to the eight-hour day for children, and also for adults except in cases where special conditions require the ten or twelve-hour day; provisions for rest periods and holidays; safety and health measures; welfare measures for childbirth and education of child workers; compensation and benefits for sickness and accidents. No minimum wage law was enacted, but certain regulations were indicated as to regular payment of wages and enforcement of contracts, as well as regulations for apprentice labor. The principle of equal pay for equal work for men and women was also indicated.

The Factory Inspection Act was enacted February 10, 1931, to become effective October 1, 1931. It was not until September, 1933, however, that the Central Factory Inspection Bureau was established. This Act was subsequently amended, and has never been actually enforced.

The provisions and application of the Factory Act have been the subject of much discussion and criticism from all points of view. The salient fact is that it has not been enforced, and in the opinion of many authorities is unenforceable, though it was intended to come into effect only by stages.

On the subject of labor legislation, Miss Augusta Wagner of Yenching University made an excellent and thorough analysis in her book *Labor Legislation in China*. She says:

"Between the idealism of the Factory Act and the practical social situation, which the Act purports to govern, there exists a wide gap. It is undeniable that conditions need reform but the question which arises is whether in view of this wide gap the law is at all enforceable in part or as a whole.... We may ask if the law as it stands offers any possibility of serving as an effective instrument for reform."

[1] The amended form of the Factory Act in English may be found in *China's Labor Laws,* published by the Ministry of Industries, Nanking, 1934, edited by Leonard Shih-hsien Hsu.

Her long and detailed answer is in general in the negative, and is recommended for reading by those interested in the subject. She concludes: "A most real danger lies in the possibility of postponing indefinitely all attempts at seriously enforcing the Act. It is now almost ten years since the Act was promulgated. Little has as yet been achieved. Although there are difficulties in the way, it is urgent that the Government make a real beginning at enforcement."

In June, 1936, the Central Factory Inspection Bureau reported the number of factory workers coming under the definition of the Factory Act as 181,461, in six cities, Nanking, Tientsin, Tsingtao, Peiping, Hankow and Weihaiwai. No later figure is available.

Factory inspection work was carried out chiefly in Shanghai. The Act applied to all factories where power was used and where in ordinary times thirty or more workers were employed. Under this definition, Augusta Wagner quotes the survey made by D. K. Lieu in 1933, showing that there were in Shanghai 1,186 such factories, under Chinese ownership, employing 214,736 workers, 115,373 being women (53.7 per cent), 18,266 children (8.5 per cent) and 75,693 men (35.3 per cent); 2.5 per cent being unclassified. Foreign-owned factories numbered about 250, employing possibly 100,000 workers, according to Miss Wagner. The Annual Report of the Shanghai Municipal Council for 1935 listed 3,421 factories with 170,704 workers in the International Settlement—not all of these would be of Factory Act definition.

The best factory inspection work was done by the Industrial Section of the foreign-controlled Shanghai Municipal Council, headed by Miss Eleanor M. Hinder. Shortly after the Factory Act was passed, the Council announced its willingness to adhere to it and Miss Hinder was appointed to the staff. In 1933 the Industrial Section was created. Rewi Alley, a New Zealander, was Chief Factory Inspector until 1938, and a competent Chinese staff was employed. Due to the controversial and ambiguous status of sovereignty in Shanghai, the Industrial Section had no defined legal standing in attempting to enforce industrial regulations. What was accomplished was done largely through an epic example of diplomatic persuasion and reasoning, at which Miss Hinder was very adept. Miss Hinder has told the very interesting story in her book recently published, *Life and Labour in Shanghai*. Extraterritorial privileges in China were given up by Great Britain and the United

138

States on October 10, 1942, so the whole complicated post-war Shanghai situation is now somewhat clarified.

The principal achievement of the Industrial Section was in carrying out measures for hygiene and safety against accidents and fire hazards. Miss Hinder comments in her book: "While industrial conditions at the close of the decade were in many cases still thoroughly bad, within the limits of authority and capacity a not inconsiderable progress had been made prior to December 1941, laying the foundation of improvement in the lives and livelihood of workers in Shanghai."

Augusta Wagner also made a useful study of this subject in *Labor Legislation in China*. She concludes: "In this review of the Council's efforts to regulate industrial conditions in the International Settlement, we can see that only the bare beginnings have been made ... (yet) it must still be said that the Council has made a promising beginning in the first actual regulation of industrial conditions in China."

Industrial welfare work was also done by Christian organizations in China, notably the National Christian Council, the Y.M.C.A. and the Y.W.C.A. "Mission industries," social centers, educational classes, etc., were created from year to year. In a few cases, the mill owners carried out welfare work and education among their employees, and also the labor unions did what they could.

It is not the province of this study to examine educational, welfare and charity projects for factory workers, but the work of the Y.W.C.A. demands special mention. As such a large percentage of China's workers are girls and women, the Y.W.C.A. has had a real influence in its contacts with women workers. Both the foreign and Chinese Industrial Secretaries of the Y.W.C.A. during recent years have happened to be exceptionally competent in this type of activity. Miss Cora Deng, for example, a Y.W.C.A. Industrial Secretary, is one of the few experts in the field of Chinese labor problems. Her thesis on the "Economic Status of Women in Industry in China," finished in 1941, is a first-rate study of the subject.

The Y.W.C.A. has provided hostels, educational facilities, library services, medical advice, recreation and clubs for working girls and women. Hundreds of girls, year after year, have learned to read and write in Y.W.C.A. classes and had their first experience of

139

social life in their centers. I once asked an American Industrial Secretary of the Y.W.C.A. what she considered the most valuable part of their work in China. She answered promptly: "Training in group leadership."

It may be noted that Lowe Chuan-hua, whose book *Facing Labor Issues in China,* has been quoted in these pages, was a Y.M.C.A. Industrial Secretary.

In her study, *Labor Legislation in China,* Augusta Wagner summed up the early legal status of labor unions in the following words:

"At the end of 1923, in spite of the agitation to legalize unions, no statutory rights had been granted to the workers of China. The only exception was the lifting of the prohibition on strikes by the Canton Government for the workers within the limited area of its jurisdiction.

"It was in 1924 that the first regulations legalizing labor unions were promulgated in China by Sun Yat-sen's government in Canton. With Communists in the commanding position, the Kuomintang was to enter on a stage of definitely putting into general practice the policy of previously tentatively undertaken, of organizing workers and strikes to promote the political revolution."

These 1924 regulations, which have already been described in an earlier chapter, governed the policies of the Canton and Hankow governments until the forcible repression of labor began in 1927. When the open street fighting was over and the Nanking government had more or less established itself, it turned to repressive labor union legislation.

On June 9, 1928, Nanking promulgated the Act Governing the Settlement of Disputes between Employers and Employees, which was amended March 17, 1930, and again September 27, 1932. This is the law governing labor disputes.[2]

At the same time the Standing Committee of the Central Executive Committee of the Kuomintang adopted a set of Regulations for the Organization of Labor Unions on July 9, 1928, which formed the basis of the new Labor Union Law passed October 18,

[2] For the text see *China's Labor Laws,* 1929-1935, p. 95. See also pp. 53-69, for the text of the Act Governing Labor Unions.

1929, and amended December 12, 1931, and again on July 20, 1933. Regulations concerning the Organization of Special Trade Unions were also passed by the Kuomintang Committee on July 26, 1928, applying to such unions as those of railway workers, seamen, postal workers and miners, which were later incorporated into the general law. On October 5, 1932, the Administrative Yuan issued four sets of regulations governing unions of seamen, railway workers, postal workers and telegraph workers, but these did not remove the restrictions on such unions to any extent.

Concerning the law on labor disputes, we may quote briefly from Miss Wagner again (page 230) : "Arbitration boards are to be composed of five members. The designated government authority, the Kuomintang, and the local law court, are each to be represented by one member. The remaining two members are to be appointed from employers and workers not directly involved in the dispute, chosen from panels registered with the Ministry of Industries."

No appeal is allowed from an award of such a board. Employers and workers in public services are prohibited from engaging in lockouts or strikes of any kind.

The "proper administrative and supervisory authority" was defined as "the Provincial Government and the authorities of the District (Hsien) and Municipality (Shih) where the union is located." On July 1, 1933, the Kuomintang Bureau of Social Affairs was designated as the "competent administrative authority" in special municipalities not under any provincial government but under the Central Government, as in the case of Greater Shanghai. As more cities came under the Central Government, the Bureaus of Social Affairs (controlled by the Chen brothers' party machine) took over more and more control.

Miss Wagner concludes : "As the Government consolidated its position and as more stable municipal administration became established, the Bureau of Social Affairs in each municipality was charged with responsibility for instituting the conciliation and arbitration procedure outlined in the law for the settlement of disputes. These Bureaus took a prominent part in attempting to carry out the Central Government's policy of peace for industry." She also points out that later on older methods of settlement were used "without any reference to the Bureaus or to the law."

As to the Labor Union Law, the comment of R. H. Tawney [3] is of interest: "While recognizing the right of association, it surrounds it with such restrictions which appear to a western observer to deprive it of much of its value. A union, as a condition of enjoying such protection as the law offers, must lodge an application for registration with the proper authority, which may either grant or refuse it. No conclusion, revision or cancellation of an agreement ('collective contract') between a union and employer or employers is valid unless approved by the proper authority. No interference, a highly ambiguous word, with the work of non-unionists is permitted. No strike shall be declared unless (a) attempts have been made to settle the dispute by conciliation and arbitration, and (b) the case has subsequently been referred to a general meeting of the Union, at which at least two-thirds of its members have voted by secret ballot in favour of the strike. It seems clear that, if such rules are enforced in practice, no union disapproved of by the political authorities of the day can come into existence, and no union which exists can make agreements other than those which such authorities approve."

Miss Wagner sums up the Labor Union Law in these words:

"Freedom of association and the right to strike and to enter into collective agreements have been granted but the provisions for supervision associated with these are so extensive that the unions are completely under government control. Although unions may be formed at the wish of fifty workers in a trade or one hundred in an industry, they may not be formed without the approval of the specified government authority. Registration is compulsory. Under serious penalty of fine and imprisonment, a record of the membership and the names of union officers with a statement of their previous activities must be submitted regularly for approval. Notice of meetings must be filed in advance and a report of all deliberations submitted. The authorities may order a change in the constitution or declare null and void any elections or resolutions of which they do not approve. Only such directors and supervisors of the union may be elected as are acceptable to the authorities. The amount of dues which may be assessed is also under government control. By the close supervision and control made possible

[3] *Land and Labour in China,* by R. H. Tawney, London, 1932.

142

under the law, the government officials thus determine the pattern on which these unions may develop.

"Officials are appointees of the Kuomintang.... It is to such government authorities that the unions are subject. It follows that only such unions as are acceptable to them may be established. Any free development is impossible. (p. 237)....

"Under the provisions of the law the area of a union's activities may not extend beyond the administrative areas of the city or district in which it is located, with the exception that under special circumstances the governmental authority may specify differently....

"On the affiliation of any union with an international labor organization, the law is explicit. This may not take place without government approval....

"The chief effect of the labor union laws has been to retard the development of a real workers' trade union movement.... Only inactive unions and innocuous leaders have been acceptable and have dared to register with the authorities.... Workers were forced to organize government-controlled unions. These unions provided Kuomintang officials with jobs and incomes. The officers did not call meetings of the membership; they published no accounts and made no reports. They threatened workers and used intimidation to prevent strikes. The dues that the employers deducted twice a month from wages were turned over to officials who rendered no accounting. It has not been difficult to find labor union officials who have become comparatively well-to-do in the service of the workers....

"Inactivity is typical of most of the reorganized unions. Independently-minded workers or unions can carry on their activities only underground."

I have nothing to add to the above comments, except a general endorsement. The recent regulations and the new Labor Union Code of the Chungking government I have discussed in the chapter dealing with the present situation in the section "Labor Under the Central Government."

VIII. CHINA AND INTERNATIONAL LABOR

UNTIL 1929 the principal point of contact between organized labor in China and the rest of the world was through the international Communist organizations, though in recent years this has been very limited. As soon as the first All-China Labor Federation was formed in May, 1925, it voted to affiliate with the Red International of Trade Unions.[1]

In 1927 an International Workers' Delegation came to China, composed of Earl Browder, representing the Trade Union Educational League of America; Tom Mann, Chairman of the National Minority Movement of England; Jacques Doriot, a member of the French Parliament; and Sydor Stoler of the Soviet Union, "who acted as secretary and translator to the Delegation." [2] There were also about this time other good-will visitors, such as Indians, Javanese, Japanese, Koreans, Formosans and others.

On April 3, 1927, over fifty thousand people gathered at a mass meeting in Hankow to welcome the International Delegation. On May 20, 1927, the first Pan-Pacific Trade Union Conference, with sixty delegates, was held in Hankow, and created its Secretariat, of which Earl Browder became first Secretary and remained in China during 1927 and 1928 carrying on this work. Others on the Secretariat after its organization were Jack Ryan, of Australia; Crisanto Evangelista, of the Philippines; Su Chao-jen, Chairman of the All-China Labor Federation; Huang Pin, also representing Chinese labor; K. Kawasaki of the Japan Trade Union Congress; and George Hardy of England.

The second Pan-Pacific Trade Union Conference was held August 1, 1929, at Vladivostok, though in the meantime the Secretariat

[1] Chinese workers were present as delegates at the Red International Conference in Moscow in August, 1924, and a number of workers were admitted as students at the University for Oriental Labor in Moscow during several years.

[2] An account of this Delegation is given in the booklet *Civil War in Nationalist China,* by Earl Browder, Labor Unity Publishing Association, Chicago, 1927.

144

held various meetings. Little was heard of this organization after 1930.

The Soviets and their labor unions in the interior were blockaded and cut off from the rest of China after 1928. It may be noted here that excepting an Indian, who attended the Soviet Congress in 1931, and some Koreans, only one foreigner ever entered the Soviet regions until 1936. This was "Li Teh," a German officer, who served as military advisor to the Red armies. He penetrated secretly through the blockade in 1933 and was on the Long March to the northwest. The only other foreigners who accidentally had contact with the Soviets were a few missionaries who failed to escape as the Red armies moved into their towns.

China had been a member of the International Labor Organization [3] set up in Geneva after the World War from its initiation, but the first time a full Chinese delegation was sent was in May, 1929, to the twelfth session. Previous to this China had usually been represented by resident diplomats in Europe. After 1929 co-operation with the I.L.O. improved, though there have been many difficulties in the way of making full use of such co-operation. Some of these are indicated by Augusta Wagner in a long chapter devoted to the I.L.O. in her book, *Labor Legislation in China* (p. 175):

"... It was not until 1929 that a complete delegation appeared at Geneva. Since then, in addition to the government representatives, workers and employers have supposedly been represented at every annual conference, except the one in 1932. But since sufficiently well-organized employers' associations, interested in an international conference on labor, or well-established labor organizations, such as are characteristic of the industrialized countries of the West, do not exist, the employers' and workers' delegates at the conferences were such representatives in name only."

She concludes:

"The I.L.O. has left its mark on China in spite of its general failure to improve labor conditions either by convention or more realistic measures. The contribution of greatest importance was the assistance, already noted in a previous chapter, which Dame Ade-

[3] Information on the relations of the I.L.O. with China is easily available in the records of that organization, so I have not gone into detail on this subject.

laide Anderson and M. Pône rendered in attempting to bring about a settlement between the authorities of the International Settlement at Shanghai and the Chinese Government. Although no agreement has yet been made, efforts of the I.L.O. have not been wasted, for the negotiations which have taken place pave the way for a solution in future.

"The second contribution of importance was the help given to the Chinese Government at the request of the Ministry of Industries in the organization of a factory inspection service for the enforcement of the Factory Act.[4] ...

"Almost twenty years of participation by China in the I.L.O. and of interest by the I.L.O. in China have had very little tangible result in the regulation of industrial conditions. The conditions which existed in 1919 still largely prevail."

Dame Adelaide Anderson, a Factory Inspector in England, first came to China in 1923 to assist the welfare program of the National Christian Council, and was co-opted for the Child Labor Commission appointed by the Shanghai Municipal Council in June, 1923. In 1924 M. Pierre Henry of the International Labor Office visited China and Japan and in 1926 Colonel L'Estrange Malone of the British Independent Labor Party also visited China. These were followed by Albert Thomas, former director of the I.L.O., in 1928, who carried on many discussions with the Chinese government.

All these visits were useful in stimulating interest in labor legislation and workers' welfare.

In July, 1930, a Correspondent Office of the I.L.O. was opened in Nanking which made available information on labor conditions in China. The next year it began publication of *International Labor Information* in Nanking and later *International Labor News* in Shanghai.

In 1936 Max Eastman, chief of the Extra-European Section of the I.L.O., visited China, and his trip resulted in furthering closer relations with the I.L.O.

Since 1938 much the same Chinese personnel has been sent to recent I.L.O. conferences, the Chinese government delegates being Lee Ping-heng and Pao Hua-kuo and the workers' delegate being Chu Hsueh-fan, President of the Chinese Association of Labor,

[4] The I.L.O. sent Dame Adelaide Anderson and M. C. Pône for this purpose in 1931.—N.W.

with credentials from the Chinese government. Although no national labor union federation has existed since the destruction of the All-China Labor Federation of 1925-1931, the C.A.L. is at present empowered by the Chinese government to represent Chinese labor at I.L.O. conferences, pending the proposed creation of a national organization. In fact, this was the principal function of the C.A.L. after its organization in 1938, though since the new unionization drive by the Ministry of Social Affairs in 1942 and 1943 it has become more active in China.

While Chu Hsueh-fan was in the United States as I.L.O. delegate in 1942, American labor unions were planning their war relief program for allied countries. After consultation with Mr. Chu and others, it was decided that the C.A.L. was a suitable recipient for such funds. Chu Hsueh-fan returned to China and a Board of Custody of the American Labor Fund for Aid to China was set up, with Mr. Chu as Chairman, and Dwight W. Edwards, of United China Relief in Chungking, as Treasurer. At present relief funds from the Allied War Relief Committees of the C.I.O., A.F.L. and Brotherhoods of Railroad Trainmen are transmitted to this Board through United China Relief. In 1943 $600,000 was sent, and the budget for 1944 is $650,000.

The 1943 funds were used to set up recreation centers for workers, to provide supplemental feeding for soldiers in base hospitals, and to transfer skilled workers to the interior. The Board of Custody has given no share of American labor funds as yet to the workers in the Industrial Cooperatives nor to the labor unions of the North China Trade Union Federation in guerrilla areas, these being the other two principal labor organizations in China aside from the C.A.L.[5]

As the sending of relief funds is the first direct contact the C.I.O., A.F.L. and Brotherhoods of Railroad Trainmen have had with China, this step was one of considerable international importance, though its significance was not fully recognized in the United States. It does not, of course, imply approval of the type of labor organization represented by the C.A.L. nor of the present government policy toward Chinese labor. The intent of American labor

[5] In some instances, individual unions have contributed to the American Indusco Committee and the China Aid Council in New York for the coperatives and guerrilla areas.

147

was merely to reach a helping hand to Chinese workers, in accordance with its general policy of sending funds to labor unions in allied countries, and the C.A.L. was the only available recognized agency in direct sight, with *bona fides* from the Chinese government. This intent would be much clearer to the Chinese, however, if funds were fairly and impartially given to the two democratic labor organizations—the Industrial Cooperatives and the North China Trade Union Federation—as well as to the unions organized under the anti-labor Ministry of Social Affairs, which is an instrument of the Chen Li-fu political machine. At a delicate moment when angels feared to tread in Chungking, American labor rushed in without regard to the tense political situation in China, much to the alarm of all who watched on the sidelines and to the friends of labor in China.

As soon as she learned of the plan to send American labor funds to China, Madame Sun Yat-sen sent a cable to her American committee, the China Aid Council, on June 8, 1942: "Heartily welcome CIO and AFL efforts in behalf of Chinese labor. Please request Messrs. Murray and Green together with UCR (United China Relief) to organize a representative committee for funds to China through representative here for disbursement impartially to Chinese Industrial Cooperatives, government unions, and China Defence League for guerrilla labor, etc."

In China Madame Sun Yat-sen is the symbol and spokesman of the pro-labor and democratic forces. She also stands for unity in China against Japan and the fullest co-operation between China and the United Nations. She speaks for the people of China, and her voice cannot be ignored when the cause of Chinese labor is in question. Through all the troubled times in China, she has never failed to champion the rights of labor, year after year. To the Chinese worker, she is his one steadfast friend in Chungking today, whom he can always depend upon to defend his interests.

Madame Sun Yat-sen, Chinese labor and all popular forces are today carrying on a difficult struggle for democracy and mobilization of the people against the Japanese. They need international support and most of all understanding of the issues involved. On January 2, 1944, Madame Sun Yat-sen sent a message to American workers, which should be quoted here:

"Every American worker, and every thinking worker throughout

148

the world, now understands his stake in strengthening democracy in the war against the Axis.

"Labor is fighting in this war, and producing for it, because its hope for a better life is bound up with the beating down of blackest reaction, represented by Fascism—Fascism that begins by reducing its own workers to helots and then goes on to reduce the peoples of other countries to slavery.

"Labor works and fights for the extension of democracy everywhere because only under democracy can workers organize and move forward toward the fuller enjoyment of the fruits of their own efforts. The nightmare of Fascism in Axis strongholds and the slave farms of their "New Order" have shown the workers of the United Nations the value of democracy at home.

"China has one-fifth of the world's people. For years she has stood as the great barrier to Japanese Fascist domination over all Asia which holds half the people of the earth. Today United Nations forces, as well as her own, are striking at Japan from her soil. The more effectively she fights, the shorter the war against Japan will be, and the less the cost in American lives. That is why American workers have an interest in China's resistance.

"Chinese resistance has been greatest and most effective at times when and in places where democracy has been strongest, where the people's initiative has been encouraged, and where the people's war—the only weapon with which an economically backward and relatively unarmed country can beat back a better equipped invader —has been given the freest rein.

"China's resistance has faltered and failed at times when reactionary forces have committed open treason by going over to the enemy or made the enemy's task easier by suppressing the people and their initiative, and by fearing and sabotaging the democratic effort of all.

"That is why American labor has a stake in China's democracy.

"The Chinese people are strong in defense of their own soil as proved by their resistance through seven years. But reaction and Fascism in China are strong also. This is proved by the betrayal of Wang Ching-wei and of many army generals, by the increased ease with which the Japanese can operate in different parts of our country, by the diversion of part of our national army to the task of blockading and 'guarding' the guerrilla areas, by the fact

149

that some still hold private profit above the national interest, by the oppression of the peasantry, and by the absence of a true labor movement in most of our territory.

"American labor can best express its interests in China's resistance by insisting that the products of its efforts and the gifts it makes be equally distributed to every force in China, wherever situated, that is actively engaged in operations against Japan—and to no force that is otherwise engaged.

"It can express this interest in China's democracy by going on record against the threat of civil war which some Chinese reactionaries are preparing in order to destroy a democratic sector of our struggle. That sector is the guerrilla bases in North Shensi and behind the enemy lines where the labor movement is fostered and encouraged and where many detachments of armed miners and railway workers cooperate with the guerrilla fighters to pry Japan loose from her main continental base in North and Central China.

"Our government has promised—not for the first time—that we shall have constitutional government, and that one year after the war all parties will be equal and compete politically through the ballot. We need democracy during the war because we must have equal treatment for all anti-Japanese forces. Let the first step be the lifting of the inhuman blockade which prevents wounded fighters of the guerrilla armies, that have inflicted such a large part of all Japanese casualties, from receiving vital medical supplies. Talk of democracy cannot be worth much at a time when even this first step towards a simple humanity has not been taken.

"American labor needs no praise from me for what it is doing for fighters against Fascism everywhere. American workers know, as we all know with warmth, fellow-feeling and gratitude, that ships built by their hands are carrying the weapons they have forged to many fronts of our common struggle. I ask American labor to make known its desire that the men who fight Fascism behind Japanese lines get a share of its efforts commensurate with the task they are doing."

American and British labor have, in the past, paid too little attention to the problems of the labor movement in China, and to the general political and economic situation there which so profoundly affects not only the allied war effort but the whole question

150

of post-war development. The calling of a world labor conference has been proposed, in order to bring together the labor movements of the United Nations for the first time. Such a conference would be of historic importance in laying a solid cornerstone for future international co-operation. For example, it is no accident that the I.L.O. is practically the sole remaining vestige of the League of Nations. In the field of labor, internationalism finds its greatest possibilities.

Looked at in perspective, the rise and fall of the labor movement in China is a remarkable chapter in the history of labor. In 1920, the year that organized labor both in Britain and the United States reached a peak unsurpassed until World War II, the first Chinese unions were tentatively created. As a result of World War I, British trade union membership rose from 4,135,000 in 1913 to 8,337,000 in 1920, dropping later to 5,208,000 in 1926. American membership increased from 4,135,000 in 1913 to 5,047,800 in 1920, declining to 3,546,500 in 1927. Yet in this period of post-war decline, from 1920 to 1927, 3,065,000 Chinese workers organized into unions for the first time, of whom 2,800,000 were solidly united in the All-China Labor Federation. In 1927, the British Trades Union Congress, started in 1868, had 4,163,994 members; the American Federation of Labor, started in 1886, had less than 3,000,000 members.

The Chinese movement rose on a wave of revolutionary activity and fell when the reaction came. It was defeated in its first attempt, as others have also been. Its present situation is dark but not without achievement. Though labor has no independence and no voice in Chungking as yet, it has organized the only democratic movement in government territory—the industrial co-operatives. And what underground labor movement during this war has grown from infancy to a network a million strong as the North China Trade Union Federation in guerrilla areas? In this region, the strength of labor unions is growing as part of the liberation of a nation from the double chains of feudal oppression and Japanese exploitation; this development is highly significant. As industrialization progresses in post-war China, the strength of labor must grow with it, and the achievement of 1920-1927 will not be forgotten.

APPENDICES

I. FACTS AND FIGURES

SURVEYS in China on a national scale have always been confronted with immense difficulties, and no figures can be considered more than nominally accurate. This is taken for granted in China. The only reliable statistics are those collected by researchers in various limited investigations, which are seldom kept up to date. Even the total population is not known. To quote a recent book:[1] "There is no accurate census of the population of China. The most generally accepted estimate is 450,000,-000, but the true number may be nearer to 500,000,000." It is usually said that about 80 per cent of the population is agrarian. A recent estimate puts this at 71 per cent.[2]

"Manufacturing industries may be classified into four different systems, namely: household, craftsman, merchant-employer, and factory; but co-existence and overlapping of industrial systems constitute a notable feature of the transitionary state of economic development. Thus, in China we may find all the four industrial systems, and their transitional forms, in existence in different parts of the country. The prevailing systems of industrial organization in China today, however, are those of the craftsman and merchant employer, although the factory system is fast growing...."[3]

As I have said in a previous chapter, no useful estimate has been made of the total number of handicraft workers or cottage industries, except a rough guess of about twelve million handicraft workers in 1927 and 1931. An interesting study was made by H. D. Fong in 1933, showing the decline of rural industries. He concludes: "The above six industries, namely cotton spinning, tea preparing, paper making, flour milling and oil pressing, have either declined considerably or disappeared entirely as rural industries. Meantime, foreign productions have taken their place either in China or in foreign countries."[4]

---

[1] *The Making of Modern China,* by Owen and Eleanor Lattimore, New York, 1944.

[2] According to Lieu and Chen, the agrarian population in China is estimated at 345,780,000, which is 71 per cent of the total population of 485,508,-000 (Chinese Post Office estimate in 1926).

[3] "Industries," chapter by Franklin L. Ho, in *Symposium on Chinese Culture,* 1931.

[4] *Rural Industries in China,* by H. D. Fong, China Institute of Pacific Relations, Tientsin, 1933.

1. STATISTICS ON INDUSTRIAL WORKERS

The most generally accepted figure on the number of industrial workers in China before the 1937 war began was "about two million." Augusta Wagner concludes that "the workers in industry constitute less than a fifth of one per cent of the total population.... For her manufactures China relies chiefly on handicraft production." [5]

The Ministry of Industries of the Chinese government presented two figures in 1933,[6] giving the reader his own choice. One stated there were 2,190,409 factory workers in China and 370,731 factories; the other 2,000,256 factory workers and 363,322 factories. Handicraft industries were included indiscriminately, and the number could only have been generally estimated. Another figure gives 29,269 factories and 1,120,215 workers.

Under the Factory Act of China a factory is defined as an industrial establishment "using machines driven by motor power and regularly employing thirty or more workers." This Act applied only to 2,787 factories and 786,716 workers, according to the Ministry of Industries in 1930.

In 1934 the Central Factory Inspection Bureau of the Ministry of Industries reported that there were, in 1933, 6,076 factories and 562,665 workers, of whom 170,905 were men, 137,838 women, 7,444 children, 28,463 apprentices, and 218,015 unclassified. These were identified as under application of the Factory Act. These figures, however, did not include the foreign-owned factories, and D. K. Lieu [7] pointed out that only 1,186 of the 5,186 factories included for Shanghai could be called factories according to the Factory Act definition.

One can only conclude with Miss Wagner: "Of establishments conforming to the Factory Act definition of a factory there are probably not many more than 2,000. In Shanghai a census of 4,234 factories in 1934 showed that only 375 factories, less than a tenth of the whole number, averaged over a hundred workers. In another survey it was estimated that there were only 2,750 factories in Shanghai which employed as many as ten or more workers or used motive power. In all China, there are probably not more than five hundred large factories." She adds: "In Shanghai there are probably more factories than in the other parts of China combined."

Factories were concentrated chiefly in Shanghai, Wusih, Tsingtao,

[5] *Labor Legislation in China,* by Augusta Wagner, Peking, 1938.

[6] *Labor Year Book,* 1933.

[7] "The Growth and Industrialization of Shanghai," China Institute of Economic and Statistical Research, by D. K. Lieu, 1936, pp. 64-71.

Tientsin, Hankow, and Dairen (in Manchuria), with others scattered in Kiangsu, Chekiang, Hopei and Shantung.

The basic survey from which estimates on the kinds of industrial workers in China are usually derived was made in 1930 by the Ministry of Industries. It excluded 417,602 unclassified workers in Canton.

INDUSTRIAL WORKERS IN 28 CITIES AND 9 PROVINCES, CLASSIFIED BY INDUSTRY AND SEX, 1930

	Men	Per cent	Women	Per cent	Children	Per cent	Total
Textiles	118,080	23.7	337,546	67.9	41,794	8.4	497,420
Food	53,333	77.0	14,843	21.4	1,107	1.6	69,283
Chemicals	32,310	74.2	8,627	19.8	2,635	6.0	43,572
Education (Printing)	39,309	98.2	78	0.2	665	1.6	40,042
Machinery	32,957	97.0	136	0.4	872	2.6	33,965
Clothing	24,751	84.3	2,373	8.1	2,250	7.6	29,374
Furniture	23,578	87.4	1,207	4.5	2,185	8.1	26,970
Building	20,472	96.1	108	0.6	719	3.4	21,254
Art	1,142	14.3	5,864	73.2	1,004	12.5	8,010
Public Utilities	3,486	97.3	81	2.3	15	0.4	3,582
Communications	1,226	95.5			58	4.5	1,284
Miscellaneous	21,571	85.8	1,974	7.8	1,611	6.4	25,156
Total	372,170	46.5	372,837	46.6	54,905	6.9	799,912

In an analysis of the above the Nankai University Weekly Statistical Service[8] attempted to classify part of the workers excluded, leaving out only 239,365 unclassified in Canton, with the conclusion that of 964,953 workers, the totals could be given as 468,728 men or 49 per cent; 432,940 women, or 45 per cent; 63,287 children, or 6 per cent.

The large percentage of women and children employed in industry is characteristic in China, notably in textiles and "art." As shown in the Ministry of Industries table, 46.6 per cent of the total industrial workers were women and 6.9 per cent children. The *Complete List of Cotton Mills in China*, 1937, showed that 62 per cent of the workers in cotton spinning and weaving mills (excluding hand loom weaving) were women. Another study by Dorothy J. Orchard[9] indicated that in some of the textile mills in Shanghai and Wusih, 78 per cent of the labor employed were women. Mrs. Orchard also reported that of 1,600 workers in 20 cotton-weaving establishments visited in 1931-1932, 41 per cent were apprenticed; and that in 41 transition and handicraft shops

[8] IV, No. 9, March 2, 1931, p. 53.

[9] "Man-Power in China," by Dorothy J. Orchard, *Political Science Quarterly*, Vols. 50 and 51, December, 1935, and March, 1936.

154

in other industries 25 per cent of 8,076 workers were apprenticed. The term usually lasted from three to five or seven years.

Studies undertaken in 1929 by the Nankai Institute of Economics of the cotton and weaving industry in Tientsin showed that "for the industry as a whole, apprentice labor represents about two-thirds of the entire working force, i.e., 5,117 out of a total of 7,873." [10]

Franklin L. Ho also stated that of the total of 2,186 factories in Tientsin in 1928: "As regards labor, Tientsin factories differ from those of Shanghai in that more men are employed than women; the former occupied 74% of the total working force, while the latter, only 5.5%. Child labor represented a larger percentage in the working force in the Tientsin industries than in Shanghai; in Tientsin, 20.5% of the workers were children while in Shanghai, only 9%. Most of the child labor in the Tientsin industries is found in the textile industry (21%), while the textile industry in Shanghai has a predominance of women labor (66%)." [11]

In the same study, Franklin L. Ho states: "In the carpet industry in Peiping and Tientsin, apprentice labor is the mainstay. In Tientsin the proportion of apprentices to adult workers is 0.4 to 1, while in Peiping there are as many as 2.8 apprentices to every worker ... in the cotton spinning factories in Tientsin child labor represents 37% of the total number of workers employed. The Shanghai Child Labor Committee made an investigation into the factory industries in 1925, and found a total number of 21,900 child workers, of whom 92% were employed in the textile factories, chiefly cotton spinning and silk reeling factories."

The general constitution of Chinese labor and industry is reflected in its productive capacity. Franklin L. Ho comments that: "The average efficiency of a Chinese miner for instance, is about twenty times lower than that of an American coal miner, and about four times lower than that of a coal miner in Europe. In the manufacturing industry, some idea of the inefficiency of the Chinese laborer may be obtained from an analysis of the number of operatives per 10,000 spindles, and the number of looms per weaver in a cotton mill. In Chinese-owned mills in Shanghai, for instance, the number of operatives per 10,000 spindle 20's runs from 550 to 600; whereas in Japanese mills in Japan, the number of operatives per 10,000 spindle 20's averages 350. In the case of weaving, the Chinese mills in Shanghai have, in average, two looms per weaver, but in Japan they have 5.5 looms per weaver." [12]

[10] Quoted from the chapter on "Industries," by Franklin L. Ho, *Symposium on Chinese Culture*, 1931.

[11] *Idem.*

[12] *Ibid.*

155

2. HOURS AND WAGES

The hours, and in some cases the wages, of handicraft workers have carried over into the more modern factories in China. D. K. Lieu [13] found that in 1929, women's wages in Shanghai ranged from 24 cents a day in the match industry to 89 cents a day in silk weaving. In the cotton spinning industry the average daily earnings for women were 45.2 cents; in silk reeling 53.9 cents.

T. Y. Tsha, in "A Study of Wage Rates in Shanghai, 1930-1934," [14] found that the average actual hours of work in Shanghai were as follows:

	Hours per Day
Shipbuilding	9.00
Printing	8.34
Silk Weaving	10.49
Machinery	9.26
Underwear knitting	10.25
Hosiery knitting	9.84
Oil pressing	11.16
Tobacco	7.83
Wool weaving	10.74
Enameling	9.27
Paper making	11.07
Cotton weaving	11.23
Flour	11.50
Cotton spinning	11.50
Silk reeling	10.96
Match making	7.46

Another investigation made by the Ministry of Industries in 1937, [15] showed the variance in different cities:

	Hours per Day
Shanghai	9.5
Soochow	11
Pengpu	11
Tsingtao	12
Tangshan	11
Hankow	10
Chefoo	11

[13] "The Growth and Industrialization of Shanghai," by D. K. Lieu, (*Ibid.*).

[14] Published in the *Nankai Social and Economic Quarterly*, Vol. 8, No. 3, October, 1935, p. 501.

[15] *Chinese Year Book*, 1937, "Labor Conditions," by Lowe Chuan-hua.

Tientsin	12
Tsungchow	13
Peiping	10
Chinghsien	11
Langchi	11.5

This survey would seem to indicate that organized labor activities in Shanghai had had some effect, as compared with the more backward cities.

The most comprehensive study of wages in Shanghai was published in 1936,[16] covering the period from 1929 to 1934. According to this, the "average wage for adult male workers was found to be from 50 to 80 cents a day. In the two industries in which women are chiefly employed, cotton spinning and silk reeling, the average wages were 45.2 cents to 53.9 cents respectively. In cotton spinning child workers averaged 30 cents a day. The highest piece wages were obtained in silk weaving where the highest earnings for men were $1.65 and for women 89.4 cents. The highest wage for child workers was an average of 41.8 cents in printing and 41.6 cents in the cigarette factories."

3. COST AND STANDARD OF LIVING AMONG WORKERS

In general the Chinese worker receives only enough for food, clothing and shelter on the basis of a minimum standard of living. Certainly industrialization in China has done little as yet to increase real purchasing power among the working population for the goods produced, though the wage system has naturally stimulated the development of a money-exchange economy. Real wages are so low that no reservoir of purchasing power can be built up to stimulate the market for anything but daily necessities, food and clothing. Hence the standard of living has not risen to any extent and purchasing power *per capita* among the working class is so limited that it has not created the demand for modern commodities that would stimulate quick modern industrial growth. In fact, China appears to be still in the stage of primitive accumulation of capital squeezed out of human labor, and has not arrived at the stage where return of part of the surplus fruits of labor to the producers themselves can create a new capitalist market. Accordingly, foreign trade is also limited.

A rise in the cost of living has also prevented a rise in living stand-

[16] "Wage Rates in Shanghai," Bureau of Social Affairs, City Government of Greater Shanghai, Commercial Press, 1936. I have quoted the summary given by Augusta Wagner, *Labor Legislation in China.*

ards, as wages have not kept up with the trend. The following table shows this rise:

	1926	1927	1928	1929	1930
Food	100.0	106.7	92.1	98.4	118.8
Clothing	100.0	96.8	95.1	97.7	99.9
Housing	100.0	100.8	101.1	102.1	104.4
Fuel & Light	100.0	131.4	114.6	118.2	122.5
Miscellaneous	100.0	104.4	130.0	136.4	145.1
General Index	100.0	106.7	102.5	107.9	121.8

Annual distribution of family expenditures among factory employees in Shanghai was shown in 1931 as follows: [17]

	Value	Per cent
Food	$218.59	56.03
Clothing	36.70	9.43
Rent	25.06	6.42
Fuel & Light	29.35	7.52
Miscellaneous	80.35	20.60
Total	$390.05	100.00

In 1931, Franklin L. Ho wrote of the rising cost of living: "The Shanghai index has increased by 21% between the present year and 1926, while during the same period the Tientsin index has increased by 19%. One dollar's worth of the workers' necessaries of life in 1926 would cost now one dollar and twenty-two cents in Shanghai, and one dollar and twenty cents in Tientsin. The present purchasing power of a dollar to the laboring class is only equivalent to that of $0.83 in 1926. He who earns ten dollars a month today is receiving only $8.30 in terms of the 1926 purchasing power." [18]

The basic and most accurate study to date of the cost and standard of living among Chinese workers was made in Shanghai by the Shanghai Bureau of Social Affairs for the period of twelve months from April, 1929 to March, 1930. This survey covered 305 families whose heads were manual workers. The average size of the family was found to be 4.62 persons, equivalent to 3.28 male adults, and the average number of gainfully employed persons was 2.06 per family. Average annual in-

[17] *A Study of the Standard of Living of the Workers in Shanghai,* by Simon Yang.

[18] Chapter on "Industries," by Franklin L. Ho, *Symposium on Chinese Culture,* 1931.

158

come was $416.51, of which the combined earnings of all family members was only 87.3 per cent; of this the principal wage earner provided only 53.3 per cent, other members contributing 34 per cent. The remaining 12.7 per cent had to come from borrowing or other activities, such as peddling or subletting rooms.

The average family expenditure was $454.38, leaving a deficit of $37.87 annually. If only the income from wages of all family members is included, leaving out all other sources, the average annual deficit was found to be $121.23.

Thus it is seen that regular hours and wages in factories do not show the whole picture of poverty and the hard work necessary merely for the Chinese worker to keep himself and his family alive. He is continually in debt and harassed by extortionate money-lenders.

Eleanor M. Hinder wrote on this subject: [19] "It may be assumed that the 1929-30 standard of living remained virtually unchanged until the end of 1936, the last normal year before Sino-Japanese hostilities. The cost of living index (1926-100) was at 101.98 in 1929, 116.79 in 1930, and 105.04 in 1936. In other words, costs in 1936 were approximately what they had been in 1926 and below the 1930 level."

A re-study was made of the expenditures of 101 families during the period December, 1941, to January, 1942, and a new index calculated with average prices of 1936 as 100. This showed the following: 1936-100, 1937-119.08, 1938-150.62, 1939-197.52, 1940-425.35, 1941-826.24. The index had reached 2,663.21, due largely to currency changes. From 1936 to 1939 the cost of living had doubled, it will be noted. The June, 1942, index figure derived from prices expressed in the old currency reached 3,870.48; in the new currency of the Nanking Government's Central Reserve Bank, it was 1,935.24.

The re-study undertaken in 1941-42 showed the increase of unemployment. The principal wage earner contributed 66.28 per cent of the income as compared with 53.3 per cent in the 1929-30 survey; other family members contributed only 13.21 per cent as against 34 per cent previously. Earnings of all family members showed that 20.51 per cent had to come from outside sources, as against 12.7 per cent in 1929-30. Working-class families were able to survive only by borrowing at high interest rates and continuously re-borrowing to pay off the debt.

At this time the position of industry is shown in figures quoted by Eleanor M. Hinder (p. 49): "On a 1936 base of 100, the earnings index of Chinese-owned plants in 1941 stood at 457.65, an increase of almost 100 over the earnings index of 242.65 in 1940. In foreign-owned plants the earnings index was 465.54 in 1941."

[19] *Life and Labour in Shanghai,* 1944, p. 45.

The following table compiled by the Shanghai Bureau of Social Affairs shows the real wage indices in Chinese-owned plants from 1930 to 1935, which has not been kept up to date:

INDICES OF ACTUAL EARNINGS, COST OF LIVING (REVISED), AND REAL WAGES: 1930-1941

New Base: 1936 = 100

	1930	1931	1932	1933	1934	1935
Actual earnings	106.95	107.34	106.08	103.21	98.10	90.49
Cost of living (revised)	108.75	106.63	100.64	92.32	92.52	93.45
Real wages	98.34	100.67	105.41	111.80	106.03	96.83

	1936	1937	1938	1939	1940	1941
Actual earnings	100.00	84.83	92.38	119.09	242.47	467.65
Cost of living (revised)	100.00	119.09	155.28	202.99	430.61	871.89
Real Wages	100.00	71.23	59.49	58.67	56.31	53.64

I have not been able to secure a specific wartime study of the cost of living for industrial workers in interior China, though one is now in preparation by Nankai University in China. Other classes of the population have been analyzed, however. The general situation may be seen from the following statistics, obtained through courtesy of the Institute of Pacific Relations in New York:

A study of the effect of rising prices in Chengtu, made by the University of Nanking, showed that from 1937 (1937 = 100) to April, 1943, index numbers of city wages advanced to 4600, farm wages to 4202, professors' salaries to 955, soldiers' cash allowances to 550. During that period, however, the index of *real wages* (1937 = 100) had declined as follows: real city wages stood at 79.4, farm wages 50.7, salaries of professors 13.8, soldiers' cash allowances 3.0. The study showed that in general the rising price level had resulted in making landlords slightly better off than in prewar days, small merchants and farmers not so well off; wage earners after 1941 at a much greater disadvantage; persons on fixed salaries, such as teachers and soldiers, suffered most. An example given was the merchant-storekeeper class, showing that average family income had increased 18.5 times, but cost of living was 21 times the prewar level. In the case of the merchant-official-educational classification purchasing power had been reduced to 52 per cent of the prewar average; cost of living had increased by 20.69 times while family income increased only 10.83 times.

Statistics collected by the Nankai Institute of Economics showed that the index numbers of wholesale commodity prices in Chungking based on market rates had risen as follows (July 1936–June 1937 = 1):

	All Commodities	Food	Clothing materials
1937	1.10	1.08	1.13
1938	1.33	0.95	1.58
1939	2.15	1.22	2.68
1940	5.94	3.83	8.20
1941	16.86	15.66	16.50
1942	50.97	37.79	66.70
1943, May	111.79	79.76	194.39

Another study by the Nankai Institute showed that the index numbers of the cost of living for government officers and schoolteachers in Chungking (July 1936–June 1937 = 1) stood as follows in June, 1943: General index: all commodities 110.97; food 101.65; clothing 231.61: fuel and light 143.00; rent 69.71; miscellaneous 93.10.

The condition of the Chinese worker is, of course, determined by the whole economic complex surrounding him. His wage and standard of living can only be raised permanently as part of a general improvement. This problem of raising the standard of living and increasing purchasing power in China is one of the gigantic post-war economic questions, that vitally concerns not only the Chinese but all industrial countries which want to trade with China. It is one of the tragedies of the present war that it has not stimulated renewed development of industry in China, as occurred during World War I and as usually comes about in most countries during war years. If the devastation of a civil war should follow the impoverishment already caused by the Japanese invasion, the poverty of the four hundred and fifty million potential customers can well be imagined.

It is difficult to see how the standard of living in China can be raised until the stable foundation of a new and workable economic system is firmly laid, a process which began long ago but is still far from completed. This foundation can only be built on widespread industrialization and modernization of the present semi-feudal agrarian system. The fundamental reason why industry failed to develop in Free China during this war is this hangover of feudal controls, which is stifling agricultural production as well. The fact that sufficient American machinery has not been brought in is only a secondary reason. If other countries had waited for ready-made machinery, where would they be today? The situation is clearly shown in the history of the industrial co-operatives, which have been hampered and limited at every turn by conflict with

161

the local authorities. They have improvised all their own machinery from the materials at hand, even though they are forbidden to operate mines to secure the scarce metals required.

4. STRIKES AND UNIONS: A SUMMARY

Figures on the number of strikes, workers involved, unions and membership, are never accurate in China. Sometimes they are incomplete; again they may be exaggerated. There are many reasons for this, aside from the difficulty in securing any kind of statistical information in China.

Newspaper reports of strikes, for example, are seldom accurate, written quickly without correct information being easily available. Reporters were ordinarily unable to get in touch with strike leaders, who usually worked secretly to avoid arrest.

Another reason is that few well-trained investigators in China have taken an interest in the organized labor movement with careful day-to-day observation and study. The use of the term "union," even among those who have written on the subject, is so careless that one is never sure exactly what is meant by the word.

One important reason for the difficulty is lack of proper government apparatus to check such information. From 1919 to 1925 figures are especially fragmentary. There were two governments operating, one in the north and one in the south, and neither had good statistical bureaus, especially on labor matters. During 1925 to 1927 labor activities were open under the liberal Canton and Hankow governments, but the development was so rapid and the organizers so busy, that they could hardly keep pace with the changing situation.

After 1927 a period of disruption ensued and nobody was able to collect intelligible figures until about 1929 and 1930, when the Nanking government secured more control. Since then government figures are highly suspect on the subject of unions and their membership, as for political and other reasons these were vastly exaggerated. In 1932 the China Branch of the I.L.O. took responsibility for collecting figures on organized labor, but their delegates were more anxious about making a good impression abroad than in minimizing the number of unions and members in China and describing what had actually happened to the organized labor movement. The figures they collected included all kinds of labor organizations under the heading "unions," and membership was never assessed accurately even on this basis.

Figures on strikes and disputes, however, are more accurate, and

162

these may be found in the government records and Year Books of the various years. The only good information available since 1927 is on labor in Shanghai, where statistics were more carefully kept and easier to check.

One must always bear in mind that during this whole period under review China has been in a state of transition, and that organized labor has been a very delicate subject where angels fear to tread. Real labor activities, from the very first, have been secretly organized in China except during the brief days of the Canton and Hankow governments. Organizers were not likely to divulge inside information to public authorities. Since 1927 the "open signboard" labor organizations under the Kuomintang have been open to government inspection, though their membership figures have little meaning in a study of real labor activities. The "secret" organizations, however, have been very difficult to get at, and even the Communists who usually organized these secret activities have lost many of their records and most of those with inside information have not survived to tell the story.

I have drawn up the following tables to give a picture of labor activities generally. Though the figures are not satisfactory, they are the best I have been able to collect, and the compilation is of some interest.

Since 1929 no national labor congress has been called. After the original All-China Labor Federation controlled by the Communists disappeared in 1931, no new national organization was created. The Chinese Association of Labor, formed in 1938, is not considered a national organization, though it was indicated in 1943 that a national federation might in future be formed. In the past it was practically impossible under the Labor Union Law for an interprovincial federation to exist.

The figures below were given to me by Liu Hsiao-ch'i, who had inside information. Other figures are higher. I do not know how to explain this, except that probably the figures may have been exaggerated originally in the newspapers and reports and later corrected by the organizers for accurate information. Again, not all organized workers were represented at these congresses, yet possibly the totals were considered by some writers as included in the All-China Labor Federation. Liu Hsiao-ch'i's figure for the Third Congress seems too small, but doubtless he included only the unions actually affiliated with the Federation. He did not give me the number of unions represented for the different years.

Fang Fu-an reported for the 1922 Congress a total of 160 delegates, 200 unions in 12 cities and 300,000 organized workers; for the 1925 Congress he reported 230 delegates and 570,000 workers represented;

163

ALL-CHINA LABOR CONGRESSES

	No. of Delegates Present	No. of Organised Workers Represented	Organizing Group
1st Congress, May 1, 1922, at Canton	170	70,000	Called by Labor Secretariat
2nd Congress, May 1-7, 1925, at Canton (All-China Labor Federation organized, Lin Wei-ming elected Chairman)	About 200	200,000	Called by the 4 big unions, Seamen's Union, General Railway Union, Hanyehp'ing Union and Canton Congress of Labor Representatives
3rd Congress, May 1-12, 1926, at Canton (Su Chao-jen elected Chairman of Federation)	600	540,000	Called by the All-China Labor Federation
4th Congress, June 23, 1927, at Hankow	300	2,800,000	Called by the All-China Labor Federation
5th Congress, November, 1929, held secretly in Shanghai (Han Ying elected Chairman)	?	70,000 (3/5 in Soviets)	Called by the All-China Labor Federation

for the 1926 Congress he gave 400 delegates, 400 unions in 19 provinces, and 1,240,000 workers represented.

Most writers fail to give complete figures on the Congresses. Lowe Chuan-hua reported the same figures as Fang Fu-an for the 1925 Congress and "about three million" organized workers for the 1927 Congress. Chen Ta gave the same figure as Fang Fu-an for the 1926 Congress; for the 1922 Congress he reported 162 delegates, 200 unions and 400,000 workers.

The usual figure for the 1927 Congress is 2,800,000 workers represented, though a little earlier the total number of organized workers in China was reported by Su Chao-jen as 3,065,000. The workers represented at the 1927 Congress are also sometimes given as 2,970,000 or "three million."

After 1927 the All-China Labor Federation was secret and the 70,000 workers represented at the 1929 Congress were all members of Red Trade Unions, three-fifths being in Soviet districts.

To explain the second table: the fragmentary character of the figures reported from various sources is obvious. The figures on strikes and the number of workers involved from 1918 to 1926 are taken from Chen Ta; the rest are to be found in the various Year Books, derived chiefly from studies by the Shanghai Bureau of Social Affairs and the China Branch of the I.L.O. In nearly all cases figures are incomplete, as it was impossible to obtain information on all strikes and disputes. The number of strikes in which the figures on workers involved were reported are indicated in parentheses. After 1930, total cases of labor disputes are included and those ending in strikes are in parentheses. In a few cases no separate figures on the two categories are available. The totals are for all China unless only Shanghai is indicated; in these years no attempt to secure national figures was made. After 1928 most of the important strikes and disputes occurred in Shanghai. No detailed figures are available for 1927, and 1931 is also wrapped in mystery for no apparent reason. For the war years following 1938, national figures are also unavailable, but occasional strikes and disputes have occurred in Free China. Those noted for 1940 and 1941 were mediated by the Industrial Division of the Shanghai Municipal Council, and are incomplete.

Statistics on unions and organized workers are taken from the sources indicated at the right side of the two columns. Few of these figures after 1927 are considered acceptable.

It will be useful to the reader to indicate some of the contradictory data from different sources and to provide details on the figures compiled, as these are scattered and very difficult to find.

One of the students of Chinese labor activities, frequently quoted, is

Table Indicating the Development of Unions and Strikes in China

Year	No. of Strikes	No. of Workers Involved	No. of Labor Unions	No. of Organized Workers
1918	25	6,455 (12 strikes)		150,000 (Liu Hsiao-ch'i)
1919	66	91,520 (26 strikes)	26 "labor organizations" formed after May 4, 1919.	230,000 (P. Miff)
1920	46	46,140 (19 strikes)		
1921	49	108,025 (22 strikes)		
1922	91	139,050 (30 strikes)	91	570,000 (Fang Fu-an) 540,000 (Seng Sin-fu)
1923	47	35,835 (17 strikes)		
1924	56	61,800 (18 strikes)		
1925	318	784,821 (198 strikes)	499	1,023,000 (Seng Sin-fu)
1926	535	530,585 (313 strikes)	?	2,800,000 (Liu Hsiao-ch'i) 3,065,000 (Su Chao-jen)
1927	110 in Shanghai	230,256	1,117	1,773,998 (Ministry of Industries)
1928	120 in Shanghai	213,966		
1929	111 in Shanghai	68,887	741	(70,000 in Red Trade Unions—3/5 in Soviet districts)
Strikes and Disputes				
1930	87 (82 strikes) in Shanghai	64,130 in 87 cases		572,739 (Ministry of Industries) (114,525 in Red Trade Unions, 64,704 in Soviets)
1931	145 strikes	?		100,000 in Soviet Trade Unions

Year	Strikes and Disputes	No. of Workers Involved	No. of Labor Unions	No. of Organized Workers
1932	317 (104 strikes)	306,160 in 109 cases (128,325 in 41 strikes)	647	421,329 (China Branch, I.L.O.)
1933	296 (79 strikes)	119,943 in 84 cases (60,605 in 37 strikes)	695	422,730 (China Branch, I.L.O.)
1934	261 (84 strikes)	135,656 in 93 cases (49,955 in 36 strikes)	759	462,742 (China Branch, I.L.O.) (310,000 in Soviet Trade Unions)
1935	300 (141 strikes)	323,884 in 121 cases (176,993 in 68 strikes)	823	469,240 (China Branch, I.L.O.)
1936	278 (134 strikes)	258,672 in 131 cases (215,490 in 72 strikes)	872	743,764 (China Handbook, 1937-1943)
1937	207 (141 strikes)	199,718 in 153 cases		
1938	81 (23 strikes)	92,164 in 54 cases		
1939	Figures unavailable			
1940	111 in Shanghai International Settlement	35,000 in 111 cases		
1941	138 "			
1942	Nothing available	45,000 in 138 cases	4,033	1,053,565 (China Handbook, 1937-1943) (1,000,000 in Guerrilla areas)
1944	"		2,867	1,044,462 (Ministry of Social Affairs)

167

Chen Ta (surname Chen),[20] a professor at Tsinghua University and also at one time visiting professor at the University of Hawaii. Most of his information before 1929 was taken from newspaper clippings, of which he kept a file in the Department of Sociology at Tsinghua University from 1923 on. In general his studies lack first-hand inside information, and some of his interpretations of events are not always well-informed.

Chen Ta made a useful study of strikes in China from 1918 to 1926. The early strikes occurred among the guilds, but also some appeared in modern industry. Chen Ta mentions one strike as early as 1912 among the workers of the Tsing-yang Railway on the Lunghai line. This seems to be the earliest known instance of a strike in modern industry. In his 1927 article, Chen Ta says:

"Prior to 1918 or 1919, most manual workers unquestioningly submitted to the traditional social hierarchy graded according to the rank and wealth of the old society, and rarely did they raise a voice of protest against the existing social order....

"The trade union movement of a really national character dates from the first National Labor Conference held at Canton from 1 to 6 May, 1922, at which 162 delegates from 200 unions in 12 cities, representing about 400,000 workers were present....

"Between 1918 and 1925 there were in China 698 strikes; in 49 per cent of these 1,273,606 working men were involved."

In his "Analysis of Strikes in China from 1918 to 1926," Chen Ta states: "This study covers 1,232 strikes in the nine-year period from 1918 to 1926, including 135 strikes arising directly from the May 30 incident in Shanghai in 1925. Disregarding, for the present, this incident, it thus appears that between 1918 and 1926 there were 1,098 strikes, or an average of 122 per year....

"For the whole period, the total number of strikers in reported cases was 1,431,804, the average number of persons per strike being 2,524.56. If the May 30th [21] strikes are included the total number of strikers was 1,813,291."

[20] References are: "The Labor Movement in China," by Ta Chen, *International Labor Review*, March, 1927.

"Labor in China During the Civil Wars," by Ta Chen, *Monthly Labor Review*, Vol. 31, July, 1930.

"Fundamentals of the Chinese Labor Movement," by Ta Chen, *Annals of the American Academy of Political and Social Science*, November, 1930.

Analysis of Strikes in China from 1918 to 1926, by Ta Chen, Bureau of Industrial and Commercial Information Booklet No. 4, Shanghai.

"Labour," by Ta Chen, *The China Year Book*, 1933.

[21] Chen Ta says 135 strikes followed the May 30 incident: 104 in Shanghai; eight in Peking; four each in Hankow and Tsinan; two each in Tsing-

As the material was taken from newspaper reports, only about half the cases indicated the number of workers involved. Of the strikes reported, 53.08 per cent indicated the number of persons involved, including the May 30 Incident, or 50.91 per cent without the May 30 strikes.

I have adapted the following table from Chen Ta's statistics. The figures in parentheses include the strikes arising out of the May 30 Incident.

NUMBER AND DURATION OF STRIKES IN CHINA, 1918-1926

Year	Total No. of Strikes	Strikes for which No. of Strikers was Reported	Total No. of Strikers	Average Duration of Strike (Days)
1918	25	12	6,455	8.27
1919	66	26	91,520	5.65
1920	46	19	46,140	7.14
1921	49	22	108,025	7.38
1922	91	30	139,050	8.37
1923	47	17	35,835	6.38
1924	56	18	61,860	9.27
1925	183 (318)	103 (198)	403,334 (784,821)	5.32 (18.88)
1926	535	313	539,585	6.87
Total	1,098 (1,232)	560 (655)	1,431,804 (1,813,291)	6.81 (9.18)
Annual Average	122.00 (136.88)	62.11 (76.66)	136,867.11 (179,254.55)	- - - - - -

Chen Ta mentions the principal causes of early strikes as the high cost of living and depreciation of copper coins in which wages were usually paid. For example, 200 pounds of polished rice in Shanghai sold for $7.78 in 1916, while in 1923 it had risen to $12.45.

He says further: "During the year 1921 a successful strike occurred in almost every important industry in Canton....

"About 60,000 workers in 100 trades in Hong Kong are unionized, some following the rules of craft guilds while others have adopted those of labor unions." (As this study is not dated, one cannot tell exactly what year is referred to, but it must be some time after 1922.)

"During the nine years successful strikes have constituted 40.80 per

tao, Kaifeng, Chiochow and Nanking; one each in Fengtien, Tientsin, Chekiang, Suikowsan, Kongmoon, and the big Hong Kong-Canton Strike and boycott. Most of these occurred in textiles and food industries. Of the 135 strikes, the number of strikers was reported in 94 cases, totaling 381,387 men or 4,057 men per strike; and the duration of the strike was reported in 25 cases, totaling 1,664 days or 66.6 days per strike.

cent of the total, excluding the May 30, 1925, affair, or 36.41 including it; partially successful strikes constituted 11.75 per cent excluding the May 30 affair, or 13.31 per cent including it; failures constituted 10.38 per cent excluding the May 30 affair or 9.34 per cent including it." The other 37.07 per cent were unknown.

"...during the last nine years the successful and partially successful strikes have amounted to 83.51 per cent of the total (excluding May 30)."

As to methods of settling the strikes during the nine year period, Chen Ta gives the following information:

Mediation

Strike settled by:	
Persuasion and settlement by management	85 strikes
Mass meetings of strikers	121 strikes
Meetings of employers	43 strikes
Joint meetings of representatives of employers and strikers	121 strikes

Arbitration by

Local officials	134 strikes
Chambers of Commerce	42 strikes
Student unions	4 strikes
Own guild or union	68 strikes
Disinterested guild or general union	43 strikes
Disinterested individuals	65 strikes

Strikes for the right to organize unions or for recognition of unions began in 1922.

The largest number of strikes was in textiles, 369 in nine years (or 400 including May 30). It is interesting to note that the establishments having the greatest number of strikes during the period were these: The Nagai cotton mills in Shanghai, owned by Japanese, had 34 strikes during the nine years; the Sino-Japanese Cotton Manufacturing Co. mills in Shanghai had 22; and the British-American Tobacco Co. had 10 strikes.

During the nine years Shanghai had 638 strikes (including the May 30 strikes), Hankow 81, Canton 54, Wusih 41, Soochow 40, Chekiang province 34, Peking 30, Fengtien province 18, Tientsin 14, Swatow 14 and Hong Kong 10.

In another article, "Labor in China During the Civil Wars," Chen Ta said (p. 8):

"Between 1918 and 1926 there were 1,232 strikes in all China about which there was some information. Out of this total, 283 strikes, or 23 per cent of the total, were due to alleged ill treatment of the workers by

170

the employers, which illustrates the strained relations between capital and labor under the new industrial situation. . . .

"Between 1924 and 1927 the growth of radicalism in parts of China was astonishingly rapid. Its influence was first noted in the rise of labor unions. In Canton, for example, there were only about eighty unions in 1922, but in 1926 they had increased to more than 300. The strikes were also more numerous. In 1923 the number of recorded strikes in all China was 47. There were, however, 56 in 1924; 318 in 1925; and 535 in 1926. The character of the strikes also changed. Before 1924 the workers' demands were largely economic and social, but between 1924 and 1926, political and patriotic demands began to assume importance. These changes were not wholly due to radicalism, but radical propaganda played an important role. . . .

"Up to 1927, radicalism in China had been a disturbing factor in the labor situation. Uncompromising and destructive radical activities seemed to have caused great damage to Chinese industry and society. Recently, Communist propaganda has been suppressed and the labor movement has swung back to the conservative side."

Of the partial figures available for the disrupted years following Chen Ta's study of strikes, the Shanghai Bureau of Social Affairs provides a source of information. According to the Bureau, there were in Shanghai 169 strikes in 1926, involving 165 factories and 202,297 workers, as compared with 110 strikes in 1927 (excluding the March 21 uprising), affecting 1,173 "factories" and companies and involving 230,256 workers (500 children, 19,520 women are included among the strikers). The loose use of the word "factory" may be noted; the large number of establishments given included a strike among the employees of 350 piece goods shops in Shanghai in September, 1927. In 1927 it was reported that in 23 cases all demands were granted to the workers, in 26 all were rejected, and in 35 some demands were granted. In 1928 there were 120 strikes in Shanghai involving 213,966 workers, of whom 22,431 were children, 122,807 women and 68,728 men.

The Shanghai Bureau of Social Affairs published a report on "Industrial Disputes in Shanghai since 1928," concerning disputes, exclusive of strikes, settled by the Bureau or in which it took some part from 1928 to 1932. According to this, of 1,491 disputes during the five years, two-thirds were concerned with dismissal of workers, one-tenth with wages and less than one-tenth with collective agreements. The detailed report showed that these settlements became increasingly unfavorable to the workers. This was explained as due to the economic depression and gain in strength of the employers' associations, and also to a change in government policy toward labor: "As the Government became more firmly entrenched and dependent on the support of industrialists, it was led to give less sympathetic consideration to labor's demands." The decline of unions was also listed as a factor. This report showed that the repressive legislation had not prevented strikes in Shanghai; during 1928 to 1932, 517 strikes were reported, one-third concerned with wages, one-fourth with dismissal of workers, and one-seventh with collective agreements.

The China Branch of the I.L.O. collected information on mediation in strikes and disputes in 1937, showing that about half the disputes studied resulted in strikes.[22] The survey showed the following:

Methods	1934	1935	1936
Direct negotiation	35	24	42
Mediation by a third party	16	12	7
Conciliation Committee	60	35	91
Arbitration Committee	4	5	5
Other organizations	80	51	41
Unsettled or unknown	66	173	92
	261	300	278

Of the 278 industrial disputes during 1936, 134 were strikes, five factory closures, six sabotage cases, 133 industrial disputes. In 134 cases known 258,672 workers were involved, including both disputes and strikes, etc. Of the 278 cases 61 occurred in the textile industry; 20 per cent occurred in textiles and transportation (57 cases, 35 strikes in textiles and 25 in transportation and communications).

During 1936, 2,724 industrial accidents were reported. At the time of the survey working hours were noted as being from eight to thirteen hours, averaging about eleven hours.

As to unions and membership:

It is hard to find any figures at all on the earliest period of labor organization in China. One frequently encounters the comment that "26 labor unions existed in 1919." This originated with a statement by Tayler and Zung in 1923 (already quoted), that the "student agitation of the spring of 1919 led to the formation of 26 labour organizations." Some of these were undoubtedly only workers' clubs or committees, and must have been organized in 1920 as well as 1919. I cannot find any record of any actual labor unions formed before 1920; if such existed they may have been temporary. Tayler and Zung also said as of 1923: "There are more than 50 labour unions in Shanghai."

P. Miff in *Heroic China* reported (p. 14) "... in 1918 the number of workers who took part in strikes was 6,500; but in 1919 the number grew to 91,500 (according to incomplete figures) and in 1921 it had

[22] See *Chinese Year Books,* 1936-1937, section on "Labor."

risen to 108,000." On page 38 he says: "Nearly all the urban workers joined trade unions. For example, in 1923 the number of organized workers in China was 230,000, in 1926 it was 1,264,000 and in May, 1927, the number was 2,800,000."

A similar source, Seng Sin-fu,[23] reported a figure of 170 delegates at the 1922 Labor Congress, and said that in May, 1924, there were 270,000 trade union members in China; 540,000 in May, 1925; and 1,023,000 in May, 1926, in 499 unions. He comments that only half the membership paid dues regularly.

James H. Dolsen in 1926 [24] said that of 21 strikes occurring in 1921, only one failed. He quotes figures for the May, 1922, Labor Congress as having 160 delegates, representing 200 unions and 300,000 members, and the May, 1925, Congress as having 285 delegates and 450,000 organized workers represented. He states there were 279 strikes in the International Settlement in Shanghai from 1919 to 1923. Dolsen also says there were over 300 unions in Canton in 1926 and 200 in Hong Kong; and that in 1925 Shanghai had 100 unions and 80,000 members.

One can read whole books and pamphlets on revolutionary activities in China and find only a few sentences referring to unions, and a few scattered figures without reference to the source. Even the books on Chinese labor have only isolated and fragmentary figures and some are useless.

Fang Fu-an in his book *Chinese Labour* reported that in 1922 there were 400,000 members of the Federation of Labor in Canton alone; and that toward the end of 1922 the "workers' federation" in Shanghai had 24 unions and 40,000 members. The Canton figure would include guilds.

For some reason, total figures on unions in China are very elusive, though membership is plentifully reported. The most accurate I know of for the early period was Liu Hsiao-ch'i's statement to me that there were about 91 unions in China in 1922, with 150,000 members, and over 100 strikes during the year. It will be noted that Liu Hsiao-ch'i, who was one of the organizers of the labor movement, gave me much smaller figures than those reported elsewhere. The Chinese Communists usually do not include any organization under the term "union" except those strictly so organized, and perhaps they do not list separately some of the small locals under general city unions, which may at times account for the smaller number of union members reported. Again in the case of newly-organized industrial unions, there may be transitory locals

[23] *China: A Survey,* by Seng Sin-fu, printed by the Communist Party of Great Britain, London, June, 1927.

[24] *The Awakening of China,* by James H. Dolsen, 1926, *Daily Worker* Publishing Co., Chicago.

or workers' clubs still in existence but not listed separately by the Secretariat, whereas outside observers may have included them all indiscriminately as well as guilds. One must also remember that clubs were often considered the same thing as unions in the early period.

Another explanation of the variance in figures may be that the underground period from early 1923 to the Second Labor Congress in 1925 resulted in the disorganization of the railway unions and suppression of other labor organizations, though all the facts may not have been known except to those on the inside. Many of the active labor organizations were educational clubs and study circles, though there were said to have been 80 unions in Canton in 1922 (Chen Ta) and 50 in Shanghai at the end of 1923, with 84,000 members.[25] These may have included guilds and transitory forms, especially in Canton, which Liu Hsiao-ch'i did not consider "unions." The big Kwangtung mechanics' guild, for example, and its affiliates were not yet unionized and did not become the Mechanics' Union until January, 1926.

Many temporary unions were destroyed in the early period. For instance, at the beginning of 1921, a "General Workers' Union" had been organized in Peking, including 300 engineers, 400 telegraph operators and 50 printers. It was suppressed within two weeks and not revived until 1925.

Another example of the slow development of unions in backward cities is Swatow: in 1920 one union was reported; in 1921, two; in 1925 eight; and in 1926, nine.

In the labor upsurge after the May 30 Incident in 1925, it was reported that during the general strike in Shanghai in the middle of June over 200,000 workers were on strike. The Hong Kong-Canton Strike involved about 160,000 strikers during the 15-months' period and was said to have affected from 200,000 to 250,000 at its height.

Following the May 30 Incident the Shanghai General Labor Union was formed, and 72 new trade unions were created during a brief period.

If separate studies on each industrial city were available, it would be of great interest to analyze the rise and fall of the labor unions. However, I have not been able to find the necessary data. Canton, for example, is reported to have had 80 unions in 1922, 250 early in 1926, and 300 later in the year with 195,000 members. The Ministry of Industries reported that in 1928 Canton had 80 unions with 89,539 members.

Shanghai had 50 unions with 84,000 members in 1923; 149,000 union members in 1926 and 502 unions with 800,000 members in 1927. After the suppression of 1927, only 429 Shanghai unions were registered

[25] *Papers Respecting Labor Conditions in China,* Cmd. 2442, London, 1925.

174

with the Bureau of Social Affairs with a total membership of 215,958, including 11,964 children, 50,833 women and 144,087 men. Those listed according to specific industries were:

Industry	No. of Unions	No. of Workers
Clothing	178	73,903
Food and drink	35	20,339
Tea and tobacco	12	18,382
Transportation	81	36,985

The underground unions, of course, did not register and are not recorded.

Liu Hsiao-ch'i told me that in early 1927 there were in Hunan 400,000 trade union members, in Hupeh 500,000, in Shanghai "700,000 or 800,000" and in Kwangtung province "several hundred thousand." For all China he gave a total of 2,800,000 as represented at the Fourth Labor Congress in June, 1927.

In the following table the figures on organized labor for May, 1926, are taken from Seng Sin-fu's booklet *China: A Survey*, printed in 1927. Those for 1927 are taken from the report of Su Chao-jen, Chinese delegate, presented at the Pan-Pacific Trade Union Conference in May, 1927.

REGIONAL FIGURES ON ORGANIZED WORKERS IN CHINA, 1926-1927

City or Province	May, 1926	May, 1927
Shanghai	149,000	800,000
Canton	195,000	
Kwangtung Province	111,000	400,000
Hankow	42,000	
Hupeh Province		450,000
Hunan Province	80,000	350,000
Hong Kong	207,000	250,000
Chihli Province	103,000	
Honan Province	60,000	6,000
Shantung		4,000
Nanking		50,000
Wusih		120,000
Shensi		15,000
Kiangsi		200,000
Kwangsi		50,000
Chekiang		300,000
Tientsin		10,000
Chinkiang		30,000
Szechuan		45,000
Three Eastern Provinces		5,000
Total	947,000	3,065,000

At the Pan-Pacific Trade Union Conference in 1927, Su Chao-jen also reported the number of organized workers according to industries as follows:

NUMBER OF ORGANIZED WORKERS IN 1927 CLASSIFIED ACCORDING
TO INDUSTRIES

Cotton mills	180,000
Seamen	160,000
Telegraph	15,000
Transport	150,000
Metal works	30,000
Tobacco	30,000
Rickshamen	60,000
Silk Factories	120,000
Railroads	35,000
Printing	50,000
Architecture	120,000
Employees	250,000
Chemical works	15,000
Miners	60,000
Post office	18,000
Customs	3,000
Rice selling	50,000
Tannery	5,000
Police, etc.	80,000
Other industries and factories	634,000
Total	3,065,000

When the unions were broken and reorganized in 1927 and 1928, it was impossible to estimate figures. The Ministry of Industries gave out one report as of 1928 of 1,117 unions in all China with 1,773,998 members. The Department of Labor of the Ministry of Industries gave out another report for 1928 of 999 unions representing 1,860,030 workers and eight "special unions" with 41,412 workers, a total of 1,007 and 1,901,442 organized workers. According to the latter, Shanghai had 429 unions with 207,492 members; Nanking, 114 unions with 23,763 members, Canton, 80 unions with 89,539 members; Honan province, 77 unions with 27,036 members; Kwangtung province, five (sic) unions and 1,423,058 members. A year later a figure from the Kwangtung provincial government gave a total of 234 unions in the province in 1929, and 272,631 members.

Although the "reorganization" of unions in other cities had disastrous effects, in north China new unions were created and guilds reorganized for the first time by the Kuomintang. This occurred after Peking was

176

captured by the Kuomintang troops in 1928. In 1929 it was claimed that Peking had 11,269 union members, and Tientsin twelve unions with 29,542 members (all men). A survey made by the Social Research Institute in Peking showed that from January, 1927, to June, 1929, 134 industrial disputes occurred in Peking and Tientsin. Of these, eleven disputes occurred in the first half of 1927 and four in the second half. In 1928 six disputes occurred during the first half of the year and 45 in the second half. During the first half of 1929, 68 disputes occurred. The sudden jump in the last half of 1928 was due to political causes. In August, 1928, the military commanders in Peking and Tientsin ordered all unions disbanded, and the workers protested through strikes and other forms of opposition.

The only other figures I can find on this period are a report that in 1929, 187 labor unions in Shanghai filled out questionnaires for the Bureau of Social Affairs on the unemployment situation, showing that 6.45 per cent of the 155,069 registered members were unemployed. Hence, apparently 187 "legal" unions existed in that year, with small membership in each.

In the general industrial survey by the Ministry of Industries in 1930, 741 unions were reported for the whole country with 572,739 members.

From 1928 to 1931 there were both "Red trade unions" and "Yellow trade unions" in the cities, after which the Red trade unionists had a policy of joining the other unions. Lo Chao-lung [26] reported that in 1928 there were "three types of trade union in China": (1) the Black Trade Unions of the Kuomintang, having no masses and mercenary leaders; (2) The Yellow or Gray unions, real workers' organizations but having formal relations with the Kuomintang to avoid suppression, such as the "Big 7" unions in Shanghai; (3) The Red Trade Unions under the All-China Labor Federation, outlawed by the Kuomintang.

According to Lo Chao-lung, the "Black" unions had been found by the authorities to be useless and were being liquidated, and the leaders of the "Gray" unions were being "corrupted by the Kuomintang." He says further: "Outside of the cities of Shanghai, Canton and a few coast ports, practically all organizations are the 'Red' trade unions. In Honan and Shensi they exist half-legally, but in Hunan, Hupeh and Kwangtung they are absolutely outlawed, and open workers' organizations exist only in such disguises as aid clubs, etc., primitive organizations of small groups with limited aims."

He mentions that 99 strikes occurred in Shanghai from April to Sep-

[26] "The Chinese Trade Union Movement in 1928," by Lo Chao-lung, *China Tomorrow,* Feb. 20, 1929.

tember involving 126,185 workers, and tells of the Postal Workers' Strike in 1928 of 3,000 men when troops occupied the post office and the strike was crushed and the "leaders bought off." He also mentions a strike of porcelain workers in Kiangsi in May, 1928, when 300,000 workers went on strike for wage increases and had a victory, driving away the troops sent to check the strike.

Another Communist source, Ting Yu-ling [27] reported in 1929: that the anniversary of May 30, 1929, was celebrated on the streets of Shanghai, and that during July and August about 20,000 workers were on strike every day. According to him the "pillars of the Red trade union movement" then were the Shanghai Trade Union Association, the Hong Kong Workers' Association, the Miners Association at Kailan, Tongshan. He also mentions the principal Red unions in Shanghai as the Telephone and Telegraph Operators' Union, the Arsenal Union, the Textile Union, the Ricksha Pullers' Union, etc.

The Fifth All-China Labor Congress called by the All-China Labor Federation secretly in Shanghai claimed 70,000 members of Red Unions, three-fifths being in the Soviet districts. In August, 1930,[28] the Communists claimed to have 114,525 members of Red Unions, of which 64,704 were in Soviet regions and 49,821 in Kuomintang territory. Only 5,748 were reported in the large cities, however, and the rest in the provinces. By September, 1931, the Soviet unions had increased to 100,000 members, and those in "White" areas had "declined."

The separate Red trade unions in Kuomintang cities were given up in 1931, though the Communists still dominated certain unions. One of these was the original General Textile Workers' Union in Shanghai, which in December, 1932, had only 1,000 members. Another was the original General Tobacco Workers' Union, reported to have only 900 members in 1932 but dropped to an "intolerable state" in October, 1933.

As of 1934 the Soviet labor unions claimed 310,000 members. The Communist work in unions in Kuomintang cities was done individually and by small groups after 1932.

During 1936, the last normal year before the war with Japan broke out, a study of labor activities was made available by the China Branch of the I.L.O., which was analyzed by Lowe Chuan-hua.[29] This covered the period from 1932 to 1935, and the questionnaires were filled out by government authorities in various districts, or by the "unions" themselves. Mr. Lowe comments that 1935 was the lowest year for union

[27] "May First and the Chinese Revolution," by Ting Yu-ling, *Pan-Pacific Monthly*, May, 1930—October, 1930.

[28] See *Eastern and Colonial*, Vol. IV, Nos. 10-11, August-September, 1931.

[29] *Labor Conditions in China*, by Lowe Chuan-hua, pamphlet issued by the Council of International Affairs, Nanking, China, July 7, 1937, vol. IV, No. 5.

activities, being the depth of the economic depression. Though these figures are unacceptable to students of China's labor movement, I include them for reference.

The survey covered 29 districts and cities. Organized labor was reported as follows:

Year	No. of Unions	Membership
1932	647	421,329
1933	695	422,730
1934	759	462,742
1935	823	469,240

It is to be noted that several backward cities were included in the survey, which could not be said to have modern labor unions. The 29 places listed included Shanghai, Tientsin, Hankow, Tsingtao, Canton, Wusih, Hangchow, Changsha, Nanking, Peking, but also Tsinan, Taiyuan, Soochow, Chinkiang, Haimen, Tungshan, Kiashing, Kwaining, Pengpu, Wuhu, Tingling, Nanchang, Hanyang, Chungking, Amoy, Swatow, Nanhai, Waiyang and Kunming. These "unions" would include any kind of *"hui"* or labor organization, obviously.

The reader is warned that figures derived from such surveys are of no value, as little or no distinction is made between real labor unions and any variety of guild, mutual welfare association or Kuomintang setup that might or might not actually exist. For example, on receiving the questionnaire the town official would indiscriminately fill in whatever groups might by a stretch of local imagination be related to "labor." The figures collected for three industrial cities, Canton, Hankow and Shanghai, are shown in the table on the following page. The so-called unions are classified into "industrial" and "occupational" unions, the former supposedly organized by industry and the latter by craft.

In China certain categories of workers are only permitted to form what are called "special unions." These include workers in government-owned enterprises, which under the Labor Union Law (Article 23) are forbidden the right to strike. Article 3 of the law specifies such workers: "Workers in the administrative, communication, government enterprises, education and public utilities of the state may organize unions in accordance with this law, but neither the office staff and employees in them nor the workers and the office staff and employees of the military institutions and military industrial establishments."

Several of these organizations are now affiliated with the Chinese Association of Labor, such as seamen, railwaymen, postal workers, etc. As of December, 1936, government figures showed 61,545 workers employed on the Chinese railways, 26,639 in the postal service, and 23,355 in the telegraph system.

179

City	Year	Industrial Unions		Occupational Unions		Total	
		Number	Membership	Number	Membership	Unions	Membership
Canton	1932	0	0	33	31,545	33	31,545
	1933	0	0	39	32,115	39	32,115
	1934	1	425	41	32,115	42	32,540
	1935	2	3,602	43	32,541	45	36,143
Hankow	1932	0	0	11	12,416	11	12,416
	1933	0	0	11	12,416	11	12,416
	1934	4	7,900	23	32,819	27	40,719
	1935	9	10,500	38	54,147	47	64,647
Shanghai	1932	32	36,464	34	23,472	66	59,936
"	1933	38	37,741	37	24,502	75	62,243
"	1934	39	38,025	45	27,536	84	65,561
"	1935	47	32,887	72	32,731	119	65,618

Lowe Chuan-hua, in the above 1937 survey, says: "Among new special unions which have been formed during the last two years are the Nanking-Shanghai and Nanking-Hangchow Railway Workers Unions, the Canton-Kowloon Railway Workers Union and the Chinese Seamen's Union." The following table showing membership in such unions is given:

SPECIAL LABOR UNIONS IN CHINA

	Number of Members			
	1932	1933	1934	1935
Nanchang-Kiukiang Railway	2,960	2,960	2,852	2,735
Canton-Hankow Railway	1,174	1,268	1,440	1,525
Chenting-Taiyuan Railway	1,683	2,134	2,122	2,239
Tientsin-Pukow Railway	16,800	20,260	20,169	20,821
Peiping-Hankow Railway	16,299	16,707	15,435	16,130
Nanking-Shanghai and Shanghai-Hangchow, Ningpo Railway	—	—	—	9,836
Peiping-Suiyuan Railway	8,920	8,917	8,935	9,048
Lunghai Railway	7,027	7,216	7,361	8,208
Chinese Mechanics Federation	567	607	676	736
Chinese Seamen's Federation (Canton Branch)	8,300	9,600	12,000	14,000
All-China Postal Workers' Union	10,879	12,637	13,340	14,164
All-China Postal Employees Federation	7,179	7,262	7,297	7,347

In the section on "Labor" in *The Chinese Year Book*, 1936-1937, written by Lowe Chuan-hua from statistics compiled by the China Branch of the I.L.O., figures are slightly different. For Shanghai he gives a total of 76 unions in 1931 with 61,365 members; for 1932, 81 unions with 70,221 members; for 1933, 77 unions with 65,016 members; for 1934, 81 unions with 62,252 members. He says that up to March, 1934, 797 labor unions in all China had been reorganized in accordance with the Labor Union Law and recognized by the Ministry of Industries. The totals given for that year are 846 unions and *88,860 members*.

In face of the extravagant claims for union membership, the opinion of objective outside observers is instructive. Augusta Wagner [30] wrote in 1938:

"Attempts, however, to establish organizations primarily for trade union purposes have been rare. Outstanding examples are the Machinists' Union, the Postal Workers' Union, the Railway Workers' Union, the Commercial Press Union, and the British-American Tobacco

[30] *Labor Legislation in China*, p. 246.

Company Workers' Union, but these have not been completely free of political interference and influence.

"With these noteworthy exceptions and a few others, the 823 labor unions, with their total membership of 469,240 members reported in 1935, are little more than nominal associations of workers, adjuncts of the Kuomintang political training bureaus....

"A labor movement is developing but its growth has been slow. Hardly more than a half dozen effective trade unions have been established." (P. 259.)

Miss Cora Deng, Industrial Secretary of the Y.W.C.A. with an intimate knowledge of the inside workings of the labor movement, said in 1941:[31]

"With the establishment of the Nationalist Government under the power of the Kuomintang party, the unions came under the domination of the party in 1928 and 1929, and have had almost no freedom for development since then. Unions are little more than a name.

"Besides this governmental party control of labor, there were other methods, well known in Western countries too, used to prevent any effective organizations of labor. Sometimes capitalists employed gangsters to break up unions, and the police always seemed to be on the side of the employers if any trouble occurred at a mill. Military police and soldiers were often used to break up picket lines or any other activities of striking workmen. Many times workers were killed and seldom did anyone seem to pay any attention to such events. In cases where workers lived in dormitories or other buildings operated by a factory, a common method of treatment for strikers was to cut down their meager food supply, so that soon they were really starving, and under this condition might agree to give up the strike. Other ordinary punishments were dismissal from work, huge fines and imprisonment without trial.

"In the case of the closely guarded dormitories of the textile mills, Japanese and some Chinese, there is no chance to reach the workers for any purpose, and certainly it is not possible to start any union organization...."

Aside from the repressive measures taken against unions, an underlying reason for the decline of labor activities after 1931 was the general economic depression. In her report on "Labour Problems," for the *China Christian Year Book*, 1934-35, Cora Deng analyzes this situation: At this time cotton mills were not working full time, and about 87 per cent of the workers were unemployed. In 1930, there were 181 silk filatures with 44,823 reels; by August, 1933, only 107 were

[31] *Economic Status of Women in Industry in China*, unpublished thesis, 1941.

running with 18,570 reels; and by September, 1934, only 23 were operating, 32 having been closed in a year. This caused unemployment for 60,000 persons in Shanghai and possibly 600,000 in the two provinces among silk workers. At this time also, silk reelers worked only six to eight hours a day, with decreased earnings, instead of the usual eleven. However, cotton mill operatives worked 11½ or 12 hours on day or night shifts, as usual; in the hosiery trade the same 11-hour day obtained; flour mill workers had a 12-hour day; chemical trades from 10 to 12 hours; printers from nine to 15. "Men, women and children in China work from 10 to 12 hours a day."

Miss Deng reports average wages as ranging from $15 to $40 a month. Wages for cotton spinners in 1930 averaged $15.57 monthly, but at the time of this report women spinners' wages had been cut from $3 to $8 a month. Hosiery rates had fallen from 80 cents to 30 cents a day.

The match industry had suffered. In 1930 there were 185 match factories in operation, but competition from the Japanese product and increased taxation had caused many to close or curtail. The same was true of the rubber shoe industry.

Miners at the Pinghsiang mines in Hunan had had wages reduced to 15 cents per day in 1933. One mining company in North China in 1933 owed eight months' wages to its employees. Another in Anhui owed half a year's wages and finally paid at 20-40 per cent discount.

As to labor unions, Miss Deng commented: "Since the reorganization of unions according to the Trade Union Law, control and limitation have been so severe that there is little active expression of any spontaneous or genuine movement. Those existing are either a name only, or are run by people other than workers, mostly Kuomintang officials.

"Following 1931 there was some labor activity, directing its attention, however, in common with other sections of the community, to the organization of Anti-Japanese clubs, boycotting Japanese goods, petitioning for a policy against Japan, etc. There has been in addition some expression of resistance to the rigid Trade Union Law." Here Miss Deng mentions that the Shanghai General Labor Union, forbidden since 1929, sent a petition to the Kuomintang Fourth plenary congress to cancel existing legislation and establish new laws according to Sun Yat-sen's principles, but this was rejected. In 1934 the Shanghai General Labor Union was permitted a "qualified existence." In 1932 a petition was again sent to the government for a special law for public employees.

"Since 1931, also, the main effort of the Labor Movement has shifted from active insistence on raising of wages or bettering conditions to a

183

defence position to maintain what had been obtained by collective effort in former years. These facts are borne out by Professor Chen Ta's studies. Thirty-six per cent of the strikes between 1918 and 1926 were for wage increase. His study for 1932 shows that out of a total of 317 disputes, 68 were in connection with wages, 54 with treatment, 48 with system of work, 39 with employment and dismissals, 21 with stopping work or closing down. The figure for the last two specified causes, together with the number concerned with wage rates, totalling 37%, gives evidence that labor had begun to be on the defence. In 1933 this struggle to maintain former gains is shown to be accentuated: almost 60% out of 296 disputes were for the causes mentioned. Of these 296 disputes, 79 resulted in actual strikes, almost 66% of the causes of which were attempts to deprive the workers of the standards previously won."

Miss Deng points out that the longest and most tragic strike was in 1934 at the Kailan mines, when 2,000 workers at Ma Chia Kou opposed wage cuts and came into conflict with police during the lockout on January 14, resulting in several deaths and wounded.

Many strikes occurred in silk weaving, the largest being among the Mei Ya weavers in March, 1934, opposing wage cuts. No union existed, but the workers were systematically organized. On March 11, the workers gathered to see the manager of the factory in the French Concession and came into conflict with the French police, resulting in death and wounds for 80 workers. The deadlock continued a month.

In May, 1934, a go-slow strike occurred in the B.A.T. Company's No. 2 mill, protesting against the closing of the No. 1 mill. The workers were sufficiently well organized to prevent 400 Chinese and 30 Russian strikebreakers from entering the factory. Clashes occurred, but despite all efforts the No. 1 mill closed and several thousand were left without jobs.

Miss Deng pointed out that the industrial depression and rural bankruptcy had affected labor but not changed its fundamental problems, and that even if labor had unions and no depression had existed "probably the system cannot be changed." She concludes:

"It is flesh and blood on one side and money and guns on the other. In every case in recent strikes employers have won, despite the fact that workers have shown power, strength in organization and improved skill in tactics, and that they are willing to face acute starvation and flying bullets. They have, however, to give way to the employers who have on their side not only economic advantages but also the police force to turn against the unarmed workers.

"Though permanently organized unions of workers, then, are not to be found, the movement has nevertheless progressed on the wave crests of labor unrest. Workers have shown their willingness to suffer, and their ability to organize. Given a chance, a spontaneous movement of workers will emerge as quickly as bamboo sprouts. Meantime the suppressed energy has been gathering momentum and acquiring ideology underground which may well startle the world when a change takes place."

Wartime figures on labor organization have been included in previous chapters and details are given on the statistics put out by the Chinese Government of 4,033 labor unions in 1942 with 1,053,656 members. A later statement was cabled through the Chinese News Service on May 1, 1944: "According to statistics released by the Ministry of Social Affairs, there are now in China a total of 2,867 labor organizations, including local labor unions, with a total membership of 1,044,462 persons." The million members claimed by the Communists for the North China Trade Union Federation has also been analyzed in the section devoted to the guerrilla regions.

II. A PICTURE OF LABOR UNIONS IN CANTON, 1926-1927

It is interesting to study the picture of labor activities in Canton in 1926-27, during the heydey of unionism and left-wing control in that city. A commission, headed by Y. L. Lee, a Y.M.C.A. Secretary, was appointed in 1926 by the city government of Canton, Sun Fo then being mayor, to make a survey of the labor unions, which was completed early in 1927. This survey was of special value, as the information was obtained directly from the unions themselves. The findings of the commission were presented in a paper by Y. L. Lee dated January 10, 1928.[32] Edward H. Lockwood in Canton also wrote on the subject in a manuscript which I saw dated August 24, 1927, "Labor Unions in Canton."

At the time of the survey Canton had a total population of about a million or a million and a quarter. There were 250 labor unions in Canton, but information was secured only on 180 of these,[33] representing 290,620 organized union members.

Organized labor in Canton was then divided into two main factions, the Congress of Labor Union Representatives, controlled by the Communists, which dominated the situation; and the Kwangtung Provincial Federation of Labor Unions, a Right-wing organization, headed by the Kwangtung Mechanics Union, and which was in contact with Right-wing elements of the Kuomintang. There was always a tug of war between the two, though this was the principal instance of such Right-wing control in China and was due to the fact that most of the Federation unions had originated as craft guilds and still retained control from the employers in the old guild tradition. The Kwangtung Me-

[32] *Some Aspects of the Labour Situation in Canton,* by Y. L. Lee, pamphlet printed by the Canton Y.M.C.A., January 10, 1928. It will be noted that this was after the crushing of the Canton Commune in December, 1927. Mr. Lee does not bring the situation up to date except to say: "At the moment, we have in Canton four main groups of labor unions, viz., 1, Labour Congress, 2, Federation of Revolutionist Workers, 3, Mechanics Union (which had then split off from the Provincial Federation), 4, Kwangtung Provincial Federation of Labour Unions."

[33] Lockwood says that of the industries studied the total workers numbered 485,268, of which the 180 unions represented 290,620 workers. He also says that 139 were in the "Labor Union Representatives Federation" and 39 in the Federation of Labor. The varied terminology is due to translation vagaries in China.

186

chanics Maintenance Society, the former guild (which changed its name several times after its organization in 1909), was only reorganized as the Kwangtung Mechanics' Union in January, 1926, as a method of combating the influence the Communists were securing over the rank and file. In its original program the Union stated: "We must always, in the revolutionary spirit, fight against the Communist Party, and expose the intrigues of the Communist agitators so that the working class in China will not be deceived by them." [34]

During the "Paper Tigers" uprising in Canton in 1925, when the merchants tried to overthrow Left-wing Kuomintang control, the Mechanics' Guild was associated with the merchants and was afterward closely connected with General Li Chi-sen, who armed its members and tried to use them against the Left-wing unions. In January, 1926, the newly-formed Mechanics' Union demanded control of the workers in the railroad shops and terminals and the Railway Workers' Union, an industrial union, refused. The Mechanics' Union then sent armed groups to the terminal to take over, supported by a company of Li Chi-sen's troops. A pitched battle took place with the railroad workers, who were supported by armed members of local peasant unions, in which the Mechanics' Union was defeated. Several other minor incidents occurred later.

Y. L. Lee's report showed that 74 of the 180 unions had originated as guilds, and this was one cause of the different approach to political problems and tactics, of course, the right-wing unions being still dominated by guild psychology and practices. Lee commented: "Class consciousness has been greatly increased. For this the credit or blame is due to the Communists who worked among the unions.... At the time of our survey, that was the beginning of 1927, the Communist influence was predominant among the labor unions in Canton." This new class consciousness was indicated by what the workers and others in Canton were reading in 1927: "We also made a study of Chinese literature on the labour movement, or other subjects available in Canton. We discovered 134 kinds of pamphlets, etc., twenty-nine kinds about labour, six kinds about labour unions, twenty-seven kinds (about) communism, about six kinds about guild socialism, nine kinds on Cooperative Societies, nineteen kinds on social problems, twenty-six kinds on Marxism."

Of the 180 unions, 130 belonged to the Congress of Labor Union Representatives and 21 to the Kwangtung Provincial Federation of Labor Unions, eleven were independent, and four described themselves as belonging to "both wings." The committee system was used by 168 unions, and the rest used the Presidential system. Of the 290,620 work-

[34] *Facing Labour Issues in China,* by Lowe Chuan-hua, p. 61.

ers in the 180 unions, 77,932 said they were members of the Kuomintang, and 108,686 declared themselves able to read the newspapers.[35] Both figures seem exaggerated.

Y. L. Lee reported that about ten of the unions had developed from labor organizations created between 1911 and 1921. The two organized during the Manchu dynasty were the Mechanics guild and the Packers (or Wrappers) guild. The rest had been "organized in the last few years."

Thirteen of the 180 unions had 500 to 600 members; twelve had 800 to 1,000, eight had 1,000 to 1,200; nine had 2,000 to 2,500; eight had 2,500 to 3,500; five had 3,500 to 4,500; five had 4,500 to ten thousand; and five had between 10,000 and 15,000 members. Others fitted into smaller categories.

There has been much talk about the excessive and radical demands of the unions during 1925 and 1927. On this point the regulations reported by the Canton unions are instructive. According to the unions, maximum hours were reported as follows:

20 unions reported an eight-hour day;
34 " " 10 hours
23 " " 12 "
10 " " 16 "
2 " " 18 "
1 " " 19 "
1 " " 20 "

The Newspaper Sellers Union reported the above 19 hour day and the Cake Makers' Union the 20-hour day.

Out of the 180 unions, 160 reported on minimum monthly wages: 86 unions reported from fifty cents to $5.00 a month; 63 reported between $5.50 and $15 a month; nine reported from $16 to $45 monthly.

Maximum monthly wages were reported by 176 unions: 47 unions reported $4.00 to $15; 78 reported $15 to $30; 38 reported $31 to $85; 13 reported $100 to $500 (highly skilled engineers, etc.).

The minimum wage averaged $7.50 monthly, and the maximum $39. The general average was figured at $23.25.

[35] Lockwood says that 18,606 of the union members, or one in 19, was able to read: that 77,832, or 1 out of 4, declared himself a member of the Kuomintang showing Kuomintang "influence"; that "Seventy-two of the unions are an outgrowth of the seventy-two *'hongs'* (guilds)"; that 20 per cent of the unionists were unemployed; that the Ricksha Pullers' Union had 7,000 rickshas and 14,000 pullers in Canton, each paying a copper a day or $4,000 monthly to support the Union.

Of the 290,628 union members, 60,744 reported themselves unemployed (this did not include the Hongkong strikers who were then idle in Canton).

As to union dues: entrance fees, paid only once, were reported by 78 unions as from 30 cents to $1.00; 48 unions required $1.40 to $2.00; 34 unions $2.20 to $5.00; 10 unions required $6.00 to $15, and six unions had fees from $20 to $48.

Monthly dues of 118 unions ranged from two cents to 20 cents; 97 unions had dues of 20 cents; 31 from 31 cents to 50 cents; eight unions required from 80 cents to $1.50. Five unions collected one day's wage as dues.

The survey also included a study of 71 factories in Canton. Of these 39 used machines, 32 used power. They employed 4,603 workers, 2,650 (over 50 per cent) being women, 1,617 being men, and 336 were children under fourteen years of age. Of 70 factories, the average monthly minimum wage for men was found to be $8 and the maximum $25.50. Of 40 factories employing women the average minimum monthly wage was $7.00 and the maximum $15.36.

Of 29 factories employing children, the average minimum monthly wage was $3.00 and the maximum about $5.00. Five of these furnished board only and no wages.

As to hours, of 65 factories studied, 40 worked nine or more hours. The others had daily hours as follows:

2	factories worked 6 hours		10	factories worked 11 hours	
2	" " 7 "		12	" " 12 "	
8	" " 8 "		6	" " 13 "	
13	" " 9 "		2	" " 14 "	
2	" " 9½ "		1	" " 14½ "	
6	" " 10 "		1	" " 15 "	

In 44 factories board was furnished free to the workers; in 13 none was provided.

In response to the questionnaires, 57 factories stated that during sickness workers had to be responsible for their own care. Of these 32 paid wages during illness, but 25 did not.

In 37 factories 100 per cent of the workers were union members; in 4 factories 90 per cent were unionized; in three 70 per cent; in six 40 per cent; in two 20 per cent; in one less than 20 per cent. In six factories no workers were union members. In one factory the men belonged to a union, but not the women.

The above shows the situation at the height of labor's power in Canton, and the demands of the workers do not seem unreasonable. Yet the gains made by labor through organized action are graphically indicated in the following table, compiled by the Canton government, showing the relation of wages and prices from 1912 to 1926:

Year	Wages	Price Index	Purchasing Power of the Dollar
1912	100.67	99.4	100.6
1913	100.00	100.0	100.0
1915	100.19	112.1	89.2
1917	106.69	124.7	80.2
1919	106.19	136.4	73.3
1920	107.23	135.4	73.9
1921	119.34	144.8	69.1
1922	124.69	153.4	65.2
1923	131.30	161.0	62.1
1924	135.28	175.6	56.9
1925	206.63	172.03	58.2
1926	253.56	171.5	58.2

The rise in wages beginning in 1921 and jumping suddenly in 1925 was due to labor-union bargaining. After 1927 wages all over China were reduced, in some cases almost to pre-1925 levels, though unfortunately I have been unable to find any further figures on Canton to show the trend.

III. ANALYSIS OF FOUR CHINESE
LABOR UNIONS

After 1931 only a few important unions existed in China, chiefly in Shanghai. Among the principal ones were these: in Shanghai were the Commercial Press Employees' Union, the British-American Tobacco Company Union, the headquarters of the Chinese Seamen's Union and the All-China Postal Employees' Union in Shanghai and Nanking. In Canton was the Kwangtung Mechanics' Union. Various railway workers' unions also existed. The history of these unions shows the inner workings of labor organization in China and is of special interest. Such information is difficult to obtain, but fortunately Lowe Chuan-hua went to a good deal of trouble to translate from the histories of four of these unions, and I think the results of his research should be made available here.[36]

1. THE COMMERCIAL PRESS EMPLOYEES' UNION

The Commercial Press in Shanghai was the largest and finest Chinese-owned printing establishment in China, publishing books both in English and Chinese. The printers in China are among the most advanced of all workers, yet one of the leaders of labor activities in the Commercial Press told me once that hardly any of the printers knew a syllable of English and most of them were illiterate in Chinese. He himself had been a printer responsible for supervising English printing, yet he could hardly speak a sentence of it. This is a remarkable commentary on the ability of the Chinese printer, it seems to me, for the finished product contained few mistakes. The same was largely true of the printers who regularly produced English-language newspapers and magazines in China.

The management and ownership of the Commercial Press were also progressive and enlightened in labor policies, preferring a company union to negotiating with labor racketeers. They represented one of the best examples of modern Chinese industrial management. Had other Chinese firms been as modern-minded, perhaps collaboration between labor and capital might have developed to the benefit of both after the destruction of the independent labor movement in China, either as com-

[36] The direct quotations in this chapter are taken, as indicated, from Lowe Chuan-hua's *Facing Labor Issues in China,* from the section "Study of Some Leading Labor Unions in China."

pany unions or otherwise. No few unions such as the Commercial Press, however, could stand alone against the deluge, and in 1931 the union was taken over by the Kuomintang and reorganized, weakening it so much that afterward it had no independence at all and was an adjunct of the so-called Shanghai Publishers' "Union."

Although the Commercial Press was started around the turn of the century, labor organization did not begin until 1917, when a guild was created. This was not reorganized as a labor union until 1925 during the May 30 movement. A strike was called on June 3, 1925, is commemoration of the workers and students killed on May 30, and a mass meeting held at a school in the Chapei district where the plant was located. At the meeting it was decided to organize the employees in the Works Department into a modern labor union, and a committee of thirteen was selected for this purpose. On June 21, 600 Commercial Press employees gathered in a Chinese theatre on Jukong Road and the union was formally inaugurated. A manifesto was issued which stated that as other industries in Shanghai were already organized, such as the flour mills, machine shops, water works and tram-car operators, it was a matter of regret that the printing industry had not yet developed a union of its own. The manifesto stated that the purpose of the union was to protect the common interests of the workers and to promote their education and friendly relations.

The Union later published "A History of the Commercial Press Employees' Union," and Lowe Chuan-hua translated the following information from this and other sources:

"No sooner had the Union been organized than the workers presented eight demands for better treatment to the management. Unable to obtain full acceptance of their demands from the Company, the workers declared a strike on August 22, 1925, formed a picket corps and held secret conferences to enforce the strike. The demands were in brief, as follows:

1. That the management should immediately accept the demands presented by the employees of the sales agencies;
2. That the management should accord full recognition to the Union and give a monthly allowance of at least $200.00 to cover its running expenses;
3. Increase of wages and equal treatment for men and women workers;
4. Abolition of the system of contract-labor;
5. Reduction of the working day to eight hours;
6. Abolition of the system of daily premiums and institution of the system of double-pay for the last month of the year;

7. Improvement of the treatment of women workers and revision of the factory regulations with the cooperation and advice of the Union;

8. Better treatment for apprentices and provision for their education.

"After a week's strike, the management reached an agreement with the Union and the workers went back to their jobs on the morning of August 28. This was understood to be purely an economic strike and resulted in a victory for the Union. A second strike was declared on December 22 of the same year after the management had allegedly failed to carry out the provisions of the above agreement and had dismissed more than forty workers. The second strike lasted until December 26 when a new understanding of sixteen articles was agreed upon by the management and the Union, after considerable pressure had been brought to bear upon the latter by the military authorities in Shanghai.

"The most important strike in the history of the Union was the one staged at the time when the Nationalist Revolutionary Armies captured Shanghai in the spring of 1927. It may be recalled that during those days most of the labor unions in Shanghai were under the influence of the Shanghai General Labor Federation, which had planned a general strike to disrupt the positions of Marshal Sun Chuang-fang's troops in and around Shanghai, and in this way expedite the advance of the Revolutionary Armies. The first strike took place from February 17 to 19, but it was arranged a little too soon to be of any direct assistance to the Southern armies. A second general strike was declared on March 21 when the Nationalist troops came nearer the city. The labor pickets of the Commercial Press Employees' Union and several other labor organizations, who had been secretly armed at this time, actually fought against Sun Chuang-fang's men in Chapei. As a result of this clash, the Commercial Press Employees' Union lost seven members, including one woman worker. Eleven others were seriously wounded in the street fighting. The Union was also engaged in several other activities during this period, such as collecting gifts and soliciting provisions for the Nationalist Revolutionary Armies. This was perhaps the most important political strike that has ever occurred in the history of the labor movement in Shanghai.

"The Commercial Press Employees' Union, which had about 3,000 members before its destruction, was one of the best organized unions in China. Its activities included a weekly paper devoted to the Union's interests, a dramatic club, evening classes for adult workers, a school for the employees' children, a boy scout troop and a self-governing society for promoting discipline among the workers.

"The officers of the Union had always been active in the civic affairs of Shanghai, and in one year one of its executive officers had the honor of acting as the workers' delegate for China at the International Labor Conference in Geneva. In the summer of 1931, however, the Union was reorganized by the department of mass movements of the Shanghai Kuomintang branch on the ground that the leaders of the Union had developed connections with the Communists. Later in the year, the Commercial Press Employees' Union was incorporated into the so-called Shanghai Publishers' Union and was thus much weakened in its influence. During the Japanese bombardment of Chapei in January, 1932, the Union lost all its documents and property, and since then it has not been able to resume its activities."

Quite a number of printers, including former Commercial Press workers, left Shanghai when Japan took over and went to the interior, many of them to the guerrilla regions. One group started a mobile printers' industrial co-operative in Shansi, moving the presses in and out of Japanese lines and continuing publication of a regular newspaper. In 1937 in Yenan I met a group of printers who had previously been active in the Commercial Press union. They had made their way secretly to Yenan at the end of 1936 and had already set up a new union which managed and operated two printing plants, one in a disused temple on a hill. They were making wooden type when I first saw them, having no lead for the purpose. Dozens of other printers were recruited later and today they carry on quite a sizable printing activity in Yenan and the guerrilla districts. The head of the union, who had also been a leader in the Commercial Press union in previous years, was a very likeable person—in particular for a reason which I may as well relate: When I visited the Printers' Union headquarters in Yenan I happened to see a bottle of curry powder on the shelf in his office, and asked where he got it, with some interest. I did not mention that I was starving for condiments of this kind, having been on a rigid diet of rice gruel and bismuth for amoebic dysentery. He told me that he loved curry and had brought it in his pocket hundreds of miles and was saving it for the day when he felt he could no longer survive without it. He said he kept it on the shelf to look at, in anticipation. Immediately registering the fact that I also liked curry, he promptly decided that we should have a party as the "day" had arrived. I naturally refused to even permit him to open it and he tried to give me the bottle. Next day a messenger arrived from him with the bottle all wrapped up as a gift. I trotted back to the Union headquarters to return it. By this time, however, it had become an international issue in the Printers' union and they refused to take it back and escorted me home with the bottle. Nor would the owner or anyone else divide it or share in any food cooked with it. It was a little thing, perhaps, but in fact I never enjoyed anything so much as having curried chicken during the rest of my stay, against doctor's orders, and I shall always be grateful to that generous printer, believe me.

2. THE BRITISH-AMERICAN TOBACCO COMPANY LABOR UNION

The best example of the type of union developed in factories owned by foreigners in China was the British-American Tobacco Company Labor Union in the Pootung district of Shanghai, formed June 5, 1927. As in the case of the Commercial Press, the management showed a comparatively enlightened labor policy and working conditions and wages were better than in most other factories in China. The Union had its own organ, "The B.A.T. Labor Union Fortnightly." Lowe Chuan-hua translated from this and interviewed the leaders to secure the following information:

"As early as August, 1922, a recreation club was organized among the employees of the B.A.T. factory in Pootung (the factory on Thorburn Road in Shanghai has never organized any union as it is located within the International Settlement), and in order to improve the workers' treatment the club despatched several representatives to approach the factory authorities with the following demands: 1. dismissal of the Chinese *compradore;* 2. increase of wages; 3. better treatment for the workers, and 4. shortening of working hours. It was reported that the factory took a firm stand towards these demands, and as a result, the workers struck for about three weeks, at the end of which the military authorities in Shanghai intervened and forced the employees into a settlement with the management. According to this settlement, the B.A.T. Company agreed: 1. to increase wages from 35 cents to 50 cents per day; 2. to pay all wages in terms of *big money;* 3. to pay a rice allowance to every worker, and 4. to inaugurate a savings fund plan and the system of giving an annual bonus to the workers. However, the Chinese *compradore* was not removed and the working hours remained the same as they were before. Although the strike was a success for the club in several respects, many of its leaders lost their positions after the trouble and the club was later dissolved.

"During the first period of the Union's history, organizational activities were conducted secretly, as the former *tuchuns* or military governors were entirely opposed to labor organizations and as the forma-

195

tion of workers' associations without the permission of the authorities made one liable to capital punishment. Nevertheless, the workers obtained considerable training in group efforts and were taught the advantages of united action through the club and its ally, the Society for the Advancement of Morality through which a well-known Shanghai merchant financed several free schools for workers and their children in the town of Pootung.

"Renewed attempts at organizing the workers of the B.A.T. factory were made during the May 30th Incident in Shanghai, 1925. A labor union was formed and under its leadership all of the 8,000 workers in the factory joined in the general strike in Shanghai that spring. The workers, however, obtained practically no benefit out of this strike and at the end of three months, they had to go back to work almost unconditionally.

"The third attempt was made shortly after the Nationalist Revolutionary Armies had gained control of the lower Yangtze region. On June 5, 1927, the B.A.T. Labor Union formally established its headquarters in Pootung, and on September 30 the Union declared a general strike, the main causes of which were alleged to be: 1. opposition to the B.A.T. Company's policy of not paying the rolled-tobacco tax then inaugurated by the Ministry of Finance of the Nationalist Government in Nanking; and 2. demand for an increase of wages due to the rising cost of living. The strike developed into serious proportions and was soon supported by other labor unions in Shanghai. By January 16, 1928, after a stoppage of work for nearly four months, the management, through the good offices of the Bureau of Rolled-Tobacco of the Ministry of Finance and the Department of Agriculture, Industry and Labor of the Municipal Government of Greater Shanghai reached the following agreement (translated by the author) with the labor Union....

"While the agreement brought about a number of reforms in the treatment of the workers, the most important concession granted by the factory was its recognition of the workers' right to organize and the right on the part of the Union to represent the workers in settling disputes with the factory authorities. The management of the B.A.T. factory is understood to have adopted a very sane and liberal policy towards the Union, and has been willing to co-operate with the workers in putting their organization on a sound foundation, whereas the overwhelming majority of other foreign and Chinese industrial enterprises have been quite intolerant towards organized labor.

"The B.A.T. Labor Union is now conducted by a standing committee of seven persons (one woman worker) appointed by its executive committee which, in turn, is created by the workers' representatives'

196

conference. The term of service for members of the executive committee is one year, but they may be re-elected. During the time they are in office, they may secure a leave of absence from the factory authorities, and at the end of the year they may return to their original jobs. During their term of office they are paid a certain salary by the Union, but receive no wages from the factory. Under the standing committee there are organized four departments to take charge of the affairs of the Union: 1. organization; 2. training; 3. propaganda, and 4. general affairs. The membership fee of the Union is 20 cents *small money* per month. Although there are supposed to be 6,000 members in the Union, the income from the membership dues has rarely been fully collected and has often dwindled to only a few hundred dollars a month....

"At present the Union is conducting, in co-operation with the factory authorities, a day school for workers' children. The school is managed by an independent board of directors, composed of one representative from the factory and twelve workers' representatives. It receives a subsidy of $750 per month from the factory authorities, has more than 10 teachers and about 620 students. In addition to the school work, the Union has a boy scout troop, organized in the fall of 1920, and issues a semi-monthly paper which has a circulation of 3,000 copies, and conducts several recreational activities such as football and basketball teams.

"The B.A.T. Labor Union, like other labor organizations in Shanghai, was originally organized on the factory-unit basis. In the summer of 1931, the Kuomintang and the Municipal Government of Greater Shanghai adopted a plan of reorganizing all the labor unions into two categories: the industrial union and the occupational union. The municipal area of Greater Shanghai, then, was divided into eight districts, and each district was to have its own industrial union. As a result of this ruling, the B.A.T. Labor Union was reorganized on the industrial basis and its name was changed to the Shanghai Fifth District Rolled-Tobacco Workers' Union. However, since there is no other cigarette-manufacturing plant in Pootung, the B.A.T. Labor Union remained more or less as a factory union rather than as an industrial union, and its officers are the same persons who have served the Union for several years.

"In case of dispute between the factory authorities and the workers, the Union representative in the particular department of the factory where the trouble happened, would make a report of the case to the Union executive committee, and the latter would then take it up with the personnel manager of the factory. If no satisfactory settlement could be reached there, the matter would be brought to the Shanghai Bureau of Social Affairs for mediation and, if necessary, for arbitration. The main causes of disputes in the B.A.T. factory are reported to be: demand for increase in wages, misunderstandings regarding leave of absence and discipline.

"In fairness to the British-American Tobacco Company, it must be added that the wages and other conditions of treatment in the said Company are much better than those obtaining in most of the other industrial enterprises in China. The B.A.T. factory works nine hours a day, six days a week, and gives the following benefits and gratuities to the permanent workers (another class is called temporary workers, who have to go through a six-months period of trial before they become regular members of the working force):

1. Four per cent of the workers' annual earnings as a bonus at the close of the year;
2. A maternity benefit of $34.50 to women workers (who have been on the factory pay-roll for at least a year), to be paid in two instalments, one before and one after childbirth;
3. A rice allowance for each worker, paid semi-monthly."

3. THE KWANGTUNG MECHANICS' UNION

The Kwangtung Mechanics' Union in Canton provides an interesting study of a conservative native Chinese type of general union and its development, and indicates what might have happened to labor in China had no Communists existed to disturb the picture. It is the best example of a union (really a semi-guild) controlled by the Kuomintang and shows the failure of that party to safeguard the interests of labor. It was unique in that it was the only important labor organization whose leadership remained arch-conservative throughout the revolutionary period and never came under control of the Communists, but continued to support the conservative wing of the Kuomintang. It was one of the instruments used in every attempt to break the Leftist control of the Canton labor movement from 1924 to the time of the Canton Commune. Its leadership was always strongly anti-Communist and also uncooperative with the general labor movement. It received subsidies from political sources and had several dubious connections, though in general it was dominated by the employers. After 1927 the membership was alienated from the Kuomintang, and in 1928 the Communists led a strike among the rank-and-file and obtained considerable influence. In subsequent years the Mechanics' Union was quite impotent in its activities.

Lowe Chuan-hua gives an account of the Mechanics' Union up to 1933, for which his information was taken largely from Huang Yi-po's "Machine Workers in Kwangtung," published by the Union:

198

"The Kwangtung Mechanics' Union, one of the best organized groups of skilled workers in China, is composed of the mechanics engaged in the various industries of Kwangtung province, such as chemical industry workers, electricians, locomotive engineers, machine operators, munitions workers, lumber mill operatives, and mechanics engaged in electric power and water works, telephone and telegraph companies. The Union originated as far back as 1909 when relations between the mechanics and their employers were informal and paternalistic. At that time a 'Society for the Study of Mechanics' was established in Canton, managed largely by the workers. In 1912, the Society moved its office to Honam (opposite the city of Canton) and changed its name into 'Kwangtung Mechanics' Research General Association.'

"In 1918 Chinese mechanics in Hongkong, due to 'imperialistic oppression,' expressed a desire to co-operate with the mechanics' organization in Canton and in June that year, representatives from both bodies met together and formed the 'All China Mechanics' Guild.' At this meeting, it was decided to build a permanent headquarters for the Guild in Canton. A financial campaign was launched, and on October 9, 1919, Dr. Wu Ting-fang laid the cornerstone for the new building, which is the present home of the Kwangtung Mechanics' Union.

"During the first decade of its existence, the mechanics' guild included both employers and employees, there being no marked distinction between the two classes. The employees had no independent organization of their own, in spite of the fact that they had passed through three different stages of development, that is, the Kwangtung Mechanics' Study Society, the Kwangtung Mechanics' Research General Association, and the All-China Mechanics' Guild.

"During the 'Canton for the Cantonese' movement in 1919, the Mechanics' Guild attempted to force the Kwangtung Provincial Assembly to proclaim the late Dr. Wu Ting-fang Governor of Kwangtung by declaring a strike among the workers in the electric power plant, the railway workers and the mechanics in several related industries. However, the strike met with total failure.

"In 1920, when the Kuomintang decided to drive the military adventurer, Mo Yung-hsin, out of Kwangtung, the railway workers again declared a strike to support the Nationalist Party's platform. Train service was stopped by the railway workers in order to disrupt the transportation of Mo's troops. Subsequently, when the Kuomintang started a military campaign to help the Nationalists in Kweichow province, the Kwangtung Mechanics' Maintenance Society (as the Mechanics' Guild is now called), together with thirty-six other labor organizations, lodged a strong protest with the Governor of Hongkong

199

against the subversive activities of the Kwangsi general, Yang Yung-tai, in the island colony. This agitation precipitated the defeat of Mo Yung-hsin and his clique.

"In 1922, when General Chen Chiung-ming revolted against Dr. Sun Yat-sen, the mechanics for the third time declared a strike to support the Kuomintang chief. General Chen, however, succeeded in keeping his position in Canton and as a result, many mechanics were forced to seek shelter in Hongkong. At the end of 1922, when Dr. Sun gathered his Yünnan, Kweichow and Kwangtung forces to resume operations against General Chen Chiung-ming, the mechanics once more organized themselves, bombarded the railways and strengthened Dr. Sun's army in various ways.

"While the mechanics in Canton and Hongkong were engaged in establishing a permanent headquarters, the employers also gathered together and formed the so-called 'Machine-Trade Mutual Benefit Guild,' precipitating a split with the mechanics. During this period, working conditions were said to be very unsatisfactory. Even in the large machine shops, the workers received only 60 to 70 cents a day at the most for a working day of eleven hours, including Sundays. They were much worse off than the workers in other public works and foreign firms. For instance, in the electric power plant, the water works and such foreign firms as the Standard Oil Company and the Asiatic Petroleum Company, the working day was only nine hours, and the daily wage 80 to 90 cents with regular pay for Sundays and holidays. The apprentice system was especially in need of reform. But during those days the mechanics were too disorganized, and could not present a united front against their employers. As time went on, they began to feel the need of independent action, and established a number of workers' clubs. By 1920, most of the machine shops and industrial works in Canton and its vicinity had organized workers' clubs. Among the leading ones were the Workers' Recreation Club of the Canton-Hankow Railway, the Self-Development Society of the Canton-Samshui Railway, the Canton-Kowloon Railroad, and the Mutual Aid Club of the Canton Electric Power Co. In the following year, branches of these clubs were organized in such places as Kiangmen, Chungsan, Taisan, Shihlung, and Fatsan. With the development of these clubs, a plan of unified control and coordination was adopted in April, 1921, which gave birth to the so-called 'Kwangtung Mechanics' Maintenance Society.' As soon as it was established, the Kwangtung Mechanics' Maintenance Society presented a demand to the employers' organization (Machine Trade Mutual Aid Guild) for better treatment and for improvement of the apprentice system. . . .

"On June 9, 1921, when a general strike was threatened by the me-

200

chanics, the Governor of Kwangtung province invited the representatives of both the employers and the employees to a conference and, as a result, the following conditions of work were agreed upon by the Kwangtung Mechanics' Maintenance Society and the Employers' Guild:"

These conditions included the nine-hour day, double pay for night work, increased wages and double pay for Sundays and holidays, and also that eight holidays a year be kept; two days at New Year, Arbor Day, March 29, May Day, May 5, October 4 and October 10.

"... The Kwangtung Mechanics' Maintenance Society, however, was only a temporary expediency, and its main supporters—the workers' clubs—were organized without any plan of coordination. With the reorganization of the Kuomintang and the admittance of the Communists into the Party in 1924, a sudden growth of labor organizations in South China took place. The Communists, through the instrumentality of the Canton Labor Representatives Association, tried to dominate the mechanical workers and win the latter into their fold. In order to meet this danger, the mechanics decided on the reorganization of their Society on a stricter basis and in January, 1926, in a conference of representatives of the mechanics in the province, the Kwangtung Mechanics' Maintenance Society was reorganized into the Kwangtung Mechanics' Union. ...

"Shortly after its formal inauguration, the Kwangtung Mechanics' Union was compelled by the rising cost of living to stage another movement for bettering the working conditions of its members. The mechanics had not enjoyed any improvement in treatment from 1921 to 1926. They had, it is true, obtained a victory in their first economic strike, but what they had gained had been practically lost because the employers had failed to carry out their part of the bargain. Thus in April, 1927, the Mechanics' Union presented seventeen demands for better treatment to the machine-shops in Honam. These demands were entirely rejected by the employers, and as a result over 1,000 mechanics went out on strike. Repeated attempts at mediation proved of no avail. ... The change in labor regulations of the Canton Government in June, 1928, had given the employers the pretext they wanted, and until today (1933) the dispute has not been definitely settled. Due to the second strike a large number of mechanics have become unemployed, and several tens of thousands of dollars have been spent in supporting them. Eventually, it was decided to establish a mechanics' cooperative workshop, and a large sum of money is reported to have been secured for the project."

4. THE CHINESE SEAMEN'S UNION

The Chinese Seamen's Union has a long and interesting history, especially as showing the relations between Chinese labor, foreign control and the Chinese Nationalist movement. As most seamen are on foreign-owned ships and travel abroad, they are the chief point of contact between Chinese labor and that in other countries, though the relation has not always been a happy one.

As Lowe Chuan-hua interviewed the leaders and translated from their organ, I shall quote him directly on this union:

"Of the few national labor organizations in China, the Chinese Seamen's Union is perhaps the most conspicuous not only because it has played a most dramatic role in the Nationalist movement in South China, but also because it commands a widespread influence at home and abroad (Data for this section are chiefly obtained from the *Seamen's Monthly,* published by the Chinese Seamen's Union at Canton and Shanghai.) Although as early as 1911 Chinese seamen in Liverpool had organized themselves to cope with the antagonism of the British sailors, it was not until 1913 that systematic efforts in organizing a Chinese Seamen's union were undertaken. When Dr. Sun Yat-sen failed with his scheme for the Second Revolution, he commissioned several of his followers to organize the Overseas Communications Department of the Lien Yi Society at Yokohama as an instrument to facilitate the transportation and communication affairs of the Revolutionary Party and to get the seamen to become active participants in the Revolution. In 1914 a branch of the Chinese Revolutionary Party was established on the S.S. Monteagle where over twenty comrades were enlisted to start an organization among Chinese seamen for the purpose of pushing forward the Revolutionary movement and of working towards their own economic emancipation. The new organization was called the Seamen's Mutual Benefit Society which immediately began its work on the S.S. Empress of Russia, the S.S. Empress of Asia and other ocean going vessels. Later, a branch of the society was opened at Yokohama while the headquarters remained on the S.S. Monteagle. Still later, the Society moved its headquarters to Hongkong and registered with the Secretary for Chinese affairs under the new name, Seamen's Philanthropic Society. It began to enlist members from among the boarding houses in the island, but as it was generally suspected of being a purely revolutionary society, it failed to obtain any extensive support.

"Prior to their organization, Chinese seamen were completely at the mercy of the labor contractors and recruiting agents. Inoculated with propaganda by the Seamen's Mutual Benefit Society and the Seamen's

Philanthropic Society, the seamen gradually developed a strong agitation against the labor contractors. A mass meeting of the seamen on the Canadian Pacific vessels was held secretly in Hongkong, at which a representative was elected to approach the Secretary for Chinese Affairs for support, and a resolution calling for a general strike was adopted.

"However, labor traitors seized this opportunity to make personal gains and arranged to supply the Canadian Pacific vessels with lower-paid substitutes. As a result, not only was the much abused recruiting system unchanged but also many of the seamen who had participated in the agitation were turned out of employment.

"Later, however, renewed efforts were made to establish a modern union among Chinese seamen. In 1920 the official name 'Chinese Seamen's Union' was given by Dr. Sun Yat-sen and was registered with the Ministry of the Interior of the then Military Government in Canton. In January, 1921, a British lawyer named Britton sent on behalf of the Union a petition to ask for registration with the Hongkong Government. On February 28 of the same year, Dr. Sun, in his capacity as Generalissimo of the Canton Government, sent a personal representative to attend the inauguration ceremony of the Union at Hongkong.

"Two or three months after its formation, the Chinese Seamen's Union created a special committee to study the question of remuneration and to make recommendations for improvement. On January 12, 1922, the Union presented its demand for a wage increase to the shipping companies in Hongkong and upon the latter's refusal to comply with this request, the Union declared a strike on the following morning. The direct loss of the British shipping firms during the strike was reckoned to be $5,000,000, while the indirect loss must have been much greater. The workers lost about $200,000 in wages during the fifty days of strike, although they were provided with sustenance grants (from 45 cents to $1.00 per day) contributed by labor unions in China and sympathetic merchants abroad. (These figures were given the author in an interview with the officers of the Chinese Seamen's Union in Canton in the fall of 1928). As the men returned to Canton, they established a branch union. On March 6, the strike was settled in the seamen's favor and the sign-board of the Union, which had been taken off by the Hong-kong authorities, was replaced amidst cheers and fire crackers. Another interesting point may be noted here. As a condition for calling off the strike, the Union demanded an indemnity of $200,000 (some reports state $360,000) to cover the losses sustained by the workers during the strike period. The demand was accepted by the shipping companies and a prominent leader in Hongkong was secured as guarantor. However, the indemnity remains unpaid up to the present time.

"Further support for the Nationalist movement in South China came from the Union shortly after Dr. Sun reorganized the Kuomintang in 1924. In remonstrance against the May 30th Incident of Shanghai and the June 23rd Incident of Shameen, 1925, the Union declared its second general strike and joined hands with Canton in a vigorous boycott against Hongkong. Once more the Union moved its office back to Canton. When on October 10, 1926, the Nationalist Government voluntarily declared the cessation of the boycott against Hongkong, the Union transformed its former headquarters into a branch union only. This branch was, however, sealed up by the Hongkong Government in the following June and has never been reopened.

"In October 1927 the Union moved its headquarters from Canton to Shanghai so as to be in closer touch with the Central Kuomintang and the National Government in Nanking, and to give proper attention to the field around Shanghai. On May 19, 1928, the branch union at Canton was closed by the authorities there for alleged Communist activities. It should be recalled that on several occasions the control of the Union went into the hands of the Communists, thereby inviting its suppression by the Nationalist authorities at various intervals. The fact that the Union has been divided into opposing camps also explains its frequent removal from one place to another. Authentic information regarding the Communists' administration of the Union is not obtainable, but it is safe to state that no other Chinese Communist played a more important role in the Union's history than the late Su Chao-jen who was one time chairman of the All-China Labor Federation and later, the Minister of Labor of the short-lived Wuhan Nationalist Government. On June 5 of the same year the chairman of the Union sent a petition to the Canton branch of the Central Political Council asking for permission to reorganize the Union there. As a result, the Department of Agriculture and Labor of the Kwangtung Provincial Government gave consent to have the Canton branch changed into the main headquarters of the Chinese Seamen's Union, and appointed a committee of seven persons to carry out the task. In October, the chairman and other officers of the Union sent another petition to the Central Kuomintang at Nanking asking for support to take over the competing Union at Shanghai. On November 6, 1928, the Department for the Training of Mass Movements of the Central Party Headquarters gave sanction to the petitioners to recognize the union in Shanghai. On January 1, 1929, the Union in Canton was transformed into a branch office, and the one in Shanghai was officially reorganized as the main headquarters of the Chinese Seamen's Union. At present, its branches are in Foochow,

Amoy, Swatow, Canton, Wuchow, Siam, Hankow, Kiukiang, Wuhu, Chungking, Tientsin, Tsingtao, Wenchow, Woosung, Yokohama and several other ports.

"As indicated above, much of what the Union has achieved in Hong-kong through the two famous strikes is now lost. The Hongkong authorities are closely watching all labor activities and even play a part in reorganizing workers' clubs and labor unions by requiring conformity with government regulations. The Chinese Seamen's Associated Union is a fair example of the 'company union' now in existence in the island. The Chinese Seamen's Union in Shanghai naturally regards the one in Hongkong as a reactionary body and a tool of the employers. It may be added that the Hongkong Government does not allow its labor organizations to have any affiliation with labor unions in China.

"Notwithstanding these obstacles, the Chinese Seamen's Union is determined to restore its Hongkong branch. On September 14, 1928, the Union created a special committee to make the necessary preparations for reopening its office in the island. In January, 1930, the Union submitted a petition to the Central Kuomintang asking for its assistance in the matter. As a result, the Kwangtung Provincial Kuomintang was ordered to make an investigation of the case. In its report to the Central Party Headquarters, the Kwangtung branch states that the Hongkong authorities have utilized notorious labor contractors to put up the 'bogus' Chinese Seamen's Associated Union which has overthrown all the previous conditions of treatment gained by the seamen, and that the Hongkong branch of the Chinese Seamen's Union should be at once restored in order adequately to protect Chinese workers. By order No. 734 of the Department for the Training of Mass Movements, the Ministry of Foreign Affairs was notified to instruct the Commissioner of Foreign Affairs in Canton to co-operate with a representative of the Union in negotiating with the Hongkong Government for a speedy settlement of the issue.

"Meanwhile, the Union endeavored to solicit the support of the International Labor Office in Geneva. At the thirteenth session of the International Labor Conference, Liang Teh-kung (labor delegate from China, and representative of the Chinese Seamen's Union) proposed a draft resolution concerning the right of association of foreign seamen. Failing to obtain the necessary quorum, the resolution was not adopted. A petition for restoring the Union's branch in Hongkong was also submitted to the legislative Council there. In November, 1929, the chairman of the Union wrote to Mr. Albert Thomas, late director of the International Labor Office, asking him to help negotiate with the Hongkong authorities for the restoration of the Union's branch there and for a speedy settlement of the indemnity question which arose out of the first seamen's strike. In reply to Mr. Thomas' unofficial inquiries, the Hongkong Government declared that although the Chinese Seamen's Union is no longer manipulated by the Communists, it still entertains political motives and that since the Chinese seamen in Hongkong are taken care of by the Chinese Seamen's Associated Union and the River Vessels Seamen's Union there is no ground for establishing any additional seamen's organization in the colony. With regard to the indemnity question, the Hongkong Government's opinion is that there is yet no responsible and representative body to take the remittance.

"In a communication to Mr. Thomas early in 1930, the Union repudiated the Hongkong Government's charges and threatened to adopt drastic steps to restore its branch, if official sanction could not be procured. Already considerable progress has been made in organizing small groups and sub-branches on the various Pacific vessels and in winning the cooperation of the seamen's boarding houses in Hongkong. The future outcome will undoubtedly be interesting."

The Chinese Seamen's Union during recent years has carried on few effective activities, and has been closely tied in with the government. It is one of the "Special Unions" coming under regulations adopted October 5, 1932, which prohibit the right to strike. About this time it was again reorganized into the Chinese Seamen's Federation, at the same time that several Special Unions among railway workers were created. The China Branch of the I.L.O. reported that the Canton branch of this Federation had 8,300 members in 1932, 9,600 in 1933, 12,000 in 1934 and 14,000 in 1935. No other figures were given. When the National Mobilization Act was passed in Chungking on May 5, 1942, under the regulations all seamen were to be forced to join government-controlled unions as well as other workers, though the seamen were mostly abroad on foreign vessels. At present the Chinese Seamen's Union (as it is again called, apparently) is affiliated with the Chinese Association of Labor. As of December, 1942, the Ministry of Social Affairs, with which it is registered, reported that the Seamen's Union had its headquarters in Chungking and 12 branch unions, 154 sub-branch unions, and 437 small units, with a total membership of 37,667. At the Chinese Association of Labor conference held in Chungking in April, 1943, the union was reported to have 89,109 seamen members. This figure is arrived at by counting all seamen everywhere, including those abroad, as members *ipso facto*. I recently questioned a Chinese seaman in New York on this and he said they had received an order to join the union early in 1944 but that few had done so thus far. Hence the figure is meaningless, for it includes seamen who are already members of various American and British maritime unions and have not joined the Chungking-sponsored union.

206

Chinese seamen in New York recently tried to form a new union in co-operation with the C.I.O. but so far have not been successful. An interesting dispatch from Sydney to the Allied Labor News, May 5, 1944, reported: "Chinese seamen working ships sailing from Australian ports this week won conditions never previously attained by their countrymen in any other part of the world. The Chinese are now paid approximately the same wages and enjoy the same conditions as members of the Seamen's Union of Australia, including overtime after 44 hours, war risk bonus and the right to hold stopwork meetings on the employer's time. These gains, and the establishment of a Chinese section of the SUA, came after two days of testimony by SUA Secretary E. V. Elliot before the New South Wales Industrial Commission."

IV. PERSONAL HISTORIES

Few names stand out in the history of China's labor movement. The period of open mass action was so brief that labor leaders had little opportunity to achieve individual fame and public recognition. Nearly all the open popular leaders of the 1922-1927 heyday are now dead. The two names best known in foreign countries, especially in the Far East, are Su Chao-jen and Han Ying. Su Chao-jen was China's representative on the international Pan-Pacific Trade Union Secretariat and Han Ying his successor, both being also heads of the All-China Labor Federation. Both were real rank-and-file labor leaders, Su Chao-jen a seaman and Han Ying a factory worker. There were many others, such as Lin Wei-ming, first chairman of the All-China Labor Federation, and Wong Son-hua, head of the Shanghai General Labor Union, but of these little record remains. Since the suppression of the mass movement in 1927, no important popular figure has risen out of the ranks of labor, except in the Communist districts. Labor union officials have been mostly appointees and no national labor federation has existed.

Of political organizers once important in the labor movement, who were originally "students," some of the names best known publicly were Li Li-san, T'an P'ing-shan, Teng Chung-hsia, Chang Kuo-t'ao, Hsiang Chung-fa and Liu Hsiao-ch'i. The only one of these still alive and active today in the labor movement is Liu Hsiao-ch'i, who now directs labor activities in guerrilla areas. Chou En-lai and Mao Tsê-tung also organized labor though their names were not so well known in this field as others in the 1922-1927 period.

The labor movement centered in south and central China. Han Ying was a key figure in central China and Su Chao-jen in the south. Their life stories outline briefly the development of several phases of the whole labor struggle, but they are most interesting as showing the rise of rank-and-file leadership.

1. THE CANTONESE SEAMAN, SU CHAO-JEN

Su Chao-jen was an ordinary seaman in 1921. Six years later he was Minister of Labor in the Hankow government and chief of nearly three million organized workers.

He was a native of Hsiangshan district in Kwangtung province, which is not far from the birthplace of Sun Yat-sen. There he was born in 1888 to a family of poor peasants, went to sea as a boy and was a seaman for twenty years. Most of the Chinese seamen come from

Kwangtung, and they were the earliest supporters of Sun Yat-sen's revolutionary program among the workingmen of China. Teng Chung-hsia [37] said he believed Su Chao-jen had become a member of the early Kuomintang (the Tung Meng Hui founded in 1905) before the 1911 Revolution. He was a member of the Lien Yi and Chuang Yi Societies organized by Sun Yat-sen, and was one of the active sailors who carried messages as they touched port in various countries and helped the transportation work of the revolutionaries. The forerunner of the Seamen's Union, the Seamen's Mutual Benefit Society, was a secret revolutionary society as well as a welfare organization, and it was most active on the Canadian-Pacific vessels. Su Chao-jen was already known as a leader among seamen before 1920, and on one occasion when he returned to Kwangtung to carry on activities, he was seized and imprisoned for a year.

After the World War it became clear to Chinese seamen that they must organize on a new basis, as the old benefit societies failed to protect their interests. They were heavily exploited by labor contractors, who sometimes retained over 60 per cent of their regular earnings. Attempts to break the vicious system always failed. Also there was discrimination against Chinese seamen on foreign vessels, and when other seamen received a raise in wages the Chinese were ignored.

Until 1920 the labor union was almost unknown in China. Su Chao-jen and his friend Lin Wei-ming were among the earliest to take an interest in this subject and during 1920 these two were busy doing propaganda among the seamen and preparing the ground for the Chinese Seamen's Union which was inaugurated February 28, 1921, in Hong Kong. A committee was set up to study the wage situation, and demands for wage increases were made to the shipping companies without success. On January 12, 1922, the Union sent an ultimatum. As this was ignored, a strike was voted and Su Chao-jen was elected chairman of the Strike Committee. He managed the spectacular affair that followed and overnight became the first noted labor leader in the country. Hong Kong was paralyzed for two months, and negotiations resulted in a great victory for the seamen, under which they received wage increases of from 20 per cent to 30 per cent. Su Chao-jen was the leader of a demonstration of some two hundred thousand people who gathered in the streets to celebrate the occasion and to watch the policeman replace the Chinese Seamen's Union sign, which had been taken down by the same person two months before.

It would be of great interest to know exactly where the underlying

[37] "The Life and Work of Sou Chao-jen," an article by Teng Chung-hsia in the *Pan-Pacific Monthly*, July-September, 1929.

urge behind this first big strike in China came from, as it marks the beginning of the first stage of China's labor movement. It is customary to deprecate the initiative and abilities of China's working people and to assume that all such affairs are either started by the Communists, the Kuomintang or some political group. Teng Chung-hsia, however, declares that this strike was not initiated by the Kuomintang, as is sometimes claimed, but by militants among the seamen led by Su Chao-jen and Lin Wei-ming. Later, however, General Li Chi-sen gave $100,000 to the strikers and the Kuomintang utilized the strike for its purposes. Several of the 1922 strike leaders, Chen Ping-sen, Chai Han-chi and Twang Tai-sen, were soon afterward corrupted and became labor traitors, according to Teng Chung-hsia; they pocketed funds and were discredited. Su Chao-jen and Lin Wei-ming, however, intensified the fight.

In June, 1924, Su Chao-jen was active in organizing the first international labor union activity in China, indeed in the whole Far East, when a Pacific Transport Workers' Conference was held in Canton, with representatives from the Philippines, Japan and elsewhere. This had been originally called, however, by a representative from the Red Trade Union International.

Although his friend, Lin Wei-ming, had joined the Communist Party in 1924, Su Chao-jen did not join until the following year. In 1925 he was the representative of the Kwangtung workers at a preparatory conference of the Kuomintang held in Peking about the time of Sun Yat-sen's death, and joined the Communists during his stay in Peking. He had stopped off in Shanghai and talked with the Communists there on his way north and decided to join. Su Chao-jen told Teng Chung-hsia that he had first tried to get in touch with the Communists during the Hong Kong Seamen's Strike in 1922, as that party had just been formed in 1921. He went to Canton during the strike and looked for some Communists, but apparently without much success, as there were few in Canton then, though they published a paper, the "Chuan Pao." He also went to the Soviet News Agency in Canton and asked it to send out news of the strike. Teng Chung-hsia reported that just before the big Hong Kong-Canton Strike in 1925, the Communist Party still had only 400 members in Canton, but immediately afterward increased to several thousand. It seems incredible that they could have had so much influence, but nearly all the key labor figures were tied up with their organization in one way or another.

Su Chao-jen was a dominant figure at the Second National Labor Congress held in Canton in May, 1925, which had been called by the "Big Four" unions, including the Seamen's Union. Su Chao-jen was elected to the committee of the All-China Labor Federation that was created at this conference, but Lin Wei-ming was elected first chairman. Soon afterward, however, Lin Wei-ming became ill, and died of paralysis in the summer of 1927. Su Chao-jen was elected head of the Federation at the Third Congress held in Canton in 1926.

The great Hong Kong-Canton strike and boycott, which lasted fifteen months from June, 1925, was directed by Su Chao-jen, Teng Chung-hsia, Huang Pin and Yang Ying,[38] all noted labor leaders, none of whom are now alive. Su Chao-jen was head of the Strike Committee and also of the Finance Committee, being in charge of 2,000 pickets and head of about 160,000 strikers. At this time there were over a hundred labor organizations in Hong Kong, mostly guilds or Yellow unions, according to Teng Chung-hsia.

When the Nationalist Government moved to Hankow at the end of 1926, Su Chao-jen became Minister of Labor. He has the distinction of being the first person to hold such an office in Chinese history and also the last to date—for the government has since had no separate Minister of Labor, but the office was placed under the Ministry of Industries, etc. Another Communist, T'an P'ing-shan, became Minister of Agriculture. At this time four million peasants were organized in Hupeh province alone, of which Hankow is the capital. The Hupeh provincial workers' organizations numbered 500,000 members, while neighboring Hunan had 200,000, according to Teng Chung-hsia.

Su Chao-jen was in charge of labor matters in Hankow at a very difficult and exciting time. The workers organized temporary management committees to take over the factories and keep industry running, as most of the owners had closed them down and run away. Prices had risen due to the disruption of war and wages had to come up to meet the rising cost of living. Labor was practically in control of the city administration.

At the first Pan-Pacific Trade Union Congress held in Hankow in 1927, Su Chao-jen was elected to head its Secretariat, with Earl Browder as secretary. This later claimed to represent fifteen million organized workers of such Pacific countries as China, Japan, Korea, Indonesia and the U.S.S.R.

When the split between the Communists and the Kuomintang occurred in Hankow in July, Su Chao-jen went to Kiukiang. He opposed the opportunist policy of the Communist Party in this period, though

[38] Yang Ying was also a Cantonese, a native of Chungshan district in Kwangtung, and an early member of the Tung Meng Hui. His regular job was the Salt Inspectorate, but he organized the Canton-Hankow Railway workers, becoming a Communist in 1923. In 1927 he was active in the Canton Commune. On August 30, 1929, he was executed at the Shanghai Garrison headquarters, together with three other important Communists, he then being a member of their Central Committee.

the other Communist minister, T'an P'ing-shan, supported it and was later expelled. Before leaving Hankow Su Chao-jen took $100,000 remaining in the treasury of the Ministry of Labor and distributed it to the unemployed.

A representative of the Comintern arrived in Hankow at the beginning of August, 1927, and Su Chao-jen and Teng Chung-hsia accompanied him to the August 7 conference of the Communist Party, at which Su Chao-jen was elected to the Central Committee. Su then carried on activities between Shanghai and Hankow until the time of the Canton Commune in December, during which he was elected chairman of the soviet created—the first in any city in Asia, outside the U.S.S.R. On this day, however, he was not in Canton but had gone to the nearby peasant districts to recruit armed forces to aid the labor uprising in Canton.

In the spring of 1928 Su Chao-jen went to Moscow as a delegate to the Fourth Conference of the Red Trade Union International in April, and also attended the Sixth Congress of the Comintern in August. He was elected to the executive of both Internationals. At the close of the last conference he became ill with appendicitis and went to the Crimea for a brief time. He returned to Shanghai in January, 1929, however, where he died a month later on February 26, at the age of 41. Teng Chung-hsia said his death was caused by overwork, poor food and general exhaustion over a period of time.

2. HAN YING: A BRIEF AUTOBIOGRAPHY

Han Ying worked in the heart of China's labor movement from the day in 1920 that he organized the first textile strike in Wuhan at the age of 22, to 1931 when he went to the interior and became noted as a military commander. His story is the story of a real rank-and-file labor leader and he exemplifies better than any other individual the potentialities of the ordinary Chinese workingman. An apprentice at the age of twelve, he was the strikers' delegate chosen to negotiate with the authorities during the general railway strike of 1923. Next year he was elected to the Central Executive Committee of the Kuomintang. In 1927 he was in command of the famous "Hankow pickets" which controlled the city. Two years later he succeeded Su Chao-jen as Chairman of the All-China Labor Federation. During the civil war he was one of the Big Three in the Chinese soviets, together with Mao Tsê-tung and Chu Teh. At the time of his death, in the prime of life, he was the leader of the guerrilla movement against the Japanese in central China.

I myself did not meet Han Ying, but he told the story of his life briefly, in 1938, to my husband, Edgar Snow, who said of him: "Although I was with Han Ying only a short time, he made an impression on me in a few hours more vivid than most people one knows for months and years. In physical appearance not prepossessing, he in fact looks like the treaty-port foreigner's idea of a 'typical coolie.' Wiry and muscular, his short figure ends with a head that protrudes dome-like in the back. The fingers of his hands are stubby and calloused; his lips and nose are broad and thick; his teeth, some of which are missing, jut out in an irregular and unbeautiful manner. But his grin is the captivating grin of laboring China."

At that time, Han Ying was leading the New Fourth Army of 40,000 men. This was attacked by Central Government troops in 1941 and 4,000 persons killed. Han Ying was wounded and captured; then killed.

In the following story, there is not a little rare inside history:

"I was born in Wuchang, Hupeh, in 1898, of a poor family. My father was a shop clerk and died when I was 10, leaving my mother destitute with two children to support, myself and a younger sister.

"My education consisted of four years in primary school, at the end of which I was obliged to go to work to support my mother. I was sent as an apprentice to a spinning factory and after three years of toil I became, at the age of 15, a salaried worker. My sister also became a mill worker and later on she joined the Communist Party. I have not seen her since 1927; probably she is already dead. She was influenced by my own struggles and took part in the great Wuhan labor movement, after which we became separated.

"I was beaten and maltreated in the factory, and was inclined to be rebellious against working conditions, which were very bad. I could read and write and knew a little more than most factory workers. At the time of the Russian Revolution I was 19 and the news of this event interested me very much. I did not know anything about the Communist Party or Marxism then but during the May 4th (1919) Movement much propaganda was conducted about revolution and the revolutionary slogans appealed to me.

"Before I had any connection with the Communist Party I wanted to organize the mill workers to fight for better conditions. I led the first textile strike in Wuhan, in 1920. After that the Communists became interested in me. The first time I heard of Marxism was through an intellectual who came to talk to me and wanted to make a connection with the workers. He had some influence on me. Later on he joined the Kuomintang and disappeared from my life.

"When the Communists got in touch with me I liked their program and agreed to work with them to organize the Wuhan working class. Soon afterward I left the spinning mill and began to carry out an assignment to organize railway workers, under Ch'ên T'an-chu and

Teng Pi-wu, who were leading Communists then. I organized and became secretary of the first railway union in Wuhan—among the workers of the Peking-Hankow Railway.

"After that I went to Tayeh and worked among the iron miners, and also did organizational work at Hanyang and P'ing-hsiang. The Han-Yeh-P'ing workers union was the third one organized. The second organized was a union of machinists in Shenchiachi, about 30 *li* from Hankow. These three unions declared a strike for improved conditions, and as a result the Governor of Hupeh (Shao Yao-nien) ordered the unions suppressed and their leaders arrested. But there were 7,000 workers militantly organized, led by the advanced steel workers of the Hanyang Works. After five days the owners of the iron works became alarmed: all the furnaces had been deserted and the cooling iron and steel were sticking to them, threatening them with destruction. Hanyang was the first to capitulate. It was the first great strike victory in China and from this time unions began to increase very rapidly.

"The workers unions of Wuhan now united in a general trade union movement, of which I became secretary. A series of strikes, nearly all successful, swept over central China. Tobacco, power, and textile workers especially won big gains. By 1923 Wuhan had become the center of the Chinese working class movement.

"Our biggest and most powerful union was organized among the workers of the Peking-Hankow Railway and through it the workers in the north began to be affected. At first the railway unions were only locals but we decided to unite these into one federation, and called a meeting, at last, to be attended by delegates of all locals, at Chengchow, in Honan. Wu Pei-fu was at that time the most powerful figure in north China and he regarded the railways as his own property, considering them part of his military organization. Naturally he opposed the unions. When he learned of our meeting he sent soldiers to arrest us. They arrived and surrounded our camp, trying to disperse us, but we resisted. At night, when we were holding a meeting, they attacked us.

"As a result of this incident we declared a general strike on the railway, in which 20,000 workers participated, all the way from Peking to Canton. This pressure finally forced the Government to ask the workers to send a delegate for negotiation, and I was chosen. On the following day the authorities attempted to force the railwaymen back to work, but in that they failed. I was arrested and held prisoner for several days and this strengthened the workers' determination. At last I was released. The strike continued until February 7, 1923, when the Government began suppressing the unions by military force. About 40 were killed at Chengchow, and more in Wuhan and elsewhere. Union leaders were obliged to go into hiding for their lives and for a time I hid in

214

Wuhan to escape arrest and death. For a while after this the labor movement was completely crushed.

"Meanwhile the entente between the Kuomintang and the C.P. was developing. In 1924 the Kuomintang Congress was held in Canton and I was elected a member of the Central Executive Committee. In the north, however, the reactionary militarists were making a terrorist drive everywhere against labor and our leaders continued to be arrested in Wuhan. In the midst of this struggle I was appointed secretary of the Workers Department in the Communist Party and went to Shanghai. At that time Li Li-san was also organizing workers in Shanghai, his area being in the Yangtzepoo or northern district. I took charge in west Shanghai. Despite severe suppression our trade union movement grew very rapidly, so that by 1925, in February, we were able to declare a general strike in which 100,000 workers participated. The movement also enjoyed a revival in Wuhan, where Wu Pei-fu's reactionary influence failed to destroy us; and I was for a brief time transferred back to Wuhan. But the May 30th Incident occurred in Shanghai, when the British police shot and killed some students and workers demonstrating against the Japanese mill-owners, in sympathy with striking textile workers. I returned to Shanghai, to lead a general strike. We had to fight strong suppression and our work became secret. Li Li-san left and I was the remaining workers' organizational leader. From the time of the May 30th Movement onward until the time of the Northern Expedition labor became increasingly powerful, reaching its climax in the seizure of Shanghai.

"(Following Chiang Kai-shek's coup d'etat at Shanghai?) I returned to Hankow where I became organizing secretary of 500,000 workers—the Hupeh Trades Unions. Workers of all kinds of industry were organized—both machine and handicraft. I also took command of the worker pickets in Hankow.

"Between 4 and 5 thousand workers were organized as pickets, and these had altogether about 1,000 rifles. The arms had been given to us by Yeh T'ing, who was commander of the 20th Army. Together with Yeh T'ing we workers ruled Hankow and when Hsia Tou-yin revolted, in April, 1927, we were mobilized to maintain order while Yeh T'ing was sent to suppress the revolt. At this time T'ang Sheng-chih had two divisions in Hankow, but he was afraid to act against us. He was watching the outcome of Yeh's fight against Hsia Tou-yin. Chang Fa-kuei's 4th Army was also in Hankow—part of it—and T'ang also did not know their political position clearly. Although we had only 1,000 rifles our position was very strong organizationally: we had unions in Wuhan alone with a membership of 280,000. If we had declared a general strike we could have armed more people.

"But our weakness was in slowness of political work in the army. At that time the soldiers had little political knowledge; we should have worked on T'ang's troops, but did not. Ch'ên Tu-hsiu was opposed both to doing political work in the army and arming the workers. His policy at that time was responsible for our eventual suppression. As it was the worker pickets really ruled Hankow for 1½ months, and T'ang did not take action against us until we were disarmed at Ch'ên's order. After the final Communist-Kuomintang split (after the expulsion of the Communists from the Kuomintang) Ch'ên was afraid even then to lead any resistance.

"I took sick and after July could not leave Wuhan for two months—during which I remained in hiding. The unions were suppressed and our leaders arrested and executed. In August Ho Lung and Yeh T'ing led an insurrection at Nanchang. Not long afterward I escaped to Shanghai, where the Party tried to reorganize the labor unions for strike action. But the White Terror had become very strong and it was difficult to mobilize the workers under the new conditions. In 1928 I was made secretary of the Kiangsu Provincial Party, and soon afterward I was sent to Moscow as a delegate to the Sixth Congress of the C.I., where I was elected a supervisory member. Returning to China I worked in party headquarters, and in 1929 I became chairman of the All-China Labor Federation. (Li Li-san was then the dominating personality in the Politburo, and remained so until 1930.) Following P'eng Teh-huai's capture of Changsha, and its subsequent loss to the Kuomintang, the Politburo was reorganized and I was sent to Kiangsi.

"In Kiangsi I became chairman of the Revolutionary Military Committee of the Workers and Peasants Red Army. This was just after the defeat of Chiang Kai-shek's First Annihilation Campaign. I entered Kiangsi after the failure of the attempt to call a general strike in Wuhan (led by Li Li-san), in connection with the Changsha campaign of the Red Army, having gone from Shanghai to participate in that attempt.

"In Kiangsi I took part in a number of battles against the Nanking forces, until at the First Soviet Congress I was elected vice-chairman. This Congress was held on November 11, 1931, anniversary of the October revolution. (November 7, 1930, was the date originally set for the convention of the First All-China Soviet Congress but because of the military situation it was impossible for the delegates to reach Kiangsi and it was postponed until November 11, 1931, according to Han Ying).

"Mao Tsê-tung was elected chairman of the Chinese Workers and Peasants Soviet Government and I became vice-chairman. Chu Teh was elected chairman of the Revolutionary Military Council and Commander-in-Chief of the Workers and Peasants Red Army. Until that time Mao had been preoccupied with military duties and even afterward, until 1933, he spent most of his time at the front, while I remained in the rear as acting chairman of the Government. When Mao returned I acted as chairman of the Military Council, for Chu Teh. In January, 1933, the Second Congress was held and Chu Teh returned, and remained at Juichin, as the Fifth Campaign of Annihilation was beginning.

"Mao Tsê-tung now became head of all the ministries. Before this time I had acted as minister of various departments, including labor, land, finance, investigation, etc. In 1934 the decision was taken to evacuate the main forces from Kiangsi and Mao and Chu went to the west, leaving me in command of the party and the army in Kiangsi. I remained as the leader of our rearguard in Kiangsi until March, 1935, when we were finally forced to retreat to the border districts of Fukien, Kiangsi and Kwangtung, based on the Wu Ling mountains. This was the beginning of a period of terrible hardship for us, which lasted for over 2½ years.

"From that time on we lost touch with the main forces and our news of the outside world became more and more fragmentary. Our radio units were lost or destroyed; our communications were narrowly limited by the enemy's blockade. After Fang Chih-min was killed the two remaining army commanders in this area were myself and Chien Yi. We many times despaired of our future and the possibilities of survival but refused to give up, despite numerous offers and blows from the Nanking forces. Considering our position we decided to de-centralize our forces into small partisan bands based on the most mountainous districts, and continued, with these new tactics, to fight some successful battles and seize enough arms and supplies to maintain ourselves. But gradually our position was becoming more and more serious. For two years I never undressed at night, nor did my men: we had to be ready to act on a few minutes' warning. We could not sleep in towns or villages but made our beds in the forests of the mountains. We learned the hills of the Fukien-Kiangsi border foot by foot; we knew every corner of them, and we became agile and strong as savages.

"Many times the enemy were within a few miles of our encampments, and came near to capturing us. During these three years of hide-and-seek partisan warfare my most dangerous moment was in May, 1937 (five months after the Sian Incident), when Chien Yi and I were resting at the foot of a mountain. Some Communist traitors led one battalion of enemy troops to our resting place to surround us. Just before the encirclement was completed Chien Yi escaped with his four guards, but I, being some distance away, did not hear the alarm until too late. Seeing Government soldiers approaching I hid under some tall grass. Searching for me the Government troops came to within 10 meters of where I lay and were examining the place very carefully, when suddenly it started to rain. It was a terrific downpour, with great thunder and lightning, and the rain was so heavy it drove the soldiers to look for shelter. In their confusion, creeping through the grass on all fours, I spent the whole day in making good my escape. There was a total of four battalions surrounding that mountain. My own troops were some distance away, as I had gone over personally, with a few guards and Chien Yi, to reconnoitre the enemy.

"In these difficult years we never had enough to eat. Had it not been for the help of the peasants we would have starved. They always helped us, and gave us enough rice to meet our needs. We were clothed in rags; for three years I did not have any new garments, wearing only my cotton uniform. We were constantly moving and were unable to build a base anywhere. Our ammunition ran very low and our guns became old and poor. We were very careful with our bullets. If a soldier had as many as 20 rounds, that was considered very wonderful. We never fired a shot without being virtually certain of getting several bullets in exchange. Sometimes the farmers would get ammunition for us. Frequently we went without any food at all for two or three days and several times even longer. After nearly three years of such a life no trial of war could frighten us.

"The Sian Incident resulted in the cessation of civil war between the Kuomintang armies and the Communist forces in the Northwest, but that truce did not affect us. Nanking's war against us never stopped. In fact it increased, as the Nanking forces were enabled to turn their main attention to suppressing us. The last 'surrounding' campaign began in 1936, coincident with the preparations for the drive on the Northwest, and was renewed again in 1937, following the interruption of the Sian Incident. From 30 to 40 divisions were engaged in the task of annihilation, including forces under Chang Fa-kuei, Yu Han-mou, Yo Hsin, Hsiung Shih-hui (Governor of Kiangsi), Chien Yi (Governor of Fukien), and many less well known commanders. They tightened their blockade of the Wu Ling Mountains, began to depopulate the villages, burned down the forests, and tried to entrap us. Ch'en Tiao-yuan was then in Chekiang and led in this work. They were determined to destroy us, and did not want any 'truce' as in the Northwest. Because we were the last Communist forces in the southern provinces they feared us and our potential influence; they did not want any Communists left there nor any trace of the Soviet regime. We could not get any news or instructions from Chu and Mao, but when we finally heard of the settlement of the Sian Incident we issued a manifesto calling for a cessation of war. This was ignored and the campaign continued.

"My forces at the time we parted with the main Red Army consisted of about 10,000 troops—3,000 regulars and 7,000 Red Guards or local militia. In addition we had some 20,000 partisan irregulars. Altogether we did not have more than 10,000 rifles. At the end of nearly three years of partisan warfare, following the capture of Juichin, our forces had dwindled to about 5,000, all told, with a rifle power of about 3,000. Many of our partisan districts had been depopulated and our peasant guards scattered or disbanded or killed. But those 3,000 remaining had become seasoned veterans of scores of skirmishes and battles; they were hardened warriors and nearly all of them were capable of leading men in battle as officers.

"It was not until the Liukouchiao Incident that the pressure against us diminished. Considering this our opportunity, we issued a manifesto calling for a United Front and asking for a chance to fight the Japanese. Only after the outbreak of the Shanghai war, in August, however, was there any response to this appeal. Hsiung Shih-hui, Governor of Kiangsi, began to weaken; some Kiangsi troops were being mobilized for Shanghai, and Hsiung feared we might make an incursion in his rear in Kiangsi. He first tried to send some Communist traitors among our troops and partisans, attempting to reorganize them and lead them to the front. Failing in that, he eventually had to call on me. Only after he had sent me a written communication guaranteed by General Ho Ying-ching, and sanctioned by the C.P., did I agree to negotiate. Hsiung sent a car for me to the border of our districts, and I went to call on him and on Ho Ying-ching. From that point on Po Ku (then at Nanking) took up negotiations. From Kiangsi I went to North Shensi and there received orders concerning the reorganization of our forces as the New Fourth Army, under the chief command of Yeh T'ing, with myself as vice-commander. A tentative agreement was reached in October, but my troops retained their arms and command until the end of the year. Only after I returned from Shensi, with instructions from the Party, was the New Fourth Army finally organized in January, 1938. We then moved from our old bases northward to our present area in the lower Yangtze Valley, to begin partisan warfare against the Japanese.

"During our years of severe hardship and trial our cadres never changed their minds and never gave up hope. They never abandoned their faith in Communism; they listened only to the orders of the Party. The majority of our fighters are peasants. What remained of our army, after this ceaseless fighting, is almost pure iron. The faint-hearted and the traitors have cleaned themselves out. Our New Fourth Army is politically and militarily the pick of the old Kiangsi veterans."

V. CHRONOLOGY OF EVENTS AFFECT-ING THE CHINESE LABOR MOVEMENT

1890　Opening of first cotton mill in China marks successful start of modern industry though first attempts date from the 60's.

1911　October 10, "Double Tenth," fall of the Manchu Dynasty, followed by the establishment of the Republic of China.

1912　Earliest instance of a strike in modern industry; occurring among workers of the Tsing-yang Railway on the Lunghai line.

　　　National Labor Party formed with 700 members at Tongshan; dissolved in the same year, 1912.

　　　Provisional Penal Code of Peking government makes strikes illegal.

1917　January 18, first contingent of Chinese Labor Corps sent to France to aid World War, resulting in knowledge of modern labor organization.

　　　Beginning of the "Literary Renaissance," led by Hu Shih, Ch'ên Tu-hsiu and others, which popularized the *pai hua* vernacular instead of the former classical writing, thus making popular education possible. Ch'ên Tu-hsiu's followers soon become interested in Marxist theories.

　　　Fushan mine explosion in Manchuria, killing 900 workers and 17 Japanese, creates public interest in labor safeguards.

　　　November, Bureau of Overseas Workers established.

1918　Socialist Youth organized in China among students.

1919　"May Fourth" student movement, followed by first significant strikes and boycotts among labor; "26 labor organizations" of various kinds reported growing out of May Fourth movement.

　　　Chinese "Work-and-Study" students arrive in France, soon numbering 3,000. They work in factories part-time, join unions and are influenced by Socialism, Anarchism and Social-Democracy. Other students go to Russia, Germany, etc. On their return to China they organize unions and strikes.

　　　Comintern organized in Moscow, which soon makes contact with Ch'ên Tu-hsiu and other radicals in China.

September, Chinese Returned Laborers' Association created in Shanghai by workers returning from France.

1920 January, Labor Federation for Chinese Workers in France set up in Paris with 6,000 members and 36 branches.

May 1, Labor Day first observed in China.

July, nucleus of Chinese Communist Party formed by Ch'ên Tu-hsiu and Li Ta-chao, publishing first newspaper for workers in China.

Unions, clubs, workers' study groups, etc., formed during 1920 and 1921, one permanent union being the first Ricksha Pullers' Union organized by Ssŭ Yang in Hankow. Chinese Seamen's Philanthropic Society reorganized into the Chinese Seamen's Union in 1920 or early 1921.

Hong Kong Mechanics' Strike, first significant strike in south China, involving about 9,000 workers. This was an action of a guild, not a union.

Chinese Socialist Youth joins Communist Youth International and begins to recruit workers for membership.

1921 Communists organize Labor Secretariat in Shanghai (date uncertain, possibly in 1920), which plans and directs first systematic drive for unions in China.

July, founding of Chinese Communist Party, which concentrates on labor activities.

Strike wave in Japanese-owned mills in Shanghai and Tsingtao.

1922 January 13-March 5, Hong Kong Seamen's Strike, involving about 50,000 workers, marks beginning of first stage of the organized labor movement in China.

Many students return from Russia, France and elsewhere, participating in labor organization work; 104 Left-wing Chinese students deported from France, among whom are several who become important labor organizers.

May 1, First National Labor Congress called by the Labor Secretariat, representing about 70,000 organized workers.

High-tide of labor activity begins about the end of May with a successful Peking-Hankow railway strike that spreads to all principal railways. About 100 strikes occurred during 1922, and some 91 unions were in existence.

Kwangtung authorities repeal local application of Article 224 of Provisional Penal Code which outlaws strikes.

221

1923   February 1, Chengchow Conference of Peking-Hankow railway union locals creates a general union; has conflict with authorities.

February 4-9, general railway strike involving 20,000 workers led by newly-formed General Union of Peking-Hankow Railway Workers.

February 7, "Pinhan Incident," Wu Pei-fu begins to break the railway strike by armed force and closes unions, causing labor activities to go underground until 1925 except in Canton.

1924   January 20, First National Congress of the Kuomintang, resulting in reorganizing that party for the purpose of co-operating with a mass movement of peasants and workers and with the Communists, who are admitted to membership. Liao Chung-k'ai made head of a new Kuomintang Labor Department.

February, General Union of Railway Workers organized secretly in Peking, the first national union in China.

November, Sun Yat-sen's government in Canton promulgates Trade Union Regulations, giving legal protection to unions and protecting the rights of labor for the first time in China.

1925   January to May, strike movement rises in Hsiao Sah Tou cotton mill district in Shanghai against Japanese and British, during which the leader of the movement, Ku Tsen-fung, is murdered by a Japanese foreman at a Nagai Wata Kaisha mill, resulting in renewed protest strikes. Students take up the cause, organizing demonstrations, etc.

March 12, death of Sun Yat-sen in Peking.

May 1-7, Second National Labor Congress held in Canton, which votes to establish the All-China Labor Federation. This is soon formed, with a seaman, Lin Wei-ming, as chairman, and votes to join the Red Trade Union International.

May 30, "May Thirtieth Incident" in Shanghai, in which British fire on a demonstration of students and workers. This is the signal for the rise of revolutionary activity throughout the country and the direct cause of 135 strikes.

June, Shanghai General Labor Union is organized and about 200,000 workers go on strike lasting a month.

June 12, British marines fire on demonstration of workers in Hankow, causing further resentment.

June 23, "Shakee Road Massacre" in Canton, when a mass demonstration is fired on by British and French troops in Shameen.

June to October, 1926, Hong Kong-Canton Strike and boycott

against the British, involving from 160,000 to 250,000 strikers.

August 20, assassination of Liao Chung-k'ai, pro-labor and Left-wing leader of the Koumintang.

1926   May 1-12, Third National Labor Congress held in Canton, representing several hundred thousand organized workers.

July 9, Northern Expedition starts from the south to establish the Kuomintang government all over the country, reaching the Yangtze Valley within six months; hundreds of strikes occur to aid the military occupation.

November 10, Nationalist government moves to Hankow from Canton.

December 15, Bureau of Public Safety in Canton adopts repressive policy toward labor unions and is denounced by the All-China Labor Federation.

1927   January 3, Hankow workers occupy British Concession which is later returned to China after diplomatic negotiations.

March 12, uprising of 600,000 Chinese workers in Shanghai results in occupation of the Chinese part of the city and disarming of Sun Chuan-fang's troops.

April 12, Chiang Kai-shek's *coup d'etat* in Shanghai resulting in three days' fighting in which several thousand workers are killed and wounded and many leaders arrested and executed. The Shanghai General Labor Union is closed and "reorganization" of labor unions begins. This marks the split between the previous united revolutionary forces.

April 15, Chiang Kai-shek sets up the Nanking government in opposition to the Leftist Kuomintang Nationalist government at Hankow.

May 20, first Pan-Pacific Trade Union Congress held in Hankow and the Pan-Pacific Trade Union Secretariat created.

June 23, Fourth National Labor Congress held in Hankow with 300 delegates claiming to represent 2,800,000 union members.

July 15, split between the Left-wing Kuomintang and the Communists in Hankow, followed by the dissolution of the Hankow government.

August 1, Nanchang Uprising of 20,000 Kuomintang troops under the Communists Yeh T'ing and Ho Lung, many workers being in these regiments. This marks the beginning of the Red Army and the period of open civil war between the Communists and the Kuomintang, lasting nearly ten years.

August 7, Chinese Communist Party Congress votes to change

223

opportunist policy of Ch'ên Tu-hsiu and to use armed resistance.

November, first soviets in China set up in Hailofeng near Canton.

December 11, Canton Commune uprising of armed workers and cadets holds the city three days but is defeated.

December 15, the Nanking government breaks off diplomatic relations with the U.S.S.R.

1928　June 3, Nationalist armies take Peking, following which guilds in Peking and Tientsin are reorganized into labor unions.

June 9, Nanking government promulgates the Act Governing the Settlement of Disputes between Employers and Employees; amended later March 17, 1930, and September 27, 1932.

July 9, Kuomintang adopts Regulations for the Organization of Labor Unions, forming basis of the Labor Union Law passed in 1929.

July 26, Kuomintang issues regulations governing "special unions" of seamen, railway and postal workers and miners.

1929　May, China sends first complete delegation to an I.L.O. Conference.

August 1, Second Pan-Pacific Trade Union Conference held in Vladivostok.

October 18, Labor Union Law passed; later amended December 12, 1931, and again July 20, 1933.

December 30, Factory Act promulgated by Nanking government to come into effect February 1, 1931, later postponed to August 1, 1931. The Act was amended December 30, 1932 and again March 27, 1935.

1930　July, Correspondent Branch of the I.L.O. established in Nanking.

1931　February 10, Factory Inspection Law promulgated, to come into force October 1, 1931.

September 18, Japanese occupation of Manchuria creates political crisis in China.

November 7, Provisional Government of the Soviet Republic of China formed in Juikin, Kiangsi.

1932　January 28, Sino-Japanese hostilities at Shanghai begin, causing industrial destruction.

June, Shanghai Municipal Council announces willingness to adhere to the Factory Act.

224

October 5, Administrative Yuan issues four sets of Regulations Governing Special Unions of seamen, railway, postal and telegraph workers.

1933 September, Central Factory Inspection Bureau established in Nanking.

Industrial Division of the Shanghai Municipal Council created with Eleanor M. Hinder as chief and Rewi Alley as Factory Inspector.

1936 Max Eastman, Chief of the Extra-European Section of the I.L.O., visits China, creating closer relations with the I.L.O.

December 12, Sian Incident, the settlement of which results in stopping the civil war.

1937 July 7, Marco Polo Bridge Incident marks beginning of Sino-Japanese War, followed by the Japanese occupation of Shanghai, Wusih and other industrial centers.

September 22, Chinese Communist Party issues manifesto announcing its co-operation with all anti-Japanese groups and support of the Central Government; change of Soviets into democracy for all classes.

1938 August, Chinese Industrial Cooperative movement inaugurated in Hankow which soon creates a network of industry owned and managed by the workers themselves.

Chinese Association of Labor created at Hankow under official auspices, claiming to represent 422,652 organized workers in 1943.

October 25, Central Government evacuates Hankow and Wuchang, followed later by fall of Canton, marking last of important industrial cities to be taken over by the Japanese.

December 29, Wang Ching-wei issues statement on co-operation with the Japanese, followed by his becoming head of the puppet government in Nanking.

1939 Kuomintang Bureau of Social Affairs becomes Ministry of Social Affairs of the Chungking Government and labor affairs are placed under its control in 1940.

1941 August 21, Provisional Regulations Governing the Control of Labor Unions in Time of Emergency promulgated under which all qualified workers are to be forced to join unions, a provision later carried out under the National General Mobilization Act.

December, Japanese occupy foreign-administered areas in China in Shanghai, Tientsin, Hong Kong and elsewhere.

1942   May 5, National General Mobilization Act enforced in Chungking, under which new labor policy is outlined October, 1942, at First National Social Administration Conference.

October 10, governments of Great Britain and the United States announce relinquishment of extra-territoriality in China.

1943   North China Federation of Trade Unions organized in guerrilla areas claiming to represent a total of a million union members, including some 700,000 members of six local federations.

Allied War Relief Committees of the C.I.O., A.F. of L., and Brotherhoods of Railroad Trainmen send $600,000 to Board of Custody of the American Labor Fund for Aid to China in Chungking.

November 20, Chinese government promulgates new National Labor Union Code under which membership of workers in unions is legally made compulsory.

1944   January 2, Madame Sun Yat-sen appeals to American workers to support unity and democratic mobilization in China in the political crisis.

United Nations labor conference proposed, China to be one of the participants.

May 17, Lin Tso-han (Lin Pei-ch'u) arrives in Chungking to negotiate with the Central Government on behalf of the Chinese Communists for a new working co-operation, the first important step in this direction for several years.

VI. REFERENCES

Long bibliographies of articles on Chinese industry and labor may be found in the books by Lowe Chuan-hua and Augusta Wagner, and the list need not be repeated here. For annual information the reader is referred to the various *China Year Books,* to the records of the China Branch of the International Labor Organization, of the Industrial Section of the Shanghai Municipal Council, and of the Shanghai Bureau of Social Affairs. A recent government source is the *China Handbook,* 1937-1943, compiled by the Chinese Ministry of Information, The Macmillan Company, New York, 1943.

References to useful articles and studies on general labor and industrial conditions are listed in foregoing pages.

No previous attempt has been made to write a history of the organized labor movement in China. The only books on Chinese labor problems are the following:

Tso, Sheldon, S. K., *The Labor Movement in China,* Commercial Press, Ltd., Shanghai, 1928.

Fang Fu-an, *Chinese Labour,* Kelly & Walsh, Shanghai, 1931. Published by the Bureau of Industrial and Commercial Information, Ministry of Industries, Commerce and Labour. This contains a chapter on "The Unionization of Labour in China" and one on "Strikes in China."

Lin Tung-hai, *The Labour Movement and Labour Legislation* in China, China United Press, Shanghai, 1932.

Tawney, R. H., *Land and Labour in China,* George Allen & Unwin, Ltd., London, 1932. Mr. Tawney discusses labor organization in the section "Problems of Social Policy."

Lowe Chuan-hua, *Facing Labor Issues in China,* China Institute of Pacific Relations, Shanghai, 1933. This has a chapter on "The Labor Movement in China" and another on the "Study of Some Leading Labor Unions in China." Mr. Lowe has also contributed to the labor section of the *China Year Books* and analyzed material collected by the China Branch of the I.L.O., references to which are given in previous pages.

Wagner, Augusta, *Labor Legislation in China,* published by Yenching University, Peking, 1938. This book, which is an excellent discussion of general labor problems in China as well as of legislation, has one chapter dealing with organized labor, "Militant Labor."

HINDER, ELEANOR M., *Life and Labour in Shanghai,* A Decade of Labour and Social Administration in the International Settlement, Institute of Pacific Relations, New York, 1944. Miss Hinder has only eight pages on "Labour Organization" in the Settlement, but it is of special interest as it deals with wartime conditions in Shanghai following 1937.

A useful pamphlet on the early period is the *Analysis of Strikes in China from 1918 to 1926,* by Ta Chen, Booklet No. 4, published by the Bureau of Industrial and Commercial Information, Ministry of Industry, Commerce and Labor, Shanghai. This is undated but was probably printed in 1930. Mr. Chen has also contributed to the labor section of the *China Year Books* and published several articles on labor.

Some Aspects of the Labor Situation in Canton, by Y. L. Lee, a pamphlet printed by the Canton Y.M.C.A., Canton, 1928, gives an interesting picture of the labor union situation in that city in 1926-1927.

Labor Conditions in China, by Lowe Chuan-hua, a pamphlet issued by the Council of International Affairs, Nanking, China, July 7, 1937, Vol. IV, No. 5, contains an analysis of a survey made by the China Branch of the I.L.O.

Economic Status of Women in Industry in China, by Cora Deng, an unpublished thesis written in 1941 by the Industrial Secretary of the Y.W.C.A. in China. This is a first-rate study of the subject, the best that has been done.

Organized Labor in Asia, special edition of *Amerasia,* May 12, 1944.

Allied Labor News dispatches, from their correspondent Israel Epstein in China, contain good recent information on labor there. These are available at the office, 1133 Broadway, New York 10, N. Y.

On the guerrilla areas in China, the following give some information on labor activities:

North China Unconquered, June, 1943, a pamphlet published in China by the Chinese Communists.

"The North China Front, Chinese Guerrillas in Action," by Michael Lindsay, *Amerasia,* issues of March 31 and April 14, 1944.

228

Economic Reconstruction in North China Border Regions, pamphlet published in China by the Chinese Communists, August, 1943.

In Guerrilla China, Report of the China Defence League, Chungking, September 15, 1943, printed by China Aid Council, 1790 Broadway, New York City.

Two books dealing with the Chinese industrial co-operatives are these:

WALES, NYM, *China Builds for Democracy,* A Story of Co-operative Industry, Modern Age Books, New York, 1941.

HOGG, GEORGE, *I See A New China,* Little, Brown and Company, Boston, 1944.

INDEX

232